DOWNED BY FRIENDLY FIRE

Downed by Friendly Fire

· · · ·

BLACK GIRLS, WHITE GIRLS, AND SUBURBAN SCHOOLING

Signithia Fordham

University of Minnesota Press
Minneapolis
London

Portions of chapters 3, 5, and 6 were published in a different form in "Competing to Lose? (Black) Female School Success as Pyrrhic Victory," in *The Social Life of Achievement*, ed. Henrietta Moore and Nick Long (Oxford: Berghahn Books, 2013), 206–29. Portions of chapters 4 and 6 are adapted with permission from Signithia Fordham, "Passin' for Black: Race, Identity, and Bone Memory in Postracial America," *Harvard Educational Review* 80, no. 1 (Spring 2010): 4–29; copyright 2010 by President and Fellows of Harvard College; all rights reserved.

Published by the University of Minnesota Press
111 Third Avenue South, Suite 290
Minneapolis, MN 55401-2520
http://www.upress.umn.edu

Printed in the United States of America on acid-free paper

The University of Minnesota is an equal-opportunity educator and employer.

23 22 21 20 19 18 17 16   10 9 8 7 6 5 4 3 2 1

LIBRARY OF CONGRESS CATALOGING-IN-PUBLICATION DATA
Names: Fordham, Signithia, author.
Title: Downed by friendly fire : black girls, white girls, and suburban schooling / Signithia Fordham.
Description: Minneapolis : University of Minnesota Press, 2016. | Includes bibliographical references and index.
Identifiers: LCCN 2016034580 (print) | ISBN 978-0-8166-8966-8 (hc) | ISBN 978-0-8166-8967-5 (pb)
Subjects: LCSH: African American girls—Education (Secondary) | African American girls—Social conditions. | Discrimination in education—United States. | Suburban teenagers—United States. | Youth and violence—United States. | United States—Race relations.
Classification: LCC LC2779 .F673 2016 (print) | DDC 373.182352—dc23
LC record available at https://lccn.loc.gov/2016034580

This book is dedicated to the memory of my parents,
both of whom worked nonstop, albeit unsuccessfully,
to keep us, their children,
safe from the unacknowledged, pervasive violence in our lives,
and to my sister-moms, whose love and guidance is
essential to my survival.

Contents

Who Has Seen the Headwinds?

The headwinds come in blistering, unrelenting waves, varying in intensity and endurance, their roar too powerful to ignore. They sting and restrain, penetrating every crevice and corner, disheveling and rearranging all objects and bodies in their paths. Individuals caught in their massive strength reflexively lean forward, twisting and contorting their bodies, genuflecting in the presence of such awesome power. To refuse to acknowledge the superior power of the wind is to risk one's very survival; leaning forward (or walking backward) is a sign not only of respect but also of adaptation.

Disregarding the headwinds is not an option. Unlike the dry, dusty harmattan winds that form annually for several months in parts of the African continent, in the American context, headwinds are an invisible constant in the lives of females socially identified as having African heritage—regardless of where they live, work, worship, study, or play. These winds alter everything in their lives—including scientific claims regarding their DNA—from the time they leave their homes in the morning until they return at night.

African American females who achieve a modicum of societal success live in the shadows of these winds, as if they were stowaways, vigilantly seeking—largely unsuccessfully—to limit their visibility and avoid confrontation. But in order to survive, they must risk being seen and must elude altercations when they leave home to look for work, to go to school or to work, to attend church services and other religious activities, to buy groceries, to shop at the mall, to go to the gym or the library or private and community meetings, to visit relatives and friends, and the like. When they do leave their homes, these females seek to minimize the power of the winds by deflecting their deviation from dominant, gender-specific normality, rejecting all aspects of their "hood" lives that suggest difference, including language and speech, dress, foodways, religious practices, the styling and care of their wind-disheveled, arrogant hair, their dark brown skin, and their nonangular facial features. However, the power of the rapacious, penetrating winds is nonnegotiable. It exposes their bodies to the voyeurism permanently ingrained in society, lifts their skirts and dresses, twists and tightens their pants and jeans, rearranges their coats, hats, and scarves, aggressively ignoring all personal boundaries, the universally recognized benchmarks of personal (and even cultural) integrity. Like oxygen, the one constant these females can count on is the ubiquitous presence and intensity of the headwinds.

The coexistence of the unprecedented scale of the dreaded head-winds and the misguided belief that these winds are a historical relic and no longer a reality in American life undermines draconian efforts to embrace what is defined as normal. Black females' health and life trajectories are intimately implicated in these social, cultural, and economic phenomena. These winds propel them not only to walk differently (fueling the fear of early-onset arthritis and other debilitating chronic diseases), but also to adopt a posture and a gait that enable them to remain standing despite the power of the winds; to wear their arrogant hair in an array of styles— including "natural," covered, braided, dreaded, twisted, permed, straightened—in order to minimize a disheveled appearance and the default perception that they are angry (an inappropriate emotion if one is gendered female, regardless of ancestry) and therefore not "nice people." Moreover, because one of the consequences of long-term headwinds exposure, especially in the winter, is the adverse effect it has on their eyes, ears, and throats—not to mention the liquid that drips from their noses—they constantly police their appearance, repeatedly looking in the mirror. Smiling, a quintessential symbol of femininity (and, some would argue, subordination) is something they do infrequently, primarily because to open one's mouth is to involuntarily take in too much oxygen, running the risk of choking and inadvertently reinforcing the widely believed allegation that they are not "good girls." These winds also force them to talk louder and to speak not with uncertainty but with certainty, to use language directly and parsimoniously not simply because they like to "be loud," but because they want to be heard. If one wants to hear or be heard in a headwind, talking softly is not an option (not to mention that the possibility of early hearing loss makes a lowered voice even more problematic). The headwinds are also implicated in African American females' increased appetites—and larger bodies. In order to withstand the crushing wind power and the inordinate stress they experience, these females eagerly and repeatedly seek the fuel and emotional gratification that food provides.

Home, "the hood" broadly defined, is only a temporary respite, for that space is penetrated and breached episodically not only by wind-sanctioned surveillance officials and other uninvited, legal, wind-supported outsiders, but also, paradoxically, by all females, regardless of race or ethnic identity. These intragender incursions, especially between and among Black and White females, are misrecognized as culprits in the relentlessly reported school achievement gaps, attributed primarily to (historical and contemporary) single motherhood and other familial dysfunctions, the reported Black-on-Black criminal behaviors leading to incarceration and long-term prison time. Elite, designated surveillance officials repeatedly award headwinds funding to educators and other professional and academic researchers to thoroughly interrogate gendered and racialized populations for their nonconforming behaviors and practices. The goal is to assign reasons for inability to compete successfully, to eliminate gender and racial discrimination, and to discover how the intersectionality of race and gender inequities alters or eliminates achievement gaps. Why, they ask, for example, do (White) girls often speak with uncertainty ("I think the answer is . . ." "Wasn't that the birthplace of Abe Lincoln?" "Don't you think you should be doing your homework?") rather than certainty ("I am not gonna do that." "What?" "What you want?" "Where you at?")? Why do girls experiencing the headwinds mispronounce the words "this" and "that" as "dis" and "dat," say "ax" rather than "ask," fail to conjugate the verb "to be," talk too loudly, not know how to swim? And on and on.

Inarguably, the culture's third rail, Americans whose ancestry includes a history of enslavement, are rewarded, perhaps un-wittingly, for denying the historical trauma embedded in the ongoing power of the headwinds. By slavishly conforming, consuming, and entertaining the wind-sanctioned surveillance by officials, their families, and their friends, the "blurred lines" of their historically complex relationship is elided by a national obsession with literal binaries and the eschewal of the potential moral panic that official acknowledgment of this complication might invoke. Hence, denying the power and/or existence of the headwinds is tantamount to describing rain by an absence of wetness and water, lightning by a dearth of light and electrostatic impulses, and thunder by a lack of sound. Yet since virtually no one outside "the hood" is negatively affected by the headwinds, the privileged voices of nonhood citizens categorically denying the presence of the headwinds (the trade winds are their stock in trade) often unintentionally reinforce existing social, cultural, and economic inequities. Fully embedded in every corner of the American cultural landscape and continuously bloviating for more than four hundred years, these winds repeatedly and successfully deflect all social and economic incentives to disappear. (By the way, thank-yous are here offered to Sara, Zora, and Maya: yes, Sara, we regret that there were no abolitionists and only unadulterated capitalists in your life; belatedly we understand, Zora, why you warned us about our slavish tendency to mimic the seductive behaviors and practices of the "white mare"; and admittedly, Maya, we are a little late to the table in understanding why the "caged bird sings"—is it really in celebration?) Typically what happens, at least today, is that the country's major sociocultural and economic institutions "admit . . . , but [do] . . . accept" a few academically successful stowaways who manage to survive the headwinds' blistering psychic and physical blows. Paradoxically, these survivors, like their nonhood peers, are rewarded for denying and misrecognizing the presence and power of the winds, so much so that when asked, *Who has seen the headwinds?*, they eagerly, albeit quizzically, respond, sans hesitation, Who? Wind? What wind?

Violence—by Another Name?

Upstate New York. It is about 7:30 a.m. on a windy Tuesday in the middle of January; the light of the much-desired sun, but not the snow, is MIA—again. In the semidarkness, the sleepy, sullen, and distracted suburban high school students disembark from the yellow school bus slowly and reluctantly and make their way to the front door and to the areas where their lockers are located and where their first-period classes routinely meet.

This part of New York State, widely known for its harsh winters, habitually overcast skies, and ubiquitous blistering white snow, unevenly trimmed in a mawkish cement gray, is not the most desired location in the state, at least not during the winter.[1] In order to survive the coldest months of the year (January, February, March, and sometimes April), most residents permanently don their survival uniforms (long substantial underwear, heavy coats, hats, boots, and gloves) and, like robots, hang on until the arrival of spring; others, the "snowbirds," leave for warmer places until the missing sun, the quintessential harbinger of spring, returns.

As a consequence of their habituated practices and behaviors, on this dark wintry morning only one of the students on the bus recognizes that the new bus driver is unintentionally taking them to the wrong location: the junior high school instead of the high school where they are supposed to be. Sleep deprived, morose, and habituated to this morning routine, belief, not empirical evidence, propels them to misrecognize their geographic/spatial location.

Enique, a tall Black eighteen-year-old senior, a tad oversized, embodies the widely shared perception that in any gender-specific conflict, the Black girl is the assailant, not the victim. Characterized as "bossy," "pushy," and "mean" in the wake of her involvement in an interracial conflict with a White girl the year before the study reported here began, she is the only visibly Black person on the bus and is the self-appointed, unofficial sentry. Unlike the other students, she is alert (even aware of the howling winds) and on duty, her caramel-colored skin serving as a sunless spotlight in the bus, which speeds so fast past the remote trees and farm animals down the semirural graveled roads that she experiences the images outside with something closely approximating vertigo. (BTW, she says she knew the bus was not headed in the right direction but opted not to advise the driver, fearing that she would be disbelieved.) She assures me that she is never off duty on the school bus (or anyplace else, for that matter), and this is even truer now since the physical fight. Experience has taught her that because she is identified as a fraudulent or at least a second-class citizen of this school community, no one will believe what she says, so she deliberately keeps her mouth shut until she is directly asked for information, and even then she is extremely circumspect in her verbal responses. She could cope with this uncomfortable situation if it were a fair fight between her and one other student, she reasons, but it never is. As she experiences it, she is up against not just the student with whom she had the fight, but the entire school community, except for the small smidgen of the Black students who don't cower in fear and blame her—totally—for having got in the fight in the first place. She assures me that it is both the entertainment (read desire for drama and conflict coupled with the unequal power relationships) and the largely hidden involvement of these bystanders—her school-age peers as well as the adults and their masked support for one side or the other—that scrambles her school life options.[2]

Enique is impeccably dressed today and every day, her hair carefully styled and her long nails dipped in an array of beautiful designs to show off the expensive gold watch her father (with whom she now lives) gave her on her most recent birthday. She repeatedly shared with me the numerous ways she is consistently misrecognized, branded a "bad seed" (especially after the physical violence the year before had subjected her to both unrelenting surveillance and un-needed rehabilitation at an alternative school site several days a week). She loathes this official definition of who she is and the shame and humiliation implied in the partial assignment to a remote school site. She also revealed that she was emotionally disfigured when she reported that she was responding to a devastating verbal attack. During virtually every interview I had with her, she reported she could hear the n-word—stage-whispered almost every day after that conflict—if she was alone in a predominantly White space at the school. It was the fear of hearing such names, of being the target of the kind of violence embodied in widely accepted name-calling and vile language, and, most of all, of being disbelieved when re-porting female interracial conflicts that made her avoid spaces at the school that were not populated by a critical mass of the school's Black students.[3] She insisted that the teachers and administrators were virtually "useless" in combating this kind of violence because they did nothing to curb the use of such language and the affiliated violence and humiliation contained therein (see chapters 3 and 5).[4] In response to long-standing institutional practices, Black students' primary adaptation, she insisted, is to embrace the unofficial (that is, expected) racial and gender balkanization because classroom teachers and other school officials appear to be rewarded for being unwilling to challenge or breach these harmful instituted policies and practices and, in the process, to relabel this kind of language as violence—by another name.[5]

Brianna, the embodiment of what it means to be a nice (read nor-mal) girl, is one of the lower-class White girls in the study. A girl with luminous brown eyes, very pale skin, and long dark-brown hair that she tends to wear up, off her shoulders, Brianna lives with her maternal grandmother and her two brothers in a small three-bedroom town house not far from the school. One of the first things she told me when I initially interviewed her is that she is taking cos-metology classes at a school-based alternative educational site. She knows she wants to be a cosmetologist after high school and takes all those classes with adultlike seriousness. Like almost every girl in my study, she is very aware of the accepted racial differences and tensions between Black and White girls at the school, but she insists that they do not matter. Like most of the other White girls, she does not have much direct interaction with the Black girls and does not seek to interact with them because she has preconceived ideas about who they are, how they typically behave, and so on. Her responses and images of her Black female peers are based on how they are constructed through the use of language—that is, not on her personal experiences but rather on rumors, images of them from a distance at the school, and virtual images from television and other media sources. Her perceptions are typical of what I discovered about how the White girls at the school viewed their Black female counterparts (and how the Black girls viewed their White female peers).

During one of several interviews, Brianna told me why she and most of the other White girls at the school are not friends with the Blacks girls, at least "not as, like, *best* friends."

> There's not like really *good* friendships with Black and White girls. The [African American] Black girls, I notice, they stick together.[6] And they're usually really loud. (Laugh) And they—I don't know—they're always yelling at someone, or chasing someone, or talking loud. Just loud. Mm-hmm. And they're always—you always know where it's coming from, and you always know they—but it's loud and they make a scene, I guess. I mean, I don't know. Someone's always chasing someone. (Laugh)[7]

Like Brianna, most of the White girls distance themselves from the Black girls because, at least at this school, Black girls tend to be identified as "the other" and are typically seen as too aggressive, too competitive, and therefore guilty of excessive bullying, and, the coup de grace, not very nice people.[8]

This kind of violence, however, is not limited to interracial contexts. Black-on-Black and White-on-White female violence is also pervasive and is typically constructed by group members whose primary goal is both to successfully mask and to exclude inappropriate members in an effort to maintain and reproduce existing social arrangements. Among the Black girls, this feels strangely like what Alvin Poussaint identifies as "why [b]lacks kill [b]lacks," though from a nonphysical perspective.[9] At the same time, I learned from the various "shades of white" group members how valuable it is to be popular and members of a valued clique, to appear to belong to the appropriate social status.[10] The White girls whose parents are wealthy are expected to display proper breeding and class status by deftly excluding the undesired Black and (poor) White females, not just by avoiding interacting with the "wrong girls," girls who are either race and/or class inappropriate, but also by compelling the participants to misrecognize that they are being excluded (see chapter 4).

Officially constructed as paragons of virtue who are rewarded for masking and harnessing their personal ambitions to at least appear to support existing rules, White girls are, instead, as Lyn Mikel Brown persuasively asserts, "put in the untenable situation of receiving social power for acting in [socially approved] ways that [inevitably] objectify them, render them less significant, less visible, and less in control."[11] These girls embody and reflect what is defined as the core of hegemonic femininity: niceness equated with "good girlness," the epitome of what it means to be a female victim, despite their privileged race status.

Female Aggression in Black and White

My research project at Underground Railroad High School (UGRH—the pseudonym for the predominantly White suburban high school that was the site of my two-and-a-half-year ethnographic research project) examined female-specific bullying, competition, and aggression and the ways in which it is racialized. It interrogated and put on trial the prevailing notions that Black girls are aggressive but White girls are not and that aggression is by definition physical, not verbal, mental, or emotional. My ethnographic research documented those cultural mechanisms that compel girls to confine their competition and aggression both to girls inside their social groups and to girls who are "othered." In due course, the responses of girls targeted as objects of others' aggressive behaviors are revealed.

The idea that gender is a socially constructed way of inhabiting the sexed and raced body does not tell the whole story. Gender is also, more importantly, "experiences formed and performed in interactions with other people."[12] Gender is a performance, an interactive act in which the self is constructed, presented, and validated—or not. The presence and power of gender divisions in societies and the prevalence of gender-specific performances are now acknowledged by social-scientific scholarship, but how persons of the same gender compete to retain and reproduce group status or integrity is not well documented. Indeed, in the case of females in the United States, competition among women is a taboo subject that researchers have avoided scrutinizing or even acknowledging until fairly recently. This study cross-examines the gendered construction of power by looking at it through a prism of disguised contempt.

I begin with this proposition: in male-dominated social systems, females—Black or African American, Hispanic, Latina, Native American, White, or any other—subconsciously find ways to be aggressive while appearing not to be. They do this in order to attain what is socially and culturally central to femininity: desirability in the eyes of males, who are in the position of choosing them for dating, mating, marriage, and mothering.

I am convinced that the teenage girls and adult women (and the teenage boys and men) at the site of the study reported here have not inherited a meanness gene—even when their behaviors and practices appear to suggest this.[13] In addition, as the case studies in this book reveal, gender-appropriate girls fight for what females continue to be most rewarded for in our society—beauty, male attention, and reproduction—in order to avoid the designation given to highly successful professional female achievers: "spinsters" or "leftover women."[14] As careful practitioners of the cultural rules embodied in the often-repeated (albeit inartfully expressed) sentiment "I am just doing my job/following the rules," the social actors at UGRH are repeatedly rewarded for honoring the preexisting rules of the patriarchal hierarchy, including seeking to be the best at the discrete school- and society-based categories that create winners and losers.[15] When focusing on adolescent gender relations, as I do here, desire—for male (or female) attention, parent and teacher approval, academic access and success, and the like—is inarguably at the heart of the friendly fire, the intimate apartheid, and the making of frenemies that are the subject of this book.

Using tools central to anthropologists and ethnographic researchers—participant observation, interviews, field notes, long-term engagement—I unmask the meaning of the familiar, "strangifying" it, and in the process, I reveal what is culturally invisible or hidden from school officials and the students at UGRH.

Underground Railroad High is the petri dish for interrogating the issues discussed above. My findings examine both gender and the intersectionality of race and gender at the school by offering an analysis of a place that, because of the widespread societal fear of physical violence and the equally important search for security and safety by the adult members of the community, is not only a microcosm of the larger society but is also a "gated [academic] community"—that is, an insulated "walled and guarded" learning environment that goes beyond academic tracking to exclude. Thus, when talking about the instruments of bullying and exclusion, it is imperative that we realize this occurs primarily through high-stakes testing, underfunded de facto segregated classrooms, and other exclusionary forces. These forces subvert the realization of the democratic ideals of equality and of a society based on meritocracy and instead reproduce a society actively engaged in re-creating the race, class, and gender inequality it purportedly exists in order to eliminate—within that microcosm.[16]

A Gated (Academic) Community: Frenemies at Underground Railroad High

Most American adults will laughingly, but nonetheless nervously and seriously, acknowledge that they do not desire to revisit their high school experience under any conditions.[17] But why is this familiar response to an obligatory, ubiquitous childhood experience so common? Is it because so many of us did so poorly in school, at least socially, that we cannot bear the thought of having to do it again? Or are there other, more salient issues impelling this response? Did our peers readily embrace us, or was our high school experience characterized primarily by lack of acceptance and marginalization?

The ubiquity of this "never again" response is here juxtaposed with the assumption that schools are sites totally committed to the leveling of inequality in our society and the reality that inequality is not significantly erased by obtaining a high school diploma or college degree. The most common response appears to be connected to how the schooling experience made the students feel: Did they feel normal, that is, validated and/or affirmed at school? Or did they feel excluded from the inner sanctum of an institution allegedly designed to promote equality and a level playing field based on one's willingness to work as hard as or harder than the next person? Why and how these divergent responses emerge is the focus of this book.

Not only as a schoolgirl but as an American citizen of African ancestry and, most recently, as an anthropologist studying my own culture—albeit from a space of marginalization—I admit to being continually flummoxed by the uncompromising "gated" structure of American society (and, not surprisingly, of its system of schooling) and the professed commitment to "equal opportunity for all." Everyone readily acknowledges that despite our unequivocal claim to equality for all, America is hierarchically ranked by three major categories (and maybe more): race, class, and gender. We live in different neighborhoods, often based on race and class, with the size of our homes, our professions, and other indicators of achievement presumed to be accurate markers of our individual and group accomplishments.[18] Indeed, in a recently published book, *The Social Life of Achievement*, edited by Nicholas Long and Henrietta Moore of Cambridge University, a group of European and American anthropologists and other scholars challenge this narrow definition by interrogating and complicating what it means to be an achiever, questioning the widely accepted idea that equates achievement with merit and goodness or, at the very least, banality.[19] What logically follows from this narrow perception of achievement is the misrecognition of the reproduction of inequality. Driven primarily through our insatiable quest for status and normality, some Americans have a hidden advantage, with more (inherited) wealth and class privilege, not just in the larger society but especially in schools—from prekindergarten to postsecondary education. In the popular imagination, from the moment of birth, American girls (and boys) are socialized to learn different gender roles and rules and are rewarded for embracing the extant hegemonic or normative ones: males are rewarded for being achievement oriented, aggressive, and strong; girls are rewarded for needing and seeking protection, for being nice, and for eschewing (or at least masking) aggression and competition.[20] This book examines what happens to girls who violate these expectations, that is, who are recognized and penalized for their gender-inappropriate aggression, bullying, and competition, known here as violence—by another name.

As I hope will become crystal clear, the gated nature of the school community—that is, its preoccupation with status and the inevitable exclusion—is omnipresent and unavoidable, compelling all the students either to embrace or to violate official, societally approved rules. Parenthetically, there is also the presence of parental pressure, which is more effective for some groups and for some members of some groups. In all the students' responses, future consequences are inevitable. These consequences, connected to what is valued and devalued in the larger society, are deployed to suggest what will happen to the student when she graduates: Do her academic responses in pre-K through high school suggest a readiness for placement in one of the most prestigious colleges or universities in the country? Or does her performance indicate that she will be consigned to the lower rungs of the hierarchical ladder, compelled to sell her (re)productive labor to the highest (or lowest) bidder in the neoliberal capitalist market economy?

Against this backdrop, one might ask why we continue to misrecognize and officially deny the power of the legacy intimately affiliated with "the life of the mind" (that is, "academic work as the intellectual playground of the elite"). For example, in his book *Ebony and Ivy: Race, Slavery, and the Troubled History of America's Universities*, Craig Wilder documents the indelible connections that academic institutions, like all the nation's major social and economic institutions, have to the totality of the nation's history, including enslavement and hierarchy embodied in the idea of free and unfree.[21] What, then, one might ask, do we think is likely to happen in contemporary America when balkanized teenage social groups—Black and White, male and female, heterosexuals and gays, thoroughly steeped in the historical, dominating categories, norms, mores, and values of the larger society prior to coming to UGRH and having that raced, classed, gendered structural reality reinforced on a daily basis—meet at this site and are told that they should permanently forget what they were taught from birth and what they have spent the previous nine to eleven years of schooling learning (either explicitly or implicitly), that they should choose, instead, to seek to coexist as social and status equals in a predominantly White, obligatory public high school that embodies the hierarchical structure into which they have been "naturally" socialized? Should they discard their prior history and cultural knowledge and, instead, seamlessly embrace the coexisting rules—equality versus status—of engagement in this new contradictory social context? Are these teenage girls rightfully expected to adopt school-based ideals regarding equality and to lose their previously learned and largely embraced ideals of status, hierarchy, power, and winners and losers, not just in the school but in their home communities and the larger society as well? Or, alternatively, are they predisposed to resist and reject these intimately familiar social policies? Regardless of their predispositions, the "gated [academic] community" offers an ambivalent flotilla of anemic responses to female students' search for equality, and it rewards them—in spades—for their quest for gender-appropriate status and distinction.

For most parents—regardless of race, gender, or ethnicity—the idea of protecting their children is paramount, hence the saliency of the e-word: "exclusion." Nowhere is this more apparent than among White suburban parents whose unending fears of "the other" fuel their quest for safety from the Black erstwhile inner-city residents (as well as from the native-born, suburban Black students) and from the perceived immigrant hordes arriving daily in America. It is the conflation of these fears and the desire for safety and status that enables these White parents and their carefully gender-, class-, and race-appropriate enculturated children to embrace their "class-based exclusion strategies and residential segregation."[22] Hence (at least at this research site), even when a predominantly White school includes class-appropriate students from different demographic groups, White parents' long-held fears and their commitment to what one researcher describes as "opportunity hoarding" evoke a kind of moral panic that does not erase but rather reinforces their extant values and practices.[23] Further, as Cheryl Harris observes, since "Whiteness [is] property," that is, a highly valued commodity with unlimited potential, it is rarely negotiated or traded.[24]

The "gated [academic] community" confronting all female students at UGRH is gendered, multilayered, complex, complicated, and contradictory. These contradictions are fueled not by individual actors but by the gender-appropriate enculturation that is unilaterally, albeit unevenly, typically assigned to and learned by females in the American context, regardless of race or class: that is, "Be nice." Indeed, the "tyranny of [fake] niceness," laced to "meanness," melds seamlessly with what is identified as "intimate apartheid," here relabeled "frenemies," masking the amorphous, latent hostility reflected in the brief student narratives above and the five ethnographic narratives that follow.[25]

Reflections: Trespassing Backward to the Future

My collaboration with John Ogbu in the late 1980s intensified my interest in the subject matter of this book, especially as it affects

African American female achievement, both in and out of school.[26] Embedded in my interest in the larger narrative about the role of resistance in Black students' school success were concerns about gender—which I inadequately pursued.[27] Indeed, it was at Capital High that the following questions emerged organically but were unanswered: Why are African American girls and women rarely allowed the victim role, being obsessively identified with aggression, power, and other markers that make them eligible for the accusation of being "strong Black women"? Why are they routinely assigned the role of assailant, not victim—often even when interacting with their (Black) male and female peers?[28] These questions emerged in the context of Capital High, whose population was more than 99 percent African American. Not surprisingly, I was repeatedly flummoxed by what I could not explain: why these girls' refusal to be voiceless in the face of incredible economic and social imbalance appeared to negate their claim not only to suffering and the attendant anger but, more critically, to femaleness as well.[29]

I watched the (Black) girls at UGRH in ways I was unable to in my earlier research projects. I watched the way they talked: not with gender-specific uncertainty ("I don't think we have any more soup"; "don't you think you should close the door?"), but with unmediated confidence and certainty ("No, I am not going to do that"; "I don't care, go ahead and call my mama"). I watched the way they walked: as if they owned the world. I watched their bigger bodies, inadvertently suggesting power rather than weakness. I watched their compelled silence in explicitly gated spaces (especially classrooms) reeking with the scent of their marginalization and the closely affiliated absence of help and protection, the damsel in distress narrative ("That White boy hit me; make that White boy stop hitting me"; see chapters 4 and 7). And I observed their "arrogant hair," which reinforced a perception of visibility and lack of bodily control.[30]

Needless to say, when I began the study reported here, these same questions loomed larger, haunting my interactions with the Black (and White) girls and, in the process, revealing, unabashedly, my complicity. At this research site, I had comparison populations:

Black and White girls. I observed both groups of girls in ways I could not when I was at Capital High, an overwhelmingly African American school. I was curious as to why the Black girls—whose social status did not include economic and social privilege but a history of enslavement, massive historical and ongoing contemporary poverty, and race, class, and gender discrimination and other indicators usually suggesting social and economic subordination— were more often identified with unadulterated (aka male-identified) power. Inevitably this leads to accusations of being strong and to a misrecognition of why power merged to femaleness in America's hierarchical patriarchy was not (and is not?) desired. Admittedly, I was—and remain—continuously flummoxed as to why they were consistently identified as gender inappropriate, why they were labeled as aggressive and far more powerful than their typically more privileged, but seemingly less powerful, White female peers. My raison d'être as an anthropologist is to analyze (and make visible) cultural patterns in order to render conflict and tensions less problematic and, in the process, to understand and illuminate hidden or masked behaviors and practices. Thus, my inability to offer an adequate explanation for this pervasive phenomenon invoked a heightened sense of frustration, moral panic, and discipline dissonance.

Repeatedly vexed and professionally frustrated by my inability to explain these contradictory issues, the gateway to illumination began when I revisited an essay I had taught in several undergraduate courses: Michael Kimmel's "Toward a Pedagogy of the Oppressor."[31] In that essay, Kimmel compares the effects and consequences of living in an environment characterized by trade winds versus one characterized by headwinds, noting that regardless of determination, in the face of a headwind, progress is much more difficult, even unlikely. In striking contrast, individuals experiencing a trade wind are unlikely to even notice it; they can virtually float as the wind pushes them forward. Indeed, he asserts, the beneficiaries of this wind "do not feel the wind; it feels [them]," propelling them to their goals in a virtually effortless manner.

For me, the headwinds-versus-trade-winds analogy offers an appropriate metaphor for investigating the way the dysfunctional trope of a seamless sisterhood, evoking kinship and familial images between Black and White females, masks the "intimate apartheid"— "the involuntary and predictable manner in which sharply delineated segregation and conflict impose themselves at the level of everyday practices driven by *habitus*"—in the school lives of the girls I studied at UGRH and, in hindsight, Capital High as well.[32] While everyone (mis)recognizes each other's racial identity, even if he or she claims not to notice it, race—except when it is not—is almost unanimously characterized as a benign category, a historical relic that no one finds harmful (or helpful) in a postracial America.[33] However, the truth is less absolute, located in a "gray zone," sandwiched somewhere between friends and enemies, that is, frenemies, compelling the girls to be (mis)identified as frenemies and harmed—deliberately and systematically, not inadvertently or accidentally.[34]

Using a recursive process, the analysis offered in this book enables me to be more transparent, personal, and intimate than I have been in my earlier research projects, deliberately blurring the rigid distinctions between narrative and traditional ethnographies, so much so that I am likely to be accused of practicing autoethnography, a genre of ethnography that many in the discipline find concurrently alluring and loathsome.[35] I am willing to take that risk because I believe that from this stigmatized raced and gendered space, my experiential knowledge in social science research is not simply valuable but essential. Indeed, given my pedigree as a subordinate whose life history includes (stigmatized) race and gender subordination, I fear that my perspective, unlike that of most of my anthropology colleagues, propels me to interpret the "inadequacies" of the students whose narratives are included here, and which in many ways parallel my own, as embodying what Kirby Moss identifies as "the paradox of privilege."[36] For me this means that my professional training is deemed successful—at least officially—if I am not just visibly the opposite of my colleagues but also able to "*interpenetrate* and inhabit" their "assumptions and definitions."[37] More critically, acceptance of what I write is more likely if my worldview, analyses, and definitions are inevitably indistinguishable from theirs. But what about Pierre Bourdieu's assertions regarding the power of habitus? What about Paul Farmer's concept of structural violence?

Rehabilitating Violence

In this this book I argue that the widely reported differential academic performance, general decorum, behaviors, and practices of the two girl groups I studied at UGRH can be attributed not only to their individual practices but also to larger social forces, to their dissimilar habitus—Bourdieu's concept of an ever-changing practice that is part of a larger social, not individual, process that creates transferrable, enduring patterns from one context to another—not just their individual deficiencies.[38] My study reinforces this claim, buttressed by my long-held belief that although these girls matriculate at the same school, are taught by the same teachers, are expected to complete the same academic tasks, and are compelled to obey the same rules, their divergent habitus (in interaction with adults whose habitus are also dissimilar) structures their differentiated academic performance, habitus beliefs, responses, and practices.

In order to engage the reader and to fully embrace both my experiential knowledge and my professional training as an anthropologist, this book takes the reader deeply into the belly of the research site by offering this text as "something made or fashioned," blurring the distinctions between narrative and traditional ethnography by deploying James Clifford's assertion that "ethnographic texts are [both] inescapably allegorical" and "partial truths."[39] Moreover, as Clifford also asserts, "the making of ethnography is artisanal, tied to the worldly work of writing."[40] I wholeheartedly embrace his assertion that ethnographies are accurately described as "true fiction" in that "ethnographic truths are . . . inherently *partial*—committed and incomplete."[41] Consequently, through the use of practices more closely aligned with narration (or narrative writing) than with ethnography, I am able, at least partially, to rehabilitate a dominant meaning of violence. This is facilitated by the fact that during the two and a half years I spent at the research site, I was compelled to be a stranger, a permanent outsider. In this text, I am able to find my voice, first, by creating seamless composite characters, thereby protecting the identity of the key participants, and, second, by writing in the second and third person rather than the first person—enabling me to channel the students' voices in such way that I appear to be speaking *to* rather than *for* them.

This more accurate definition of violence has as a primary source an idea proffered by Laura Nader some thirty years ago in "Up the Anthropologist: Perspectives Gained from Studying Up," or studying power in a globally connected world in which dominance works best, at least in the American context, when it is masked or hidden.[42] This means that the following assumption is problematic: the absence of physical violence (including the sporadic outbreaks of "planned fights" at the research site among and between Black and White girls) in the way it is both expected and pervasive among their male peers is not prima facie evidence that girls are not aggressive and/or do not interact with each other in ways that mesh with our common (mis)understanding of violence. Moreover, the social import of the differential habitus of the Black and White girls—indeed, the simple fact of their current existence in the same or at least similar social and geographical spaces—is uncontested evidence of the stranglehold of social domination and misrecognition and of the resulting "intimate apartheid" of the friendly fire, a reoccurring claim in this book.[43]

This book, then, is not about violence—as we commonly know it—even though the language affiliated with drama, conflict, and warfare (words such as "aggression," "bullying," "competition") is repeatedly deployed. This book is not about war or peace and the resulting social and emotional upheavals. (Except when the bell rings to signal the changing of classes and the five- to ten-minute period when students are allowed in the hallways between classes, language is spoken in such hushed tones that it is almost possible to hear one's heartbeats, if one is also using one's inside voice.) It is also not about cyberspace, virtual space, or any other one-on-one conflict or small-group (that is, cliquish) skirmishes, including the current rabid focus on bullying, which is widely attributed to "mean girls" (or boys), queen bees, and the like. It showcases five ethnographic narratives of individual girls, chronicling the multiple ways they are complicit in reproducing their stigmatized "nomadic subjectivities" by their unending quest for normality, fueling what Alain de Button identifies as "status anxiety," or what I identify in this ethnography as "statusitis." It is also not about girl fighting—that is, biological determinism—or about individuals identified as inherently racist, sexist, classist, or other -ist.[44] In other words, this book is not about individuals—either those committing evil acts leading to the predictable binaries of assailants and victims portrayed in the narratives presented here, or those who embody niceness, invoking halcyon days of yore. It is not about these identified individuals and their practices because to focus on individual evil acts inevitably compels us to privilege symptoms of the problem rather than causes that are embedded and reflected in the seams of the larger society in which these issues are lodged.

Instead, this book is about the injurious impact of what Bourdieu labels "symbolic violence," that is, "everyday practices"—and the ubiquitous perception of the banality of normality.[45] In other words, *this book offers the reader an opportunity not only to interrogate the idea that normality is neutral but also to consider it as a socially approved form of violence.*[46]

Therefore, the central goal of this book is threefold: to excavate, to resuscitate, and to rehabilitate the meaning of violence, with the major focus being rehabilitation.[47] I do this because I believe the issues chronicled in the five ethnographic narratives that follow are the unacknowledged, underground fuel that animates most female violence, leading to the evolving physicality prominent at UGRH and by extension in the larger society. These girls turn their anger against each other rather than the larger society—a common practice among subordinated populations (consider the frequent reference to Black-on-Black crime)—which predisposes them to be complicit in the inadvertent reproduction of their subordination.[48] In addition, as I argue here, violence, especially among females, is much more intimate and pervasive, defying the hegemonic tropes of physicality and, among females, of a seamless sisterhood. Therefore, since there is a growing lack of consensus regarding the meaning of violence, including the porosity of its boundaries, clearly defining what it means in this context is the first task of this book.

Therefore, what I propose here is to rehabilitate the primary meaning of violence by highlighting the following point: at UGRH, the Black and White girls are frenemies, embracing, perhaps fortuitously, a kind of "intimate apartheid"—not a seamless sisterhood.[49] While this definition is not gender specific, it is nonetheless, female appropriate and female practiced—in the trenches, buttressed by the fact that at the core of all human violence, both physical and nonphysical, is the intent to harm someone. For that reason, I am reluctant to embrace the traditional meaning of violence and its claim of unconditional physicality as suggested by Frantz Fanon in his seminal works *The Wretched of the Earth* and *Black Skin, White Masks*.[50] I occupy this ambivalent space despite the fact that many aspects of Fanon's analysis—for example, deploying (physical) violence as an obligatory form of therapy for formerly colonized populations, including their descendants, in order to cure them of a pandemic cultural disease that is the inevitable outcome of colonial domination—resonate in ways I cannot find words to explain, a memory deeply lodged somewhere in my cultural DNA.[51] Hence, I seek to rehabilitate what we mean by violence not because I reject Fanon's brilliant description of the impact of global colonization on the minds and consciousnesses of the formerly colonized and their descendants but because I seek to suggest the ubiquity and "everydayness" of the kind of violence discussed in the narratives in this book.

Moreover, as the case studies in this ethnography explicitly reveal, violence—that is, the intent to do harm—is practiced daily, both consciously and unconsciously, by individuals gendered female (and male) and is as essential as (or more important than) physical violence in shaping our understanding of the persistence of race, class, and gender inequality. Perhaps it is because Fanon's texts were critical components of my coming-of-age experience and, more importantly, argued for the unconditional use of physical violence in order to re-create the lost humanity of erstwhile colonized populations, that in this text I offer ethnographic data to support a broader, more complex, and more nuanced meaning of how we might consider redefining violence and, by extension, the lives of the female descendants of the colonization experience, including both those who were privileged by it and those who were stigmatized by it.

What I am suggesting here, instead, is both a recalibration and deliberate expansion of the meaning of violence not only as a way to recognize its practice by the gender that historically was not (and some argue still is not) officially eligible for self-earned high economic status but *also* to suggest a way to talk about a taboo subject: a female form of war or fratricide.[52] In addition, it provides a parachute or way of escaping the dialectic in which violence is either physical or nonexistent. Admittedly, the examples from the research site are typically what most of us mean by violence: blood is shed, and/or one's physical survival is challenged, and for some reason the individual or group manages to survive. Beyond this kind of physical conflict, most Americans do not think they have experienced violence, even when it is labeled as "bullying," "racial or gender discrimination," or the like (see chapter 3). However, as I argue here, these are exemplars of the misrecognition so prevalent in the genre of violence that is both so common and so pervasive in our everyday lives. Paradoxically, it is social groups or individuals who are officially (and unofficially) blocked—some would say "bullied"—by state-approved rules and regulations who are more likely to misrecognize their involvement in the extant drama and, at the same time, fight the hardest to escape their perceived subjugation, their consignment to a pariah social status, *by fighting to become a part of it.*[53]

The quest for integration during the civil rights movement is a case in point. People of African ancestry embraced unconditionally nonviolent strategies in order to gain acceptance into the existing hierarchical, race- and gender-biased social system that had historically (and violently) excluded them through normalized and legal practices: enslavement, Jim Crowism, de jure segregation.[54]

Fieldwork: Among (and for) Literate Populations

As a North Americanist (like many contemporary anthropologists— but still by far a minoritized person, not just in numbers but also in status within the discipline), I have launched my primary and most significant research projects in social contexts that are profoundly literate, which differs from the dominant and dominating historical legacy of anthropology as an academic discipline. As countless anthropologists have noted, including, for example, Caroline Bretell in her *When They Read What We Write* (and all the contributors to her seminal edited volume) and Donald Messerschmidt in his collection *Anthropologists at Home in North America,* anthropologists who opt to study in and among literate populations who share their native language run a much greater risk of having their work broadly criticized, scrutinized, and interrogated.[55]

Moreover, while ethnographers habitually protect the privacy of the people who agree to share their insider knowledge (in all contexts), assigning them pseudonyms and changing identifying details about their lives, studies that are "at home" are much more likely to draw attention to these issues. Typically, in these contexts, ethnographers are obligated to create composite characters, sometimes theorizing them as Weberian ideal types that have heuristic value. I have reluctantly embraced that practice here. To unconditionally honor my confidentiality pledge to school officials to protect the study participants, their parents, the school, and school officials, I have made every effort to deeply conceal who they are.[56] For example, I would have been able to get approval of the research population and gain access to the classroom observations and diary (journal) constructions in a shorter period of time had I been willing—in exchange for the needed funds—to give the institution where I was employed the social security numbers of the students who signed the consent forms for participation in the study. I adamantly refused and funded this component of the work myself because I promised to protect the people who entrusted me with their stories.

Against this background, I have approached the task of conveying the truths of my subjects' lives while shielding them from the embarrassment and pain that being identified would entail in a particular way—and of course, with their consent. In keeping with the sense that Americans like me are displaced bodies—both literally and figuratively—I have constructed composite portraits that retain the integrity of my informants' voices while displacing their bodies.[57] The words of my informants are quoted directly as taken from their diaries, our interviews, and my field notes.[58] But their bodies have migrated. They have been mixed and merged into divisions that reflect the racial categories recognized and normalized at the school and within the society at large. Each voice is that of a single informant, confined in the privacy of her diaries, conversations with me in formal and informal interviews, and the pages of my field notes. Like me and most other Americans of African ancestry, the narrated bodies—both Black and White—in this text are composites; but each young woman's words are hers and hers alone.

Structure of the Book

As noted above, this book is not a traditional ethnographic study. Stated differently, this is neither your mother's (nor your father's or grandparents') ethnography, in that it blurs the boundary between two dominating, albeit disconnected genres, ethnography and narration, making it a hybrid of these two distinct writing traditions.

It is divided into three sections. The first section is made up of chapters 1 and 2. It frames both the violence connected to the autoethnographic narrative of the anthropologist and larger anthropologically specific theoretical issues and also provides an overview of the research site, including a detailed description of how the study was done. This personal and professional framing shapes and expands the definitions and meanings of the key concepts, adding to the debates about what it means to be violent and female, and specifically about what it means to be a successful female—as a teenager and as an adult. It is the blurring of narrative and traditional ethnographic boundaries that inform this complex analysis of how deeply ensconced gender-specific practices and behaviors fuel what is not well known as symbolic violence.

In chapter 1 I present the theoretical framework for this book. This includes the important recent anthropological and popular-culture research on traditional or physical violence and female (gender)–specific violence. I look expressively at what is best known as relational aggression (aka "intimate apartheid" and "frenemies") through the prism of symbolic violence and the way its perceived ordinariness, normality, or blandness is implicated in its misrecognition among school officials and the entire student body, especially the females who consented to participate in the study. This chapter is devoted to chronicling the anthropological theoretical claims shaping the ethnographic data presented in this book, especially as they are related to the society's major social categories: race, class, and particularly the intersectionality of race and gender. It is here that I propose a theory of gender-specific competition in which the often hidden and/or misrecognized objective of female competition is to lose—in order to win. Indeed, I argue here that in female aggression, bullying, and competition (ABC), losing is rewarded, and hence one needs to keep one's competiveness deeply hidden and masked in order to avoid accusations of being powerful and/or male identified.

Chapter 2 provides a historical and contemporary overview of the internal structure of the school and the larger community in which it is embedded. It chronicles how today's inequality in what one researcher identifies as "the promised land" (that is, suburbia) replicates the larger social, cultural, and economic forces that are implicated in the school's academic practices and racial and gender expectations.[59] Further, it is in this chapter that my "nomadic subjectivities" and positionalities as an ethnographer are recorded, propelling me to disclose how my perceived marginalization caused me both to flounder and to embrace the way I was viewed in the social context, so much so that I have elected in chapter 2 and the following chapters to write about myself as if I were she—in the third person, as either "the anthropologist" or "the researcher"—concurrently distancing and protecting the core me.[60] It is also in this chapter that I reveal how the study was done, highlighting the problems of obtaining the population of Black and White female students and showing how the teachers', school administrators', and the Black and White parents' perceptions of my identity compelled me to embrace—often unwittingly—their nomadic distorted constructions of me and those of the Black (and White) female students who participated in the study.[61]

The second section of the book is made up of five ethnographic narratives of teenage girls—Nadine, Brittany, Keyshia, Chloe, and Ally.[62] Written in the second person, each case study represents my attempt to, first and foremost, protect the identity of the study participants and their parents and my attempt to speak *to* rather than *for* them. Second, since I could not include in this book the narratives of all twenty girls who consented to be a part of the study, I have elected to condense and encapsulate the twenty study participants' stories into five distinct narratives, each a composite, highlighting the common themes in the racialized and gendered voices of the Black, White, and biracial girls. Thus, by condensing and channeling their voices in the five seamless narratives included here, I am able to reveal more about them (as well as about their parents, peers, and school officials), highlighting what I learned from them as racial and gender categories at the school.

The powder keg of intraclass and intrarace issues among Black students is seriously understudied—both at this research site and in the larger Black community—especially the intraracial, contested interactions of Black female students. I argue here that these intrarace class differences are exacerbated in this racially charged predominantly White school. Using this strategy, I am also able to chronicle and document the Black girls' class-specific interactions with each other and with the more powerful White—and biracial—girls at the school, who are, unwittingly, both victims and perpetrators with "nomadic subjectivities."[63]

In the third and final section—the conclusion—I briefly revisit the ethnographic data and chronicle what the study detailed here tells us about anthropological theory and educational practices that compel the readers to be convinced of the need to excavate, resuscitate, and rehabilitate our understanding and meaning of violence—albeit identified by another name.

CHAPTER 1

Frenemies and Friendly Fire at Underground Railroad High

Any situation in which some individuals prevent others from engaging in the process of inquiry is one of violence. The means used are not important: to alienate human beings from their own decision-making is to change them into objects.

—Paulo Freire, *Pedagogy of the Oppressed*

Misrecognition, Complicity, and Symbolic Violence

"Friendly fire" and official warfare: what do these two have in common? Harm, in an exquisite variety of forms. Death. Mutilation. Frayed reputations. The outcomes of each are damaging, regardless of whether the fire is deliberately hostile or from supposed comrades-in-arms, allies, buddies, or sisters. In warfare, harm is expected, even demanded. In friendly fire, however, harm is officially described as unintentional—a regrettable accident. In nonmilitary contexts, where physical violence is less valorized, friendly fire—known variously as "relational aggression," "passive aggression," "violence," and "bullying," among other terms—is the product of what Pierre Bourdieu termed *méconnaissance*, translated as "misrecognition."[1] In other words, members of a group, for example, female African Americans, are misrecognized as enemy others.

Méconnaissance or misrecognition best characterizes the interactions not only between and among the Black and White girls who are the focus of this research study, but also within the school administration, the community in which it is situated, and the nation at large. While both groups of girls readily acknowledge their gendered subordination, like most Americans, they fail to see how their socially ascribed racial genes compel them to be seen and to see themselves as enemy others. By misrecognizing and eschewing the interlocking power arrangements that reproduce their subordination and focusing instead on the behaviors and practices of individual members, they unintentionally perpetuate their subordination. *Méconnaissance* or misrecognition is the central frame here because bullying and violence are misrecognized and freely and willfully engaged in on a daily basis by the students and everyone else at the research site. It is the participants' ongoing, structurally sanctioned engagement in passive or relational violence that is at the center of their friendly fire.

Social theorists and community activists[2] insist that the most prevalent kind of noncombat violence among nations or individuals can be accurately defined as "symbolic" violence.[3] This takes many forms, including imagery and language, and holds numerous meanings.

Pierre Bourdieu and Loïc Wacquant's essay "Symbolic Violence" offers the most accessible and meaningful definition of this concept.[4] They insist that this kind of violence is "exercised upon a social agent with his or her complicity," with his or her consent.[5] It is important to acknowledge that these authors do not intend to negate the existence of other, more recognizable forms of violence (such as mutilation, murder, lynching) as they relate to gender. It is sometimes assumed, they note, that symbolic violence

> minimizes the role of physical violence ... [makes] people
> forget ... that there are battered, raped and exploited women,
> or worse, to seek to exculpate men from that form of violence—
> which is obviously not the case. Understanding "symbolic" as the
> opposite of "real, actual," people suppose that symbolic violence is
> a purely "spiritual" violence, which ultimately has no real effects.[6]

This symbolic domination, brought about not through conscious behavior but through habit and social normality, produces what Bourdieu terms "symbolic force." This more extensive definition is most significant in the case of Black girls at UGRH, the site of the study reported in this book. He asserts:

> Symbolic force is a form of power that is exerted on bodies, directly and as if by magic, without any physical constraint; but this magic works only on the basis of dispositions deposited, like springs, at the deepest level of the body . . . [and] it does no more than trigger [those] dispositions that the work of inculcation and embodiment has deposited in those who are thereby primed for it.[7]

In other words, symbolic gender violence is primarily effective because of its habitual character, which produces its sense of normality and "naturalness." According to Bourdieu, as we learn appropriate gender norms, these "springs" are deeply embedded in our subconscious, making it unnecessary for the individual to exert energy weighing competing options.[8] This practice promotes "nondecision-making" and produces the habitual outcome that results in the wake of a culturally prescribed normality.[9] It shapes the mind so that we are incapable of seeing that what was initially learned was one of *many* available options—not the *only* option.

Culturally appropriate humans are compelled to valorize one narrative or socialized practice over all others, and they reason that the first-learned practices are inevitably "natural." This leads unavoidably to the subordination and exclusion of all other possibilities and to an inclination to avoid change. Indeed, many researchers have argued that what we learn early in life, even if we cannot recall it, is resistant to change or unlearning, remains embedded in our memory, and influences our behaviors and practices. For example, in our male-dominated society, both males and females learn the same courtship script: males should be taller, stronger, and older, should make more money, should serve as heads of households, and should make critical public and private decisions. In this script, males learn that they are expected to dominate; females learn that they are culturally appropriate if they are subordinate. In the contemporary context, where it is claimed that 40 percent of women earn more than their male partner, these women experience their financial success vis-à-vis their partners as abnormal, and many feel guilt and/or discomfort in this position.[10] Consequently, they feel out of order—gender inappropriate. We learn this metanarrative the same way we learn how to breathe: effortlessly. Learning the rules of one's native cultural practices comes to be seen as normal and natural, and women who deviate from this script—for example, by seeking to dominate in culturally proscribed ways—lose gender capital and diminish their own value and prestige.

Indeed, one could argue that the teenage girls, Black or White, who are the recipients of passive or misrecognized violence are similar in many ways to what Lani Guinier and Gerald Torres describe as "the miner's canary."[11] Their predicament is an initial warning of the unseen and unacknowledged poisonous gender relationships between and among the Black and White girls not only at the school but also in the community, the state, and by extension, the nation. The (Black) female victims provide indisputable empirical evidence that, at least at this school—Underground Railroad High—gender relationships are deformed. School officials and the community at large often claim that they have taken and continue to take appropriate measures to revise extant educational, behavioral, and social practices in order to save the educational goals and aspirations of all female students, especially the Black girls.[12] But have they, and do they?

Frenemies and Enemies: Is It Meanness if It Is Not Seen?

As noted earlier, in most Euro-American contexts, symbolic violence is both pervasive and unacknowledged. It acts as a stealth bomber, present and invisible. This kind of violence embodies what we tend to think of as progress. It is deemed a powerful form of social control, yet cultures that regularly utilize it, even in the United

States, are invariably viewed as progressive and civilized. This is unlike the more "barbaric" underdeveloped sibling states, such as the terrorist group Boko Haram in Nigeria or ISIS in Iraq, which utilize physical force, or at least the threat of coercion. Since physical violence, as traditionally defined and identified, is both outlawed and disparaged within "civilized" societies, preferred social controls and management of individuals must be enculturated through gender-appropriate methods that disavow "barbaric" social practices such as strong or direct language, spanking, scolding, and the like. The presumed markers of civilization are the normalized "soft" rules of engagement promulgated, practiced, and sanctioned by race- and gender-defined elites.[13]

Intriguingly, the most widely used form of symbolic violence is language, in its broadest sense. According to Veena Das, language is the space where suffering is not only (mis)recognized but is even socially appreciated.[14] As used here, "language" includes images and logic as well as speech. There are many examples of gender-specific images, but some are more emblematic than others. For example, plastic surgeons are routinely deployed to perform nose jobs and eye lifts. Stylists and beauticians are charged with changing hair texture and color as part of an unending quest for long, straight, blond hair—arguably the quintessential symbol of both Whiteness and femininity.[15] Indeed, in the pursuit of hegemonic normality among adults, plastic surgery, psychology, psychiatry, therapy, and other acceptable nonbrutal means of achieving "disciplined bodies" are routinely engaged.[16]

While language is the most widely used example of symbolic violence, it is rarely recognized as such. Language, like female aggression, is rendered invisible and is seldom taken seriously when it tends toward the symbolic. Male violence, on the other hand, is readily recognized because of its overt physicality. This difference is evidenced in language when we demote "violence" among women to "aggression," although it is clearly much more. Some females treat one another as "frenemies," concurrently friends and enemies, a ubiquitous, permanent feature of most women's lives, attacking others while pretending to be their friends.[17] Frenemies are the miner's canaries writ large and are everywhere: the cashier at the grocery store; the school principal, the teacher, and the teacher's aide at your child's school; your graduate advisee or advisor; your magazine or book editor; the church ladies, church secretary, ushers, and deaconesses; your husband's administrative assistant; your biological and symbolic sisters; and even your mother in some instances. With female social boundaries being fluid, contested, and unstable, it is difficult to distinguish between who is and who is not a friend.

Frenemies, the producers of friendly fire, engage in practices that mimic Bourdieu's definition of habitus: "the space and place where structure and agency dissolve."[18] The boundaries between friend and enemy evaporate, rendering any harm that emerges as unintentional, misrecognized, or interpreted as accidental. However, is that harm really inadvertent in female-specific interactions across racial lines?

Socially constructed with highly porous sensibilities, female relationships easily hemorrhage, affecting everything and everyone in their orbit. Frenemies occupy this space primarily because, as the word suggests, they both embody and disembody the most valued currency in women's lives: intimate knowledge. Intimacy, the third rail of female relationships, is characterized by porosity—a leaky, permeable closeness bloated with details, personal knowledge, and competition—and is the engine that drives female-to-female relationships. Generally, women do not trust other women. They are even less likely to trust those who are unwilling to share the inner sanctities of their lives.[19] They are caught in a catch-22. On the one hand, hegemonic female friendship is not possible without intimacy, yet on the other, women use intimate information against each other. The individual who is willing to share intimate information about herself, to share pain, humiliation, and failure, for example, is often misrecognized as a friend. She is unequivocally assumed to be empathetic, affable, and loyal when in truth she is much more likely to be putting on friendly airs or quietly plotting the demise of others. A woman needs to know every minute detail of another woman's life in order to measure her ability to compete, to determine whether she is on a level playing field. Cross-culturally, girls are rewarded for working harder and achieving more only to lose. Subordinate advances and intermittent opportunities—vis-à-vis their male (White) counterparts—substantiate that girls, despite earnest efforts and progress, compete only to lose. Elsewhere, I discuss forms of competition as "competing to lose," which Dale Spender and Elizabeth Sarah also discuss in their book *Learning to Lose*.[20] Competing to lose encompasses recognizing the "transactions between body and language" to be able to endure the suffering that is inevitable in the construction of a life "that has to be lived in loss."[21]

This idea of "loss" or suffering is considered gender appropriate for females and is tacitly placed in categories similar to what Arlie Hochschild identifies as emotional labor, which, she insists,

> requires one to induce or suppress feeling in order to sustain the outward countenance that produces the proper state of mind in others. . . . This kind of labor calls for a coordination of mind and feeling, and it sometimes draws on a source of self that we honor as deep and integral to our individuality.[22]

Admittedly, in America's capitalist society, all citizens and noncitizens are compelled to embrace emotional labor, especially in work or the professional arena. However, there appears to be a special requirement for emotional labor on the part of women—regardless of race—and all categories of minority groups, but especially female bodies cloaked in "indebtedness."[23] Compelled to display what one writer has dubbed "commercial love" and another, "skin teeth," individuals identified as female—especially minority and female—are expected to show their gratitude in perpetuity.[24] This emotional labor takes an enormous toll on the psyche and well-being of those individuals.

Winning? The Gray Zone of Female Academic Performance

Like most social scientists, anthropologists have been derelict in addressing what Renato Rosaldo describes as "the cultural forces of emotions."[25] Traditionally, anthropologists—who until fairly recently were overwhelmingly male—have eschewed studies of social life that might claim a lack of objectivity since, in the Western tradition, to be objective is to be devoid of emotions. Instead, they cloaked themselves in what is known as logic and rationality. In striking contrast, describing an individual as being emotional is tantamount to describing her as lacking intellect, the most valued currency in academia. Consequently, to focus on the emotional aspect of social life customarily identified with women is to seek/(re)produce contempt and oblivion. Against this backdrop, the lack of understanding and analysis of the "cultural forces of emotions" is readily apparent.

This book challenges the widely practiced binary approach to Euro-American social life, arguing instead for a perspective in which the "gray zone"—a "zone of ambiguity which radiates out . . . [creating] terror and obsequiousness"—is front and center.[26] Das makes a similar claim, arguing that what is most baffling about the birth of India—the very moment official colonization and attendant domination ended—is the way the desire for nationalism was, ironically, inscribed on the bodies of native women (but not men) in the form of "brutal rape and abduction."[27] She insists that this level of violence was massive, wreaking unprecedented emotional, psychic, and physical pain. This violence was perpetrated, she maintains, not by the erstwhile colonialists but by the native peoples of India: Hindu men against Muslim women and Muslim men against Hindu women.

In the American context, a similar case can be made regarding ongoing violence, both physical and relational, against the descendants of enslaved Black women.[28] Following Gerald Early, I describe how Black women, both historically and contemporarily, are simultaneously "lure[d] and loath[ed]," their bodies sites of ghastly loss and pain.[29]

Historians, anthropologists, and many others have repeatedly documented the pain and loss that is epidemic in Black women's lives. Anthropologists have repeatedly noted the ways that humans are inevitably constrained by their society's socially approved structure and gender roles. But at the same time our analyses of the interracial, intragender achievement gap can best be characterized, at least in the case of American females, as masked by the claim of a one-dimensional—that is, one size fits all—sisterhood. Repeatedly, researchers make claims about girls' academic performance as if this gendered category were undifferentiated by such factors as race, ethnicity, class, or disability. This is standard practice—a common response of researchers—even in research studies that include subjects who self-identify and are identified as being from different social, racial, and ethnic groups.[30]

The quintessential embodiment of the "good girl" is the one characteristic that most women self-report as being critical to academic and social success. However, for the privileged female body, an additional requirement is the body image most clearly manifested by weight loss, or by being short and thin.[31] Thinness is probably the single most salient marker of femaleness and quintessential female identity, making the widely known dictum "Size matters" appropriate in reverse.[32]

In her book *Woman's Inhumanity to Woman*, Phyllis Chesler acknowledges that most of us are horrified to learn that a female has committed an act of physical violence. She chronicles some of the most egregious nonphysical acts of violence against women, pointing out, in the process, that other women, not men, committed these relational acts of aggression.[33] Women, she argues, are complex human beings whose forced subordination compels them to seek status enhancement and power while appearing not to do so and to disguise their power and prestige strategies beneath a veneer of "do-goodism" and total conformity.

In her book *The Power of Good Deeds,* Diana Kendall shares the narrative of an elite (White) woman named Sherry:

> I learned dance steps and I learned how to eat like a lady. This is true. But what I really learned is how to compete without appearing to be competitive. The underlying message that I got was that you have to compete for social recognition, you have to compete for boyfriends and for adult adoration, *but you have to appear to be cooperative rather than aggressive.*[34]

Kendall goes on to assert that one of the primary duties of elite (White) females is social reproduction: "the replication of the social structures and class relationships that characterize a society and, especially, the right to maintain the privileged position of one's family within society."[35] The widespread practice among elite and upper-class women of excluding all who do not share their monochromatic strip, she insists, is most visible in self-imposed geographic isolation, in the creation of "a social bubble," which most often is framed as a desire for safety. In this isolated space, elite women teach their children appropriate academic, professional, and social skills that will empower them to reproduce their parents' elite status and family connections. But is this a primary way to maintain not only Whiteness but also what is widely considered academic achievement?

Setha Low's research on gated communities is suggestive, arguing that the first commandment in such communities is "niceness," a euphemism that is often equated with Whiteness. She chronicles the way the fear of others built into the homogenization and racialization of geographic spaces fuels fear and the unconditional desire for "surveillance and purified spaces."[36] While her research is limited to residential communities in Texas and Long Island, New York, other researchers have noted a similar practice when it comes to the Whiteness of the most academically challenging programs in most schools, the advanced-placement (AP) and the gifted-and-talented programs, nationally.[37] It does not seem far-fetched to point out that, like the gated residential communities that Low studied, the AP and the gifted-and-talented programs in most schools are identified as property and are designed to maintain their value by excluding students generally identified as not White.[38] Interestingly, most of the work of exclusion is accomplished through the un- or undercompensated labor known as volunteerism and the efforts of White and elite women. For example, Kathleen Barlow and Elaine Dunbar studied gifted-and-talented programs, as volunteers, for fifteen years. Using Cheryl Harris's theoretical model of "Whiteness as property," and based on their observations of various efforts both to dismantle such programs and to improve the identification of appropriate Black and other non-White students for the programs, they argue that the perks of these programs are systematically reserved or held hostage to the "opportunity hoarding" of elite, or at least affluent, White families.[39] Stated differently, these families' unearned historical privilege is reinforced and maintained primarily by the uncompensated labor of the women in these families.

In their book *Corporate Tribalism: White Men/White Women and Cultural Diversity at Work*, Thomas Kochman and Jean Mavrelis document the ways the gender-specific practices of White women are generally counterproductive in the workplace as compared with the dominance of White male practices and the ongoing subordination of women who are othered. They show that the hegemonic practices of White men in the workplace undermine the goals and aspirations of White women, who in turn compel Black women and other women of color to embrace what Kochman and Mavrelis term "power dead even."[40] This "everybody is equal" positioning suggests, simply, that no one is expected to have more or be more than anyone else. Consider the White women in the corporate workplace:

> CWW [corporate White women] are preoccupied first and
> foremost . . . with what other people need or want [which] is
> motivated by their own need to be liked, loved, and accepted
> and to protect themselves against backstabbing, which leads to

loss of relationships and [forced] social isolation. [They] grew up
with direct or indirect messages that pleasing mother was more
important than pleasing oneself. This pattern was reinforced in
school by peers along with a "go along to get along" mindset. Part
of being a [corporate White woman] is to stay attuned to power
dead even. *What is important is not to have more than others. Direct
competition, which requires mastery and leads to recognition, is not
valued.*[41]

What is more interesting is that women who do not live by this
hegemonic norm of "power dead even" are labeled "bitch" or "slut."
This is a cardinal feature of White female culture.[42] Women who
are othered are forced to embrace silence and/or other markers of
subordination in order to be unconditionally acceptable.

In looking at competition between and among younger females,
a primary question is whether high self-esteem and academic success
are correlated in some way. If so, we might ask, are girls who display
hubris and behaviors that are generally associated with males and
high self-esteem (such as assertiveness and independence) and
who engage in practices such as displaying self-confidence and promoting one's accomplishments rewarded in ways that are indistinguishable from the ways their male peers are rewarded? Research
indicates just the opposite. In American culture, self-esteem is a
gender-mediated human need, differentially rewarded in males and
females, especially during early adolescence. While it has been empirically documented that high self-esteem promotes male academic
achievement, how self-esteem is implicated in female achievement
is less clear. Indeed, I argue that perhaps the only flaw in Abraham
Maslow's otherwise brilliant analysis of the hierarchy of human
needs is his failure to acknowledge that self-esteem—both as a tech-
nical concept in the psychological sense and in its more common
everyday usage—is gender mediated.[43]

In light of Maslow's significant omission, I propose this explanation for the male–female performance gap and the laceration of
Black girls' high academic achievement: when girls' self-comparisons

to other girls are examined, it appears that it is low, not high, self-esteem that fuels academic achievement.[44] These gaps in academic achievement (both male–female and female–female) exist in social contexts worldwide. This analysis teases out the entangled threads of academic achievement gaps in a more systematic manner, attempting to sort out the specific benefits and costs of Black girls' penchant—both inadvertent and deliberate—for transgressing socially approved gender-specific roles.

In my earlier works, I argued that Black American girls' visibility—their "loudness," their reluctance to hide or mask their confidence in the school context—was and is a form of resistance that, regrettably and unintentionally, nurtures their academic failure.[45] Building on this, it is easy to appreciate how Barbara Coloroso's idea of contempt as terror is smeared to innocuous cultural images of desire and protection in a male-dominated social system.[46] Of those issues surrounding the nonprevalence of achievement for Black girls, competition is the most important. In America's racialized, male-dominated society, femaleness and overt competition are like oil and water: incompatible. Binary gender division chokes off success and power to members of this culture who are socially defined as female, and power in public life comes primarily to those who are willing and able to compete. This is true regardless of gender or racial identity.

Achievement and competition, though major forces in academia, are also related to the everyday intergender and intragender symbolic violence that young girls face—especially Black girls.[47] Regarding friendly fire between Black and White females at UGRH, we could argue that friendly fire is nothing more than a sleight of hand. In female-to-female interactions, while harm is intended (all violence is intended to harm), it is not supposed to be detectable or visible. Social actors engaging in these aggressive patterns, then, could accurately be described as nonwarriors; they neither arm themselves with what is widely associated with violent combat (guns, knives, or any other traditional weapons) nor view themselves as combatants. Indeed, their weapons are widely believed to be benign: words and language, smiles, empathy, and bountiful caring, that is, helping. They are the embodiment of frenemies.[48]

The major problem with the growing body of literature on female aggression is that it is uneven, heavily freighted with issues as they affect White girls, but not Black girls or other girls of color.[49] Known variously as "relational aggression," "indirect aggression," or "alternative aggression," violence underlies all female relationships and intimacy. This female-specific anger/aggression is not well understood. The situation of Black girls in the school context is best conveyed in the title of Rachel Simmons's book, *Odd Girl Out: The Hidden Culture of Aggression in Girls* (adapted for film in 2005).[50] African American females, as "odd girls out" at UGRH, are silently bullied and excluded by the hegemonic, socially approved, and more genteel practices generally affiliated with elite White American girls. Indeed, all girls' gender-specific "warfare" is subversive, shrouded beneath an invisible veneer of politeness and civility. With this invisibility, according to a preponderance of research, persons observing these intragroup and intergroup social exchanges are led to strange conclusions. They see the perceived victims, the girls whose reactions are visible (for example, they cry and/or whine to the teacher or other school officials), as the bullies and perpetrators of the socially aggressive acts. This is a total inversion since what appears to be is not at all what it is—a classic example of misrecognition.

For instance, Simmons repeatedly notes that (White) female anger (aggression, meanness, and so on) is an inappropriate emotion.[51] She also notes that "high-achieving African American girls can and often do dissociate psychologically and make self-alienating choices, becoming silent as they move deeper into mainstream White American culture—attempting to avoid raising the ire of others who might resent their successes."[52] Similarly, Sharon Lamb notes that when talking with adult (White) women who were known as "good girls" in adolescence, she found that they repeatedly acknowledged having led "double live[s]," being "sweet, innocent, lovely and well-behaved . . . in public" while privately "playing sexual games, writ[ing] angry passages in their diaries, and act[ing] out aggressively."[53] Moreover, she claims that these erstwhile good girls, like their contemporary counterparts, admitted to behaving in ways that were limited to women whom they defined as "stupid," not as intelligent as they saw (or perceived) themselves to be.[54] These analyses are also supported in the nongendered analysis offered by Coloroso, who insists that there are "no innocent bystanders."[55] Adding insult to injury, individuals standing on the sidelines—the audience—often rapidly fuel the conflict.

By juxtaposing my earlier works with emerging popular research (that is, showing that hegemonic female aggression is inevitably hidden and shrouded in secrecy, while male aggression is direct and publicly displayed), I document that among Black and White American females at UGRH, the bully is the person who often appears to be the victim.[56] Moreover, because the victim is the bully in gender-specific, racially differentiated female competition, socially approved corrective actions, including school-sanctioned policies to limit female-initiated physical violence and other gender-specific aggressions, are misdirected. These actions only further victimize the girls erroneously labeled as bullies, and unintentionally empower their "victims." This problem is particularly relevant when comparing the norms observed primarily by White American girls and the largely White American teaching force in the public school system. Indeed, Black–White female aggression—these girls' socially defined racial apartness and their otherness to each other—exacerbates their attempts to avoid intragender conflicts and to belong to the common system of female subordination. Hence the claim made here: because African American girls are generally constructed as outsiders, they are the "odd girls out."

In her book *The Bully, the Bullied, and the Bystander,* Coloroso insists that in situations where bullying is involved, neither anger nor conflict is the issue. Instead, she asserts, contempt, which she defines as "a powerful feeling of dislike toward somebody considered to be worthless, inferior, or undeserving of respect," is the driving force.[57] Applying her definition of contempt to the school and societal divisions of the girls at UGRH (White–Black, beautiful–ugly, passive–aggressive, nice–not nice, and so on), the White girls are buoyed by binary language that substantiates their image of themselves while validating their contempt for Black girls by way of silent messages, messages that reemphasize that Black girls are not pretty, they do not have long bouncy hair, they are Black and not White, they do not observe the rules that White girls know (but are only episodically compelled to observe), and so on. In striking contrast, Black girls' efforts to marshal language against White girls' violations of school rules and practices are deliberately denied and routinely rendered impotent. The reasons vary, but much of it has to do with the inadequacy of the linguistic images Black girls attempt to evoke. For example, a Black girl calling a White girl a "slut" is ineffective because that is not an image readily associated with White girls, especially White girls who are identified as upper class. As Primo Levi acknowledges, "privilege, by definition, defends and protects privilege."[58]

Culturally prescribed powerlessness poses a real problem for all women, especially for White women. When femaleness merges with Whiteness, power is assumed, compelling females who are socially identified as White to disidentify with their Whiteness. Because Whiteness is embodied—an unearned advantage—the privilege affiliated with power is difficult, in fact nearly impossible, to avoid. For many upper-class White women, this nuanced connection to Whiteness is neither understood nor, if understood, embraced. Because they see themselves as having only one identity or gender, their disidentification with Whiteness is unmarked. They see themselves as women only, devoid of a racial identity. What is more interesting is that White women frequently deploy strategies to suppress their connection to Whiteness. These strategies include denial, marriage (and other intimate relationships) with men of color, excessive focus on gender, and a fierce commitment to social justice, denying that they benefit from the food, shelter, and wealth of men (fathers, husbands, brothers, male cousins, friends, and so on). It is men, after all, who are the quintessential exemplars of privilege affiliated with Whiteness, and by extension, masters of the universe. Thus, it is from this privileged position that White women often have the luxury of taking on social justice issues because the stakes are much lower for them.

The bodies and discourse practices of Black and White girls are diametrically opposed, as I often observed at UGRH, but they are both under surveillance. As Michel Foucault noted in *Discipline and Punish*, constant surveillance exists to produce "docile bodies," bodies that do not need external force to accept and obey existing norms of behavior, embodied in the saying "I'm just doing my job."[59] In the more literal sense, Black girls use language to resist the constraints related to their position in the social hierarchy and to reflect their desire for power.[60] By contrast, White girls use language, tone, and voice projection to concurrently embrace and distance themselves from Whiteness and its attendant affiliation with power.[61]

Because the social imagery of White girls is understood to be the exemplar of gender appropriateness and desired by everyone at UGRH (including the Black girls who resist it, primarily through avoidance), girls are rewarded academically as well as socially for embodying what is culturally defined as normality. Girls who are identified with Whiteness are forced to enter what approximates a "gray zone," mimicking and accurately reflecting the White girls' unacknowledged power.[62] Despite the White girls' efforts to disidentify with their own whiteness, their closely aligned gender-appropriate appearance, logic, and speech practices structure the lives of all girls at UGRH—if those girls seek normality. The idealization and idolization of this normality discredits other ways of constructing reality. Therefore, what is socially defined as "natural" merges with what school executives define as "official," creating, in the process, disembodied individuals. In this context, disembodied Black and Brown girls are expected to embrace practices affiliated with White girls that are also defined as "naturally feminine" and rendered neutral.

The Omnipresence, Invisibility, and Toxicity of Gendered Racism

Following Messay Kebede, my goal is to rehabilitate our understanding of violence.[63] I want to show the ways by which deeply ensconced, gender-specific practices and behaviors fuel what is widely known as symbolic violence, and how they compel young girls to replicate rather than transform these practices.

Elsewhere I have repeatedly noted the saliency of Whiteness or privilege in American society, including its impact on the academic performance of Black students at Capital High.[64] My claims have been hotly debated among a wide range of researchers in many disciplines, including psychology.[65] Popular media such as *Time* magazine, CBS's *Evening News,* the *Washington Post,* the *New York Times,* the *Boston Globe,* the *Toronto Star,* and the *London Times* have cited and reported my work in ways that do not accurately represent my anthropological research or my published findings. These researchers and journalists have enhanced, and in some instances altered, the debate.[66]

As I initially defined it, at the core of acting White is the idea of behaving as if one were entitled to integral aspects of being an American citizen. Entitlements such as living in any neighborhood one desires, matriculating at the school of one's choice, being able to obtain the job that one desires and that meshes with one's skills, marrying the person of one's choice without regard for his or her racial identity, and voting without additional qualifications beyond residence and citizenship evoke images of the American ideal. However, in the context of American racial stratification, acting White is an act of collective self-assertion, claiming as rights privileges that have previously been reserved for Whites only. For Americans whose ancestors were enslaved in this country, it means unconditionally embracing the institutions and practices created and treated as the historical prerogative of White Americans and declared off-limits to enslaved Africans and their descendants.

Acting White thus epitomizes the strangeness of being concurrently erased and embraced, displaced and calcified, perceived in both instances as bodies out of place. In addition to the academic difficulty (White) discourse styles lend to Blacks, researchers have also failed to acknowledge that for Black students, academic achievement in general is particularly challenging. Despite their historical exclusion from America's one remaining obligatory institution, they are required to be indistinguishable from their White peers in academic achievement and performance, norms, values, behavior, and practices.

Whiteness is a soft violence—a stealth bomber. In UGRH, a typical suburban school, Whiteness is purity personified. Here, without the usual images of violence—including dirt, germs, drugs, overt signs of racial animosity, vile, sexist language tethered to the commandment to "use your inside voice," and other widely recognized indicators of danger—Black girls are anesthetized, impelled to think and believe they are safe.

But they are not. What the Black girls misrecognize is that the price they are forced to pay in their quest for a nonracial identity—as promulgated by school policies, school officials, and by extension the nation at large—is loss of both a personal and a collective Black identity or integrity. Like all of America's schoolchildren, Black (and other) girls are taught a concrete version of democracy and the presumed meritocracy and even, in striking contrast, the shortcomings and evilness of other forms of social organization. Their inability to embody the goodness of Whiteness compels them to distance themselves from it. Responding to official documents and transcripts that repeatedly warn them of the dangers lurking in the schools in their native communities,[67] the Black girls and their parents, ironically, simultaneously run from the known, abnormal dangers in the Black community and, unknowingly, toward the misrecognized normal dangers that engulf them at UGRH.[68]

The absence of familiar forms of violence—physical aggression, gunfights, gang activities, open drug dealing, murder—means that the Black students, especially the Black females, are unaware of the toxin that permeates this allegedly safe social space. Because the school is modern—devoid of the debris signaling academic wastelands in their former schools and communities—they are urged to forswear their usual cultural practices and responses and ignore the real, but invisible, pathogens at the school, especially the commoditization of Black bodies in conventional pastimes (such as playing basketball or running track). In what is considered the core academic areas of the classrooms, they are compelled to act White, to disrobe culturally, completely jettisoning culturally appropriate, gender-specific linguistic practices and behaviors valorized in the Black community and closely associated with their skin color.

I argue that Whiteness is a synonym for social capital and power, and that this power often breeds unmarked violence. However, the kind of violence that is the subject of the analysis here is, like Whiteness, unmarked.

The violence that affects the Black girls at UGRH parallels what is idealized in postracial America: interactions wherein racial and gender boundaries are blurred, intimacy is highlighted, and violence, because of its habitual character, is misrecognized and invisible—like the air they breathe. The lack of air—the violence invisibly inflicted—represents being Black in a culture dominated by the promulgation of Whiteness. The soft gentleness of normative Whiteness is an appropriate metaphor for the sensibilities that dominate most social interactions at this point in Euro-American history. In America, we want human interactions to be easy, devoid of physicality and real effort, to be interactions wherein authoritative, overt physicality and hostility are replaced by a more subtle or nuanced approach to conflict in human intercourse. In our efforts to euthanize the dominant hierarchical structures and blur statuses regarding race, gender, and other formerly powerful exclusionary categories, we practice and celebrate a softer and less visible kind of discipline centered on the individual, a discipline that, paradoxically, reinforces rather than transforms existing structural social practices.[69]

In this social space, race, specifically Blackness, is constructed as a kind of "dis-ease" to be overcome.[70] This dis-ease modality permeates the ways that Black people and Blackness are perceived in the Rodman community (a pseudonym for the school district and surrounding community of my study) and in the nation at large.[71] This viewpoint is never consciously recognized, acknowledged, or admitted, which makes it impossible to provide a completely safe environment for the girls and to promote their social and academic achievement.

As a dis-ease in a social system that valorizes individualism and embraces the medicalization of social problems, race affects each Black girl at UGRH differently. However, the common social issues apparent in the girls' victimization are their self-selected racial identity and their differential commitment to that identity—both voluntarily and involuntarily. For example, Chloe's depression is inextricably intertwined with her involuntary consignment to a Black identity (see chapter 6). Indeed, she is unlikely to be depressed if not for being socially defined as Black, an identity she wholly abhors. She is unable to disentangle her Blackness from the varied threads of her identity, most critically her gender; thus, her identity as a Black person becomes a problem in search of a solution. Similar claims are evident in all the other cases presented in this book: race as privilege or stigma is the issue that each girl views as central to her predicament.

Racial Identity as Both "Nature" and Performance

The reality is that most Americans do live race-specific lives—even when they deny it. Within contemporary America, race functions simultaneously as a fluid, floating, shifting, contested, and essential socially constructed category. At the same time, it is imagined as a static, biologically immutable and distinct within-group process that compels us to believe all assigned group members share distinct racial characteristics such as constitution, temperament, and mental abilities. The ways in which the above assumptions and/or beliefs affect us are even more compelling.

As Americans, we tend to think race affects only those who are defined by or who define themselves as "not White." Even definitions of race insinuate Whiteness as favorable. Ronald Chisom and Michael Harrington of the People's Institute for Survival and Beyond define race as "the specious classification of human beings, created by European whites, that assigns human worth and social status, using White as the model of humanity and the height of human achievement, for the purpose of establishing and maintaining privilege and power."[72] Cauterizing their own fears then, everyone who does not see himself or herself as having some African or Native American ancestry is able to define race as having nothing to do with him or her personally.

However, what both Black and White Americans fail to adequately appreciate—for opposite reasons—is the inequality embedded within hidden dimensions of power that are enacted in socially constructed racial relationships. This construction leads Americans who are socially defined as Black to constantly monitor the practices and behaviors of White individuals as indicators of whether they are being treated fairly or unfairly. This is important, but minor when compared to the unacknowledged, hidden power of institutional rules and regulations.[73] Likewise, socially defined White Americans constantly monitor the behaviors and practices of "the Blacks" to make sure they follow the letter of the law (with no benefit of the doubt) and adhere to social norms and practices. This nonstop surveillance is intended to determine who is and is not a good Black and therefore eligible or ineligible for assimilation.

At UGRH, not only is race a major cultural category, but applying it is a (nearly) universal addiction. Rather than being regarded as suspect, racial categorization is taken for granted and normalized. Omnipresent physically and socially, racial ascription scorches every person who enters the school. It is misrecognized both as embodied—as belonging in bodies categorized as either Black or White—and as a performance: a matter of speech, dress, and demeanor or expressive style. People at UGRH do not seem to realize that these definitions of racial identity are contradictory; instead, they shift from one to another depending on the context.

Like race, gender is also a primary cultural category. It, too, is misrecognized, viewed both as biologically determined and as a performance. Additionally, just as race carries gendered meanings, so, too, is gender racialized. Girls from different social groups, especially those socially defined as either Black or White, are generally stripped of either their presumed gender or their racial identity, respectively. For girls defined as White, gender becomes their primary and sometimes only identity—they rarely acknowledge the White component of their identity. The opposite happens to Black girls; they lose their identity as females and become embedded in the hegemonic masculine identity that characterizes Blackness in America.

At this school, all female bodies are subject to misrecognition. Although they are racially labeled, tagged, sorted, and categorized, most of these rookie adults appear to regard this script as a meaningless benign historical relic.[74] Their color-blind stance is that the state must employ this relic for official purposes, and that it has neither immediate nor long-term consequences. Everyone has at least a rudimentary knowledge of it—even though its existence and power are often denied. This rudimentary knowledge is critical to the maintenance and reproduction of the status quo.

A White social activist highlights the Teflon-like character of race in American public and private life. His maternal grandmother, he insists, spent her entire life fighting racial discrimination and White people's denial of the humanity of people of African ancestry. Yet when she was older, suffering from Alzheimer's disease and living in a nursing home, unable to remember family members, friends, or much of anything else, she retained the ability to recall the n-word and used it repeatedly to refer to the Black workers who took care of her at the facility.[75]

I came face-to-face with these twin problems of race as a biological relic and as a performance at UGRH. The moment I entered the school I realized that I had not reached the Promised Land of a raceless or postracial America. Instead, I almost instantly became subject to misrecognition and was the target of friendly fire. My presence exacerbated the intertwined inequalities of race and gender by making visible the problems they generate.

As the only officially "raced" females at UGRH, Black and Brown girls are rewarded for abandoning their cultural knowledge and embracing the nonracial (White) school policies and practices. In this effort they become, perhaps inadvertently, complicit in threatening their own achievement. Compelled to accept the school as a nonracial White cultural space, the Black students, especially the Black girls, tend to conform to existing rules because they see that gender-appropriate conformity is rewarded, at least as it is applied to White girls.

The major issues confronting female students in general and the Black girls in particular are twofold: (1) a nonnuanced commitment to what is defined as traditional or universal; (2) an unending quest for a gender-specific normality, also known as beauty and perfection. Moreover, research suggests that both the belief that universal truths are not subject to interpretation and the desire to be mirror reflections of the most influential girls compel Black girls to see themselves as less beautiful than their White female peers, who are defined as beautiful (vis-à-vis other girls at the school) and are generally viewed favorably by their teachers.[76] This preoccupation with fitting the norm fuels the concept of symbolic violence. The Black girls are rewarded for being indistinguishable from their White female peers in dress, use of language, comportment, and, especially, hair.[77] Yet Black females whose economic class status and academic performance mimic those of their White female peers are not inoculated against or protected from the dis-ease of Blackness.[78]

The intersectionality of race and gender, especially as manifested in the lives of all females, must be included in any meaningful discussion of Whiteness.[79] Acknowledging the intersectionality of race and gender is important because of the way they affect positionality: stigma in the case of women socially defined as Black, and unearned privilege in the case of women socially defined as White. In addition, it is important because no human being has ever lived life without experiencing the desire for someone or something.

Desire, that all-encompassing human emotion, is the engine sustaining Whiteness at UGRH. As manifested at UGRH, desire is ubiquitous. But desire in all its various forms—the desire for status and validation, for comfort, for some form of legacy and continuity; the desire to discover and practice one's racial, gender, and sexual identity; the desire to practice religion without harassment; the desire to own property; and, most of all, the desire to be affirmed and/or supported—is inextricably entangled in Whiteness.[80]

Against this background, I began to see desire as a factor at the core of human exploitation. While desire is a powerful human emotion, generally wrapped in realms of banality, essentially it is the fuel of capitalism and other economic systems. In America, socially constructed race embodies desire for both Whiteness and Blackness (for vastly different reasons) but especially for Whiteness. For example, to be Black in America is to be simultaneously perceived as valueless and as a highly desired commodity or fetish, a thing. Constructed as the direct opposite of Whiteness, the cheap labor and entertainment value of the descendants of enslaved Americans is constantly revisited and evaluated. In this context, Blackness is concurrently lured and loathed, desired and despised.[81]

Whiteness, whether one sees it as a category, an ideology, or an identity, encapsulates, enacts, and embodies power, albeit invisible. In other words, it is the racial category oozing with uncontested desire. Whiteness—as a social and cultural process—operates in ways that mimic carbon monoxide: it is invisible but powerful. Its presence is often denied and/or erased and ultimately viewed as an absence.[82] Like carbon monoxide, Whiteness embodies the "presence of an absence," its omnipotence and omnipresence denied and misrecognized.[83] As something that is endemic in American society, especially in the system of public schooling, Whiteness alters everything around it with an invisible hand. Since its presence is not recognized or acknowledged, it is not considered a factor; it is presumed to be a nonfactor, an absence. Not surprisingly, individuals or groups that try to pursue the idealization of the American dream through the elimination of discrimination based on race, gender, disability, or sexuality are largely discounted, accused of being whiners, or losers, or much too sensitive.

Schlepping Around for a Cultural Explanation

Black women's institutionally defined (relative) success has blinded most people to the costs incurred.[84] The culture of Black families and communities often supports early female autonomy, which is in direct conflict with the infantilization of females in the larger society. Perceived adultification (a term used by Ann Arnett Ferguson in her book *Bad Boys: Public Schools in the Making of Black Masculinity*) has very different meanings for Black females than it does for Black males.[85] While males, regardless of race or ethnicity, are encouraged to be autonomous and nondependent, females are encouraged to remain dependent, especially on males, throughout the life course. However, when comparison is made within rather than across gender lines, the differences are broader.[86] Indeed, the visibility of Black girls—who inhabit bodies whose skin color is distinctly different from that of other females—is often equated with a kind of loudness that is totally unrelated to the level of their voices or the content of their discourse.[87] Like their male peers, young Black females are generally seen as being inappropriately mature, too worldly for their chronological age.[88]

Society (and schooling) has also prepared Black girls for essentialized female adult roles rather than nourishing them academically. Linda Grant's research in a recently desegregated school highlights the fact that Black girls are rewarded for acting in ways that reflect what are presumed to be their adult roles: mediators, caregivers, and enforcers.[89] Grant's conclusion that they are not rewarded for their academic skills is supported by other researchers, including Janet Schofield, who discusses the unacknowledged sexual tensions between Black and White junior high students in a recently desegregated school in Pittsburgh.[90]

So after inviting Nadine (Dee Dee)[91] and the other participants to be a part of my study of female aggression, bullying, and competition, I schlepped around this racially desegregated, but predominantly White, suburban school, examining female self-assertion and relational aggression across and along racial lines. My goal was to document the cultural mechanisms that teach girls, around the time they reach puberty, to avoid competition with their male peers and limit their competition to other girls. Dee Dee's narrative (see chapter 3) is a case in point. Indeed, female aggression is often directed at young women who belong to groups defined as other, a practice that reproduces the subordination of Black adolescents within the gender-specific social hierarchy and, when reinforced by the dominant culture of the school, inhibits Black females' academic performance and limits their aspirations.

Trade Wind Images and Language: Discourses of Uncertainty

School officials tend to link a child's academic acumen with her ability to speak and communicate effectively. However, Black children, especially those whose lives are ravaged by poverty, are further victimized in our society's Euro-American schools because they are perceived to lack the uniquely White speech pattern, augmented by a perception of inadequate parenting.[92] Black girls (and boys) resist this perception by maintaining a strong belief that their language skills are as good as or better than White speech patterns. That belief is constantly reinforced primarily because, during their formative and adolescent years, they are constantly subjected to negative comments directed at "Black speech patterns," their "native" communities, and as adolescents, they frequently resist the prison of conformity and obedience to these habitual images and practices, despite their parents' Herculean efforts to instill them—permanently.[93] Black children's reluctance to embrace White speech patterns and the barrage of images indicating Black deviancy leaves many of them powerless in today's school systems and, by extension, barred from participation as adults in the most prestigious arenas of the workforce—that is, in White public spaces.

In America, for example, a privileged, gender-specific discourse style is a way of speaking, behaving, and interacting based on a "veiled use of power," or indirectness.[94] Elsewhere I have described this as "the language of uncertainty" (more on this below), which is not the way most Black parents rear or seek to rear their young daughters (or sons).[95] While this discourse style is the dominant one in child rearing among large segments of middle- and upper-class White Americans and is reinforced in the public school system, the Black adolescents' peer system frequently rejects their parents' demands for total conformity. It must be acknowledged here that the language that Black parents deploy in rearing their children is not the language of uncertainty. Even more paradoxical, the language they use to teach them to obey, to conform, is flooded with affect.[96] As Ta-Nehisi Coates acknowledges in his book *Between the World and Me,* the four-letter word undergirding most Black parents' child rearing is "fear," here known as "the talk." This fear, he insists, is the pervasive, invisible shroud of Black parenting, the unbridled angst surrounding the potential loss of their children through state-sanctioned policies and practices. He chronicles the way his parents' fear, especially his father's, influenced the primary narrative they taught him:

> I can hear my Dad telling me this right now—walk like you have some place to be, keep aware, keep your head on a swivel, make sure you're looking at everything.[97]

Historically, within the African American community, language is generally not used to cloak or mask individual power. The parental role is one imbued with power, and parents' "ways with words" generally signal this perception.[98] Consequently, issuing a directive in a way that disguises the power differential between the adult and the child by appearing to offer the child more than one way to respond is not, as Lisa Delpit rightfully points out, the preferred way African American parents interact with their children.[99] Within this community, the most widely used parental discourse style makes it clear who is entitled to make the rules and who is expected to obey them.[100] Familiarity with this direct way of speaking leads many African American adolescents to misrecognize the unofficial, albeit hegemonic, discourse commandment: language is used to understate one's power, especially among women. Mistaking how power works in oral and written school-approved discourses and failing to recognize that it is routinely embraced by teachers and other school officials is a major issue in Black girls' academic performance.

In the female version of friendly fire, words—and to a lesser extent deeds—are the weapons of choice; women slay each other with words and body language. Admittedly, some of the words are provocative (the n-word, "bitch," and the combination of these two epithets), but most are not. Most of the soft words—what I call the "language of uncertainty"—are made even more benign by being framed in the interrogative. For example:

> "Johnny, don't you think you should be doing your homework?"
> "Ladies, would you consider using your inside voices?"
> "Amanda, would you like to answer question number 3?"[101]

Questions such as these, in the school context, suggest a gender-specific linguistic style that is intimately familiar to most White girls because it closely approximates the linguistic styles used by their mothers and other adult females in their lives outside the school context. Not unexpectedly, it is both misrecognized and often rejected by Black (and many other) girls, much to their social and academic detriment, because they do not understand the interrogative as a command.[102] Misunderstanding intentions leads to inaccurate conclusions. The listener believes she has a choice: to do or not do, to perform or not perform.

Because language in this broad sense is so critical to symbolic violence, its nonnormative use has serious negative social and academic consequences. But to further engage in socially approved language and to seek linguistic normalization is to participate in this unconscious and unacknowledged form of violence toward both oneself and others.[103]

Child-Rearing Modalities: "The Talk" versus "Questions as Demands"

According to John Ogbu's cultural ecological model (CEM), child-rearing formulae are adaptations and are not subject to the whims and wishes of individual members of a society.[104] How different populations opt to rear their children, he argues, is the outcome of the social and economic conditions they face.[105] One might infer from his premise that people who rear their children in the face of a headwind embrace different child-rearing practices than do people who live in a trade wind environment. For example, Black adults are much more likely to be severely punished, arrested, humiliated, imprisoned, or killed—historically and contemporarily—for minor infractions of existing laws and regulations in "White public space."[106] Their response to such harsh conditions is to focus their energies on getting their children to conform to (to obey) these environmental limitations, regardless of how uncomfortable, discriminatory, or unfair they are. Researchers have repeatedly noted that in the school context, Black kids are more likely to be punished for infractions that their White peers are routinely forgiven for.[107]

Moreover, individuals whose social histories vary will often read the symbols linked to those histories differently. This "generational imprinting"—which tends to occur and have its greatest impact during adolescence—compels them to construct the world and the future in ways that motivate them to teach their children a different narrative because they conclude that the experiences of their childhood are a road map for what their children are also likely to experience. According to a recent study, "common to all descriptions of [the gender-specific] 'the talk,' [is] a sense of the need to prepare [African American] child[ren] for discrimination . . . [and to prep them] . . . for encounters with officers of the law."[108] Social justice activists and civil rights leaders in the Black community assert that the larger goal of "the talk" is to protect Black children from all kinds of physical violence affiliated with the unconditional power of police and other legitimate state officials. Formally, these officials are paid with taxpayers' dollars (Black workers are taxpayers) to protect all children. However, Black parents and other adults are keenly aware of the discrepancy between how their children are treated by these officials and how the children of citizens who do not share their children's African ancestry are treated.

"The talk" (and its variations) embraced by Black parents is intended to protect their children by forcing them to be obsequiously obedient, to conform unconditionally to the racism and discrimination and external rules and regulations imposed by the larger society. The logic informing Black parents' child rearing, with its strong emphasis on obeying all the rules and regulations without fail, enhances the possibility that a child will be seen as a "good Black" rather than a "bad Black," allowed into the "gated community" of schools and the larger society.[109] But does the need for safety—for life itself—from those with unlimited state-sanctioned power inevitably lead to a demand for total conformity and obedience? Are public officials—such as teachers, officers of the law, judges, prosecutors, doctors, lawyers, who are overwhelmingly White—more likely to promote and reward Black girls (and boys) who obey all the rules and regulations regardless of how those policies humiliate and degrade them? Are Black children who attend de facto segregated schools or suburban private or religious schools and witness the differential treatment of their same-sex peers likely to opt to violate one of the central premises of the "the talk": obey unconditionally?

By contrast, how does the "questions as demands" gender-specific discourse style in the White community differ from the restraints central to the "the talk" embraced in the Black community? If language in the larger society is imbued with seemingly limitless options, one might expect that demands are soft-pedaled, framed as questions, such as "Amy, don't you think you should be doing your homework?" Amy is likely to understand this question as a demand. She will stop whatever she is doing and do her homework instead. ReRe, a nonnative speaker, hears the question not as a demand but as a choice of options: she can do or not do her homework. She is not a native speaker and is likely to misunderstand the demand. As I argue here, the children whose habitus is characterized by the omnipresent headwinds are likely to misunderstand the questions as demands, not recognizing the child-rearing ethos so widely practiced and understood by teachers, police, judges, lawyers, and other officials in the White community. These officials are able to speak softly and, in the case of females, to frame demands as questions because their power is reinforced by the state's penchant for hoarding power.

Neither of these child-rearing formulae is superior to the other; each is appropriate when limited to its "native" community. These discourse styles become problematic only when they are imposed or used without modification or alteration in contexts that are foreign to newcomers.

The home and community are integral parts of this study because girls' self-esteem, aspirations, expectations, and attitudes toward school are largely shaped by the prevailing cultures within the family and neighborhood. However, in families that encourage young women to achieve and to mature, there may be a serious mismatch between home-based and school-based definitions of behaviors that evince maturity. Within Black communities, young women are evaluated relative to gender-specific standards that focus on a woman's ability to be assertive, to demand respect from others, and to take responsibility for those who depend on her. Adult Black women expect respect from adult men and children of both genders, and they support older and younger people, male and female, in their extended family networks. As a Black girl matures, whether she is "grown" and deserving of the respect and autonomy due to an adult woman is evaluated relative to such a standard.

Research has shown that most Black mothers rear their daughters differently from White mothers.[110] These child-rearing practices help African American girls retain their prepubescent confidence through adolescence, unlike White girls. Consequently, they have special instructional needs, which are often inadequately served by the American educational system.

These academic needs become tangled in a web of survival issues. Kesho Scott notes that Black parents' use of discourse styles strongly reflects a desire to ensure their daughters' survival in a world generally hostile to them.[111] She provides numerous examples of Black parenting practices. A solid case in point is one she openly shares with her readers, detailing how her mother's child-rearing practices, embedded in her discourse style, shielded her from the low self-esteem affiliated with the female body and the resulting gender-specific loss:

Thirteen years tall, I stood in the living-room doorway. My clothes were wet. My hair was mangled. I was in tears, in shock, and in need of my mother's warm arms. Slowly, she looked me up and down, stood up from the couch and walked towards me, her body clenched in criticism. Putting her hands on her hips and planting herself, her shadow falling over my face, she asked in a voice of barely suppressed rage, "What happened?" I flinched as if struck by the unexpected anger and answered, "They put my head in the toilet. They say I can't swim with them." "They" were eight White girls at my high school. I reached out to hold her, but she roughly brushed my hands aside and said, "Like hell! Get your coat. Let's go." My mother taught me two powerful and enduring lessons that day. She taught me that I would have to fight back against racial and sexual injustice. . . . She taught me that my feelings did not matter, that no matter how hurt I was, how ashamed, or how surprised I was, I had to fight back because if I did not, then I would always be somebody's victim. She also taught me a lesson I did not want to learn: She taught me exactly when my private pain had to become a public event that must be dealt with in a public manner. That day my mother offered me no personal comfort for my momentary shame and embarrassment; instead, she made me see my pain as not mine. Though she spoke no words directly, she made me realize instinctively that my experience was not some expression of tenth grade girls' jealousy—not a silly, private adolescent version of "They don't like me." My experience, she taught me, was directly related to facts I could not control—my Blackness and my womanness. This was her lesson. I did not know then that my childhood had ended and my initiation into Black womanhood had begun. Neither did I know that I had experienced my mother's habit of surviving. I just knew that standing up for myself was what I had to do because it was the way Black women had to be. We had to stand up in public for what was right, and stand against what was wrong. That was our role and our achievement.[112]

As Scott so convincingly illustrates, Black mothers (and other adult Black women) are the linchpins in their daughters' culturally distinct identities. These adult Black women are extremely influential in supporting and promoting their daughters' flights to successful, gender-specific adult status. However, as Scott also points out, this "success" comes with an inordinate price: public humiliation for what would ordinarily be private pain. While the lessons Black mothers teach their daughters enable them to withstand social discomfort, embarrassment, and visibility—features that are critical markers of high self-esteem—these social skills do not produce a socially appropriate female body, a body characterized by loss. Rather, Black girls' retention of their prepubescent high self-esteem appears, ironically, to be the very weapon that subverts their "successes," both academic and otherwise.

All these standards (self-assertion, self-confidence, demanding respect, being outspoken) come into conflict with the behaviors expected of girls in many high schools, earning Black girls a reputation as "loud" and thereby out of place.[113] White female teachers, most of whom come from middle-class, racially segregated backgrounds, often expect female students to be relatively compliant rather than self-assertive, and they reward girls who conform to those expectations with good grades and encouragement to achieve academically. Those who do not conform meet with sanctions against their behavior, negative evaluations of their intellectual potential, and discouragement of their academic and occupational aspirations. This mismatch creates a serious dissonance in Black girls' lives between achievement at home and at school. Some Black families and social networks try to help young women negotiate between these two divergent and often conflicting worlds, but the burden remains on them and not on the school. Resolving this problem so that the school environment reinforces rather than undermines Black girls' path toward maturity and achievement must be a crucial element of educational reform.

This study complements existing scholarship on aggression and gender among female adolescents. It also extends that scholarship in a significant and original direction not only by considering its racial dimensions and connecting it with previous studies of academic achievement, but also by illustrating how the existing scholarship misrecognizes the intragender inequality in the ideas embodied in the claims of an overarching habitus widely known as sisterhood—regardless of race. I developed this approach through theoretical triangulation and through direct observation. In keeping with the old adage that "all the women are white and all the blacks are men," researchers have failed to investigate Black girls' academic achievement and aspirations in relation to definitions of womanly maturity that prevail in Black families and communities.[114] The reigning paradigms, including my own previous work, emphasize cultural differences between Black families and school systems in which White norms and values dominate—highlighting differences that affect male and female students alike—rather than investigating gender-differentiated norms and styles of expression.

Popular culture is rife with stereotypes of "loud Black girls," but the stereotype has simply been decried, not properly scrutinized to decode its covert messages about race and gender. My research clarifies this blind spot and advances our knowledge of how cultural factors—which are simultaneously gendered and racialized—contribute to the incompatibility between prevailing definitions of academic success for girls and the culture of (Black) female adolescents.

The analysis offered in this book (especially in the five narratives) reveals how *méconnaissance,* or misrecognition, is embedded not only in the behaviors, values, and practices of the study participants but also in deep structures of the curriculum, in the expectations of parents and local school officials, and in the ubiquity of the structural violence sanctioned by the nation at large. This revelation begins with chapter 2, where I discuss the setting and methodology.

Last Stop on the Underground Railroad, First Stop of Refried Segregation

SETTING AND METHODOLOGY

The past is never dead. It's not even past.

—William Faulkner, *Requiem for a Nun*

A Tsunami of Expectations in Monochromatic Weather

Winters in upstate New York are extremely cold, characterized by short (but seemingly endless), sunless days blanketed in blistering white snow, overcast skies, and a mawkish gray trim over all. Mention this area to anyone outside (or within) New York State, and the image that immediately comes to mind is winter and snow—on steroids.

Weather is the primary concern of the anthropologist when her alarm goes off at 4:30 a.m. in mid-January.[1] This is the first day she can officially visit the high school that has granted her permission to complete a study of female aggression, bullying, and competition among and between Black and White girls. Groggy from a lack of sleep and anxious about what she will face later that day, she finds her way downstairs to put on her coat, hat, scarf, and gloves to prepare for the daily shoveling of snow.[2] Although she worries about awakening her neighbors with the noise of the shovel as it hits the asphalt in the early-morning silence, she works rapidly. By 5:45 a.m., the job is done.

Once back inside, she removes her snow-covered clothing and remembers to put her book bag on the floor of the teacup-size mudroom so that she will not forget it when she leaves the house.

The bag is vital to her work because it contains a miniature tape recorder, her purse, a spiral notepad for recording her field notes, and various university-approved forms that potential study participants, as well as their parents and teachers, will have to sign in order to participate in the study.[3]

There will be no formal interviews or classroom observations prior to the approval of parents and students. Building an infrastructure of knowledge of the research site and its citizens, and letting them get to see her and know her, are necessary precursors to the important components of the study. She constantly reminds herself that this is why ethnography is so laborious, frustrating, and ultimately rewarding.

She compels herself to focus on the immediate tasks at hand: showering, eating breakfast, and dressing in order to get to the research site by the time the buses arrive with the students for their 7:35 a.m. classes. In thinking about dressing in clothing that is both appropriate and heavy enough to keep her warm and comfortable in her old car with its temperamental heating system, she is stymied by the widely accepted dictum, First impressions are irreversible. She desires (and needs) the students' acceptance. There is not much she can do regarding the age differential, but it is important for her to be seen as approachable by the students and as professional by the staff. This compelled her to spend an inordinate amount of time the night before worrying about how to wear her hair and selecting the appropriate attire: a long-sleeved dress, black opaque hose, a black blazer, black boots with fleece lining, and the obligatory heavy coat, hat, and gloves.[4] She concludes that the clothing she selected is appropriate and will not suggest to students that she is in the "arrival" rather than the "becoming" stage of her professional life.[5] Informed by what she learned doing a similar ethnographic study at Capital High, she seeks to limit the perception of social distance between herself and them.[6]

She reverses the car out of her newly shoveled driveway by 6:40 a.m., leaving enough time to get to the research site, park her car, get the approval of the sentries, and stand in the hallway to watch students as they enter the building for first-period classes. Looking back, she is grateful for the thirty-five-minute snowy drive to the school, which offered her a much-needed opportunity to meditate and release some of the stress affiliated with her efforts to embrace what Erving Goffman calls "impression management."[7] Later in the study, this drive will give her time to allay her anxiety, plan possible responses to situations she might encounter that day, and record any unfinished field notes from the day before. On this first visit to the research site when school is in session, she braces herself for the unknown and unfamiliar.

A "Naboh" in the Mist

The anthropologist's trepidations are relentless. Driving west on the interstate highway, she is surprised at how disoriented she feels and at how much this destabilizes the core of her identity. She reminds herself of how much she has longed for this opportunity—the chance to empirically investigate her hunch that in America, females compete to lose in order to win.

The problem, as she has repeatedly told anyone who will listen, is that female competition is misrecognized primarily because it does not replicate the male pattern of physical aggression. She fears that her audience is too small—classes of fifteen to twenty-five undergraduate and one or two graduate students once a year (or every other year)—and she wants to publish her empirical findings to engage a much larger audience. She started the application process during the spring semester[8] and submitted her application for human-subject clearance shortly after the spring semester ended the summer before she commenced the project.[9] Her army-of-one approach appeared to be insufficient, but no support was forthcoming. She resorted to asking the church ladies to do what she could not do for herself: pray that the barriers she encountered would evaporate as quickly and as mysteriously as they had appeared. They did.[10]

There is an old saying: Be careful what you pray for, because you just might get it. Driving to the school this first morning, she feels like a "naboh" marooned in an unfamiliar environment.[11] While she knows that she is entering a semifamiliar cultural and geographical space (after all, she too is American), she feels as if she is traveling from Earth to Mars. Her sense of displacement compels her to wonder if she is an involuntary participant in what could be identified as a "back to the future" project. Is this why, she wonders, it has taken so long to get clearance for this study from the institution where she works?

As her mind meanders, she realizes that she is no longer in the densely populated urban part of the city where she lives and works. She has turned off the traffic-swollen expressway, gone past the familiar gas station, and driven onto a two-lane gravel road with an uncomfortable—albeit vaguely familiar—rural vibe. Unlike the houses in the core, which were built at the turn of the twentieth century and reflect a varied, careful construction, houses in the Rodman community are situated in monochromatic, faux gated communities with cute names like Whispering Woods or Colonial Village.[12] They are more modern in design—split-levels, ramblers, and colonials—and are covered with aluminum siding or its various spin-offs to minimize upkeep. Others stand alone on larger parcels of land, with open spaces, horses, and other attributes that evoke a rural ambience and a return to a nostalgic imperialism—what James Loewen referred to as a "sundown town" history—juxtaposed with tractors and other modern farm equipment.[13]

The anthropologist brakes to turn right, and her car slowly rolls onto the UGRH campus. As she will later learn, the school is considered the community center, the place where major sports and other cultural rituals and social events take place. As she walks to the front entrance, the school building appears to be an expanded vault, perched uncomfortably in an enormous black asphalt graveyard, submerged by the cars of faculty, staff, and students and a large number of yellow school buses with motors running to keep the drivers warm as students disembark.[14] The unmarked two-lane highway in the front of the building and the lack of a surrounding neighborhood reinforce her sense of desolation, isolation, and otherworldliness.

Her anxieties are exacerbated; her heart pounds so hard in her chest that in the silence of the stark winter day, even with the clunk-clunk of her heavy boots, she can hear her nonrhythmic heartbeats. She feels small, vulnerable, and totally alone. The more steps she takes, the more the building seems to recede, compelling the black asphalt to appear to grow and potentially devour her and everything on it. Her embodied fear compels her to (mis)recognize her naboh status in her own "home"[15] as she struggles to make it to the massive front doors of the institution that, for the next two and a half years, will consume and reshape not only her personal epistemology, but also the racism embodied in the hegemonic epistemologies she will use in framing her research.[16]

The Physical Plant and the People: Unlearning What (She Thinks) She Knows

The anthropologist has been here before—at least she thought so. In preparation for her long-term field project, coupled with her en-culturated lack of entitlement, she had visited the school three times during the previous summer. Her goal was to meet face-to-face with the human resource director (her primary contact and chief supporter), the building principal, and some other staff members. She hoped to finalize her plans for a September start date. During each of these preliminary visits, she was introduced to an array of key officials, including the superintendent. Everyone was beyond polite; they were nice. They smiled constantly, asking her repeatedly about her proposed work at UGRH and her current employment. It was during this phase of her study that she learned to fully appreciate what James Baldwin[17] noted: "Every good-bye ain't gone"[18] and "Every shut eye ain't sleep."[19] In hindsight, she realizes she was expected to misrecognize the complexity of the omnipresent smile. And she did—repeatedly.

Since school was not in session during her initial visits, she met very few teachers. While there were a variety of programs in session, along with the obligatory (albeit limited) summer-school program, the modern, cavernous, three-story building was virtually empty. During those earlier visits, it had been clear to her that this massive, boxlike edifice of a school is the pride of the Rodman community.[20] The building has an array of features and modern conveniences, including an Olympic-size pool that is open to the community year-round, glass-enclosed walkways that connect the multiple wings and pathways, and an area dedicated to the fine arts, especially music and choral activities.[21] There are six fireproof, double steel doors framing the entrance, each with a small glass window running the length of the door on each side. The unobstructed circular driveway to the front door makes it easy for the bus drivers to watch students as they disembark and enter the building. As many of the adults at the school will repeatedly inform her, this cohort of children has "helicopter parents" who hover over them constantly. After the 9/11 attacks, their parents have become even more vigilant. Hence, limiting the discomfort of the cold weather for students as they get on and off the yellow school buses is not just expected but demanded.

The school's main office is immediately to the left as one enters the building. The huge, glass-enclosed space makes it possible to see everyone occupying the area without going inside. Just outside the main office—most days—is a sentry station that, the anthropologist is told, was added in the wake of 9/11.

The building consists of four major wings in response to the desire of curriculum specialists to merge, or put in close proximity, disciplines that are thought to be complementary; this is thought to lead to greater efficiency in scheduling, cross-disciplinary planning, and collaboration. According to the Rodman Fire Department, the cafeteria is designed to seat just under five hundred students with only two lunch periods. School policy compels students to eat on campus except when their parents take them away or give written permission for them to leave with a carefully vetted person. It is the only high school in this suburban community.

The spacious building is rigorously cleaned on a daily basis by individuals with skin that is never darker than brown.[22] If cleanliness were a marker of academic excellence, this school—defanged of dirt, trash, and other debris that would be markers of an absence of niceness—would receive a grade of A+. Except for two spaces that have a nefarious image—the congregation of a diversity of Black, Brown, and White bodies in the wing that is home to the "Red-Light District" and the "Black Table" in the cafeteria—the school's spatial features, its block curriculum, and the hierarchy of courses (including the AP program, Regents Exams, and regular offerings) embody what Setha Low describes as "niceness," which is the mother's milk of "Whiteness."[23]

Low locates "niceness" and nonstop smiling spatially and identifies it with physically gated communities, asserting that these country-club spaces emerge both out of a panic connected to "the fear of Otherness" and out of "the way people make moral and aesthetic judgments to control their social and physical environments."[24] Not surprisingly, UGRH embodies this phenomenon not just in its spatial configuration but, more importantly, in its expectation that everything and everybody in the building must reflect and embody the niceness aesthetic, and by extension, the dominance of Whiteness.

As Low defines it, niceness is a celebration of what is normative and embodied in our perceptions of Whiteness. She asserts:

> Niceness is about keeping things clean, orderly, homogeneous, and controlled so that housing values remain stable, but it is also a way of maintaining whiteness. Whiteness provides access to education, elite taste cultures and behaviors, and allows a group to prosper within the dominant culture. In [some] places . . . being "middle class" and being "White" overlap such that one social status can be taken for another.[25]

Niceness is so overvalued, so embodied in the perception of Whiteness, and so antithetical to the perception of Blackness at

UGRH that no matter the effort and consistency of the matriculating Black female students, they see themselves as being permanently marginalized and deliberately excluded from the safety, security, and support of the highest-ranking (racial) female group. As will become evident in the case studies in this book, the socially identifiable Black bodies that are deemed nice (especially as this identity is connected to femaleness) are seen as exceptions to rather than invalidations of the rule. The anthropologist fears that they, too, are given a naboh status that they are powerless to alter.

Similarly, Enoch Page identifies what he calls the prevalence and dominance of purified "White public space" in the American context.[26] These spaces, which include publicly supported schooling, are racialized "through the circulation and manipulation of information, knowledge, and cultural symbols and the concurrent monitoring of these same spaces for evidence of 'linguistic disorder,'" a malady from which many of the Black students suffer, at least as the adults at this school see it.[27]

There were just under fifteen hundred students enrolled at UGRH during the first and second years of the study and just over a hundred full-time and approximately ten part-time teachers, leading to an ideal student/teacher ratio of approximately 15 to 1. Only one (female) teacher was socially identified as having African ancestry. There were several counselors, a principal, and at least three assistant principals. No official accounting of the number of staff members such as engineers, custodians, and cafeteria workers is included here.

The anthropologist was repeatedly puzzled by the paucity of Black staff at the school. As initially posited by John Ogbu, "jobs below the job ceiling" are historically the only jobs available to Black workers, but that appeared not to be the case at this worksite.[28] Apparently, they just were not "qualified." The anthropologist was able to talk with three Black female cafeteria workers whom she saw repeatedly during her visits. On her first official day, she met (or tried to meet) two of the non-Black janitors—one male and one female. These workers were assigned to the cafeteria area during the two lunch hours, cleaning tables and removing debris left by students.[29] They responded to her as if she were kryptonite and repeatedly rebuffed her attempts to engage them in conversation. Hence, her sense of being a naboh was not limited to the overwhelmingly White professional staff.

Blackness and the "Paradox of Privilege"

As a researcher at UGRH, the anthropologist realized, almost from day one, that despite her academic credentials, professional title, university affiliation, and academic discipline, like Kirby Moss,[30] she was viewed with "ambiguity" and compelled to occupy a liminal professional space. Indeed, as Annegret Staiger asserts, she did not (and could not) embody the gender-specific, hegemonic "niceness."[31] Consequently, like the females who were identified as appropriate for her study, the anthropologist was routinely misrecognized, her skin color confirming her as a ghetto Black and as gender inappropriate.[32]

She remained consigned to that status throughout the two and a half years she spent there. As a state-supported institution, UGRH compelled her to embrace these racial and gender practices, to hug its (their) claims of banality (or as Amanda Lewis notes, embrace the tenacious commitment to an ideology that asserts that "there is no 'race' in the schoolyard") and its denials of inflicting harm.[33] The possession of credentials did not protect her from misrecognition. Indeed, attached to her Black body, these credentials were taken to indicate that she was a fake, unconditionally open to interrogation and friendly fire. How did she manage to obtain these credentials? Surely some sleight of hand (or at least favoritism disguised as some kind of benevolence) was involved.[34]

No one recognized (except possibly the counseling director) that what she experienced was violence—by another name. After all, no one physically abused her or called her names that are recognized as dehumanizing. She was permitted to move freely around the building as long as her outsider badge was clearly visible. She was permitted to interact with staff members; to observe students in their classes, the cafeteria, the gym, the counseling center, and the hallways; and to call or visit the students and their parents at home, provided they signed the appropriate consent forms.

The experience of being both immersed in and excluded from such a situation and the sense that there was something present that she could not quite name or define—what Pearl Rosenberg labels the "presence of an absence"—made her keenly attuned to claims regarding female competition and aggression by and about both the Black and White teenage informants.[35] She thought of it as confirming what she learned as a woman socialized in an overwhelmingly Black community but schooled in an institution that imposed values and norms that did not, for the most part, emerge organically in her native community: an omnipresent haint or ghost that she, too, often deliberately misrecognized.[36]

On this cold January morning, the researcher enters the building and goes directly to the main office. Three women (two whom she identifies as White and one whom she identifies as Black) work in the large open space. The only Black woman—the receptionist, whom she had met during the summer—greets her warmly and assures her "that she has her back" and says that even though she will not be given an office, she can leave her belongings where the receptionist and her coworkers put theirs.[37] She removes her coat and hangs it as suggested, assuring the receptionist that she will carry the book bag and purse with her throughout the day.[38]

The quizzical look the receptionist gives this naboh tells her that she does not believe that she is going to be able to walk around this mammoth building all day carrying all those items. The naboh wonders if she is violating a dominant gender norm that values weakness in bodies socialized to be female. Will she be perceived as too strong and thus ineligible for the help she desperately needs? Should she fake weakness to encourage others to help her? She makes the split-second decision that she has to continue to live in misrecognition, including perpetuating the widely accepted accusation that she is strong primarily because she is a Black woman. She wonders, again, if her misrecognition is self-imposed or externally compelled (or perhaps an asymmetrical combination). If she is open about who she is, will she be complicit in the hidden agenda of most cultural systems to reproduce themselves, and guilty of deception that would violate the ethics code of her academic discipline?

As her contradictory thoughts continue, the receptionist, Ms. Redding, shows her the office conveniences and introduces her to coworkers, who look at her strangely. Ms. Redding will prove to be her lifeline, and she knows this on her very first day.[39]

The anthropologist's naboh status is even more evident in the classroom spaces. While there are a small number of Black students—never more than five—in virtually all the classrooms she will eventually observe, their small numbers appear to undercut their influence. She learns that this is especially applicable in the case of the female students accused of aggression, bullying, and competition, who are perceived to be "insufficiently girlie."[40]

Girlie and "Insufficiently Girlie" at UGRH

A central theme in all the cases in this study is the ubiquity of violence—the intent to do harm—in these girls' lives, both Black and White. Despite its pervasive presence and deadly impact, this bloodless violence is routinely misrecognized and rarely acknowledged. How it affects—and in some instances, strangles—these young women's lives is revealed in their unique narratives. How gender-specific violence fuels their anxieties, fears, and anemic academic performance is one of the central concerns of this book.

What is most striking about the female student population is their uncanny ability to "partially" commingle modern images of femaleness ("I am woman, hear me roar"; "I can be anything I want to be") while concurrently embracing and rejecting the values, practices, and mores of their mothers, grandmothers, and female generations before. In multiple ways, they seek to embody the traditional, gender-specific elite statuses (princess/mother/wife) and the non-traditional (academic, professional, and other achievements) or inversion of the traditional statuses (princess/mother before or sans marriage). These students' commitment to the princess/mother-hood image was virtually unanimous,[41] with the desire to get married running a strong second despite the fact that most of their parents had severed their marital bonds (where such bonds existed).[42] It was their unending efforts to obtain the seemingly unchanging gender-specific prestigious rewards that these social ideals embodied that occupied the anthropologist's energy for the duration of the study.

As teenagers, these girls reflect all the joys and dysfunctions of rookie adults, including the feeling of being smarter than their parents, teachers, and any nonrookie adult with whom they interact. They are concurrently charming, curious, manipulative, joyous, morose, garrulous, adventuresome, shy, and depressed. The White girls appear to unconditionally fear the imagined physicality of the Black girls; the Black girls appear to fear the hidden power of the White girls.

Regardless of which of these categories a girl occupies, there are two common and consistent preoccupations: boys and beauty. This leads to a preoccupation with owning things (conspicuous consumption) and status. As Dorothy Holland and Margaret Eisenhart's *Educated in Romance* documents, young girls sacrifice academic achievement for male attention.[43] The centrality of male attention in their lives fuels not only the unrelenting policing of their own and other girls' sexual practices but also the constant attention to how they look. Looking good is not even sacrificed for safety. The lack of doors on the girls' (and boys') bathrooms is a case in point. Doors on bathrooms, not just in public spaces but even in our own homes, are ubiquitous because we consider privacy and safety paramount. When the anthropologist asked why there were no doors, she was told that at UGRH, a lack of exterior doors made the restrooms safer and, at the same time, lessened the possibility of smoking, including cigarettes and other "issues."

Women's bathrooms are almost never without full length mirrors; the same cannot be said for men's bathrooms. Full-length mirrors on the walls in the girls' bathrooms are nonnegotiable. One of the White girls told the anthropologist that a Black girl—with whom she had no relationship but who, as she did, took a cosmetology class at the vocational setting supported by the Rodman school district—had stated that she had *not* worn the same outfit to school the entire year. This was extremely meaningful for, and was clearly resented by, this White girl, who described it as the height of financial irresponsibility.

There appears to be an unwritten rule for White girls: thou shall not wear makeup, especially lipstick. This rule is more nuanced for the Black girls: some of them wear makeup, including lipstick; others do not. Black girls who wear makeup are not considered by their Black female peers as being sexually provocative. The White girls are not as charitable; anyone who violates the rules is open to unmitigated contempt. The monogamous imperative also applies: no more than one boyfriend at a time—even if only for a couple of weeks. Violating the informal, gender-specific commandment to always practice serial monogamy puts a girl at risk of being labeled promiscuous and a slut. Both Black and White girls are expected to follow this rule religiously.

Up South—or Mississippi on the Down Low?

UGRH is above ground, at least spatially. However, its official goals, objectives, and mission are not. In other words, its existence above ground operationalizes the *méconnaissance* that everyone routinely embraces, albeit in most instances unknowingly. Consequently, in this lower-middle-class to middle-class, predominantly White, suburban community in upstate New York, the pseudonym "UGRH" resonates because the community is near one of the registered sites of Harriet Tubman's Underground Railroad during Black Americans' official enslavement. It is also appropriate because school officials, parents, and students all misunderstand how the nation's hegemonic, ranked opportunity structure has traditionally (and continues to) shape their evolving epistemologies.[44]

The community surrounding UGRH is best defined by the intense hunger of its residents—Black and White—for both normality and status and by its "shades of White" demographic composition "on the precipice" of becoming racially integrated and culturally diverse.[45] What I call "statusitis" is the one common theme in the lives of adults and children, young and old, Black and White, rich and poor.[46] Indeed, it is statusitis that compels the White population in Rodman to unconsciously loathe the prospect of Black and White equality, compelling segments of the hegemonic White population to work diligently, albeit surreptitiously and often unknowingly, to reproduce stigma in the lives of non-White residents. This issue intensifies the achievement problem for all Black and Brown students at the school, especially Black female students.

Rodman is on the precipice economically as well as demographically, for the suburb owes its existence to the nearby industrial city that spawned it. With the decline of manufacturing, the economy in the urban core has undergone a structural transformation and a near collapse. Several of the major employers have declared bankruptcy or downsized, generating major economic insecurity and unemployment. The anxiety this situation produces is compounded by Rodman parents' commitment to giving their children the economic, educational, and social advantages they had or did not have when they were growing up and to protecting them at all costs.[47]

Many of the Black students (and other students of color) at UGRH—much to their parents' chagrin—differ in their approach to academic success, seeking not to stand out from their peers but instead to be smothered in the womb of the collective.[48] Their body language, behaviors, and practices, especially in classrooms, suggest an aversion to intellectual visibility.[49] They appear to be afraid of academic success as it is narrowly defined in this context, and they avoid—most often unconsciously—competing with White students. Outside the classroom, they are much more confident, even ebullient. They are more willing to compete with one another and with their White peers and more likely to take risks that stretch their social, emotional, and economic capacities. The Whiteness of the classroom space and the salience of what Claude Steele labels the "stereotype threat" appear to stifle their freedom to create the kind of improvised life that they exhibit in the hallways, the cafeteria, the gym, and other nonclassroom spaces.[50] School officials are not as successful in their efforts to keep all others' cultural behaviors and practices at bay in these nonclassroom spaces, and, ironically, the students who do not excel academically often enjoy higher status among their peers.[51] The classroom represents the core of the educational system, a space where Setha Low's concept of gated communities seems apropos.[52]

The adults involved with the high school girls embrace very different understandings of the nation's hegemonic democratic narrative and, consequently, of how this school and its curriculum will affect children's futures. Black parents unconditionally believe in the democratic and moral codes and want them to be reflected in their children's schooling. These parents want their children to matriculate at this predominantly White school because they think that if their children perform well in this context and successfully compete with their White peers academically, racism will disappear as a major obstacle in their adult lives. They genuinely believe that their children's academic credentials will become their master status, subverting the primacy of stigmatized race in their lives. Using this logic, they argue that if their children attend the same school as their White peers, it will equalize their chances of getting accepted into the most prestigious colleges and jobs.[53] To achieve this goal, they publicly fight the racial discrimination their children encounter at UGRH.

On 18 February the anthropologist met with the principal of the school for their first official meeting. This is an extract from her field notes:

Ms. Ferragotta, a middle-aged Caucasian woman, had just begun to offer me a snapshot of the schedule and demographic pictures of the school in her office when the director of counseling made an impromptu appearance. She introduced her as Ms. Blake, who then welcomed me and invited me to come by her office when I had a moment before saying goodbye. Ms. Ferragotta continued: there is only one African American classroom teacher and one counselor at the school. She also identified one of her office secretaries as a Black person.[54]

The anthropologist met and talked with at least three full-time Black females employed as cooks, widely known as the "lunchroom ladies" in the cafeteria. Ms. Ferragotta did not employ a single Black male employee. She noted that the school employs one school resource officer from the sheriff's office, a policeman, Mr. Sienna. She also shared the following information:

> The school is open from 7:45 a.m. to 2:45 p.m. Students work on a four-block [eighty minutes] schedule each day. The school [accepts students in] grades ten through twelve and offers a comprehensive curriculum, including special ed. There are approximately 1,400 students, [so it is smaller than Capital High by about four hundred students.[55] But it is much larger spatially and it offers many more services.] UGRH's Black student population is just under 10 percent (140 to 150 students); there are 7 or 8 percent other minorities, with less than 1 percent Native American. The ESL [English as a Second Language] program is designed to help students who speak twenty-five to twenty-six different languages. There are six counselors, three social workers, and several school psychologists.[56]

In February of the first year of the study, the anthropologist attended her first meeting of the Rodman Board of Education. Relative to the number of Black students attending the school, the Black parents made up a large portion of the audience. The overwhelmingly White (there was only one Black member, a male) board and superintendent listened to a litany of concerns regarding academic expectations from the Black parents and from a couple of White women who were parenting Black students. From the anthropologist's field notes of that meeting:

> A male parent from Africa—not a descendant of enslaved Americans—vented his frustrations with low expectations by noting that when his daughter does well, some of her teachers are surprised at her performance. Shortly after his testimony, an African American mother complained about the school board members' lip service re their commitment to eliminating the Black–White achievement gap. "This is all good, but we've heard this *so* many times before. . . . My son's teachers aren't motivated to help him. I am scared for my son. What college is going to accept him? When I try to insist that he do better work, he says, "This is fine, they'll accept this!" They don't say to him, "This is not the kind of work that I will accept." They just take it and give him an F on it.[57]

For this mother, what was most frustrating was that none of her son's teachers had called her about his performance, and there had been no official letter from the school. She reported that she and her husband had called his guidance counselor, but their calls were not returned.

From the same meeting:

> A White parent shared her painful story about her adopted Black son, who was initially in another suburban school district in the area and not doing well. She went to the school to try and figure out why. His teacher said, "Don't worry so much about his reading skills. He will be playing basketball." This mother noted that that was one of the factors that led her to give up on that school district and move to Rodman. She insisted that her son remains unmotivated, and that she feels like she is fighting a losing battle. . . . Another White mother who has also adopted a Black male child admits her life has changed immensely. Active in

the Black parents' resistance efforts, she suggested that the board expand the slots in the AP classes. Apparently, there are a limited number of slots, and they are given primarily to White students.[58] She said her son has never been approached to be in an AP class. She thinks he is a bright kid, and she doesn't understand why he is not eligible.[59]

Like the Black parents, the White parents profess to be committed to the nation's hegemonic moral and democratic narratives. At the same time, under the ruse of maintaining the "standards" that have always been a core claim in America's K–12 schooling, White parents work to maintain the privileges and advantages that they and their children have always enjoyed. They see every effort at diversification and inclusion as evidence of the erosion of these vaunted standards and attendant entitlements. Two of the White female board members (one of whom has children who attend UGRH) made the following comments regarding the issue of the Black–White achievement gap:

> It seems that a good teacher is a good teacher. Sometimes . . . the school is not at fault. It just *isn't*. . . . A huge piece of the problem is student motivation; the students who are underachieving are not motivated. The job of the teacher, and the job of the school system, is to figure out a way to motivate these kids. . . . Because they're not internally motivated, the motivation must be externally imposed.[60]

As Annegret Staiger asserts, in the postsegregation era, when many desegregation efforts have been put in place, "Whiteness" and "giftedness" are often conflated. This is especially likely to occur in contexts where school officials seek to "avoid discussions about race, do not target the racial achievement gap, and fail to make clear and decisive interventions against racial discrimination."[61]

The White parents at UGRH do what they have always done: maintain their children's connectedness to a racially segregated past that is not past,[62] which, according to Staiger, "actually constitutes a form of resegregation."[63] Unlike the Black parents, whose quest for inclusion, justice, and fairness is open and visible, the White parents pursue their goals secretly and without appearing to use race (or gender, disability, or sexuality) to retain their historical advantage. Their primary strategy is to use benign language—devoid of slurs and overt bigotry—to maintain long-standing schooling practices and standards.

For both groups of parents, the "partial truths" of their beliefs and practices elude them, compelling them to search constantly for evidence to support their positions.[64] Like the explicit discrimination that historically existed below the Mason–Dixon Line, the underground network of privileges made visible in the AP and gifted courses and with the (re)segregation of Black students into the least challenging curriculum at UGRH are indistinguishable from the earlier forms of school segregation during the heyday of the Jim Crow era. Both practices create the same outcome: a Black–White achievement gap and the logical claim that follows: Black adults are relegated to the nation's low-status jobs because they did not perform as well academically as their White counterparts.

Sentries of Surveillance: Misrecognition, Conjoined Pain, Indebted Bodies, and No Unenforced Rules

During the first year of this study (2004), fear connected to the national tragedy of 9/11 has been reinvigorated and is reflected in the increased number of fire drills and lockdowns and by the presence of an oversized community guy installed outside the school's main entrance.[65] Stuffed in a county-issued one-piece yellow jumpsuit (always unzipped from just below his waist, either because it will enable him to get in and out of it easily or because his body is too big for it) and armed with a walkie-talkie, he is a permanent fixture of the school and the embodiment of the male protector. His primary job is to screen for terrorists by checking the credentials of everybody trying to enter or leave the building. His ability to deliberately misrecognize the anthropologist is disconcerting. Every time she arrives at the front door, he (rightfully) demands to see her university ID. Even now, all these years later, she can still feel the twisted conundrum of the slime and heat of humiliation, the blood rushing to her cold face, neck, and chest, which her dark skin camouflages, as he carefully scrutinizes her ID card. She never fails to smile—or display what Lynn Bolles describes as "skin-teeth," that is, a mannerism of resistance—and to thank him as he returns it to her hand.[66]

Once inside, she has to stop at the sentry station outside the main office and show her ID again in order to obtain an ad hoc, hand-written sticker with her professional name on it: "Dr. Fordham, Researcher."[67] Inevitably, it is written with a heavy-duty highlighter in the approved neon colors, marking her as an "outsider within" and undermining her desire to minimize the imagined social distance between herself and the girls she hopes will participate in her study.[68] She is unable to change this branding or even to acknowledge that it makes her job more difficult. When she attempts to move it from her upper torso to a less conspicuous place on her body, one of the most determined sentries watches her with the eyes of a prison guard.

She is loath to ask officials to alter or discontinue the practice, so she pretends not to recognize the code embedded in it and instead continues to display skin-teeth, or "kin teet," until her face hurts.[69] She realizes how indebted she is to the school for allowing her to study their students, and she knows to grin (and grin) and bear it.[70]

However, there are times when her emotional labor fails her.[71] She diligently records these incidents with the sentries in her field notes. There is no written indication of the school's social policies and practices in this area. All the sentries are White females; most of them are in the middle to late phase of their reproductive lives. She reasons that this is the case because most of these former stay-at-home moms have children in this age range or at this school. One woman sentry is an exception. She is older than the others and more grandmotherly. She is much shorter, her hair is totally white, and her physique has a more mature contour.

On this particular day, the grandmother-like guard is stationed near the front entrance.[72] The anthropologist knows immediately that something is problematic—not because the guard is unkind but because, although she smiles generously, her arms are locked across the front of her rigid body and her gray-green eyes are steely cold; her stance makes the hair on the back of the anthropologist's neck stand up. The guard demands that the anthropologist tell her why she is at the school and everything about her planned study, a practice unheard of when a White female in a subordinate position speaks to a female believed to be a professional or higher in status. The anthropologist tries unsuccessfully to deactivate her cultural memory, struggling to be an individual version of what Eric Wolf describes as "a people without history"—an individual without cultural memory or history.[73] Is it W. E. B. Du Bois's "double consciousness"[74] or Claude Steele's more recent "stereotype threat" that is at play here, or both?[75]

The anthropologist knows she is supposed to misrecognize the guard's body language, so she smiles generously and produces the required ID. By this time, she knows the drill: in exchange for surrendering her ID, she will be given the neon name tag indicating that she has the right to be in the building—today only. This is how she records the encounter:

> As I leave the building, the sentry is not at the official sentry station. Not knowing what to do to retrieve my ID and needing to get back to the university for a meeting, I give the badge to one of the secretaries in the main office. She retrieves my ID from the sentry's desk and gives it to me. It does not occur to me to ask her why she does not put the temporary badge in the desk drawer. I do not see this [particular] sentry for several visits. When I encounter her again, she smiles and speaks so softly that I misunderstand her accusation: "You took the badge."[76] This accusation is totally unexpected, paradoxically benign and malignant. I feel lightheaded. . . . The pain inflicted by her insult penetrates my psyche—laboriously and torturously.[77]

There is a second incident involving another sentry who mis-recognizes the anthropologist as a naboh—one she labels Hawkeye. This middle-aged woman is much more intense than the grandmo-therly one. It is clear that she knows the anthropologist and could identify her in a police lineup, yet she is committed to misrecogniz-ing her even when referring to her by her professional name at a distance (for example, "Dr. Fordham, Dr. Fordham! Where is your badge?"). The anthropologist concludes that in this community her naboh status is sealed in gray cement, making it very difficult for her to become the researcher she professes to be. The following entry in her field notes records a case in point:

> I am walking with the only Black counselor's assistant, whom I meet accidentally near the main office this morning. She has just taken a job outside the Rodman school system. She tells me she is willing to talk with me off campus. I am so excited that I forget that I don't yet have the name tag. Hawkeye yells, "Dr. Fordham! Dr. Fordham!"[78] She knows who I am and can identify me at a distance. Still, I have to get the official name tag. Hawkeye is the surveillance cop par excellence, always so official and totally committed to the enforcement of every rule [even imagined or currently nonexistant ones]. She's absolutely certain that I'm the terrorist coming to blow up the building. She gives me this name tag that I paste on my body. I can feel the envy in her steely gaze and rigid body language. Sycophantically, I apologize for my thoughtlessness and I give her my ID; she gives me the dated body tag.[79]

On another occasion, this egregiously aggressive sentry becomes so upset that the anthropologist does not have her badge exactly on her left lapel that she tells the principal about the infraction. The anthropologist is summoned to the principal's office by some other adult (female) who mentions, offhandedly, having heard that the principal was looking for her. She hates getting this message from a third party and is baffled as to why she is being summoned. When she finally speaks with the principal later that day, she is informed that Hawkeye was concerned that her badge was not displayed properly. The principal assures her that the sentry is just doing her job.

The anthropologist immediately apologizes to the principal for violating the badge-placement rule, even accidentally, and explains that the badge kept falling from her lapel because of the straps on her purse and book bag and because of her cheap, damp polyester jacket. The principal appears to accept her explanation, but the anthropologist is conscious of the female-specific cultural practice that rewards women for avoiding conflict, as both of us do. The following entry from her field notes, almost a year later, details how all of this finally changes:

> The director of counseling was entering the building at the same time and as I bypassed the stairwell she said, "Why don't you go up the stairs? That way you don't have to go by the principal's office." I refused her invitation because I had to get the daily pass. Surprised, she said, "What?!" I told her, "Yes, every day I have to get a pass." Her response: "Well, that's not right. We'll see about getting you a pass like everyone else who routinely comes in the building." I was surprised and grateful because I feel dehumanized by Hawkeye's nonstop surveillance. She went to work right away, sensing that I don't feel emotionally safe. Later that day, I was given the official dog tag. As I am leaving, Hawkeye says, "Oh, I'm so glad to see that they finally gave you a pass, Dr. Fordham."[80]

The sentries have no way of knowing that the moment the anthropologist turns off the main street to enter the school grounds, she is totally transformed. No longer the self-confident professor, she becomes, instead, the sycophant who realizes that while she is described as a researcher, more eyes are watching her, eyes that are connected to powerful social and economic networks. She recognizes that some of this surveillance is occasioned by the fact that she is a Black woman completing a study in a predominantly White public suburban high school in upstate New York after the attacks of 9/11, not to mention after the shooting at Columbine High School. The hostility embedded in the daily name-tag exercise is emblematic of the hidden, gender-specific violence that is the subject of this book. It is masked by grace, kindness, and politeness, so that to even whisper that it makes her uncomfortable would validate the unvoiced perception that she is the proverbial n-bitch—an arrogant ingrate, not a victim but an assailant.

Romance and the Black Table

Since the passage of the Supreme Court decision of *Brown versus Board of Education* in 1954, one of the thorniest issues confronting Black students attending predominantly White schools is the nonclassroom behaviors and practices between Black and White students, males and females, and within these two categories— especially as these issues are connected to the potential for dating and mating. Compared to the widely studied "Black–White achievement gap,"[81] romance among and between Black and White high school students is virtually absent from the research literature.[82] Could this be a hidden factor in the inordinate focus on making sure that Black students—males and females, but especially males— follow school rules without deviation, on the almost total absence of any benefit of the doubt for young, immature, but hormonally overloaded humans? Is this fear implicated in the daily public humiliation of so many Black students? Could this be one reason for the omnipresent Black Table in the cafeteria and other highly segregated nonclassroom social spaces? Have researchers deliberately avoided this issue for fear of provoking or exacerbating racial animus and even greater eschewal of urban schools by White parents and their children? Answering these questions is important because, as is reflected in the widely reported claim that most Black kids seek to sit at what is identified as the Black Table, with whom one opts to share food is a central marker of intimacy, belonging, and equality. With the possible exception of work situations, people who see themselves as unequals socially do not eat with one another.[83]

There is virtual unanimity among Americans that since the first people of African ancestry to survive the Middle Passage arrived on North American soil, they have been intimately involved in caring for the people who compelled them to endure a permanent form of "racial indigestion."[84] During official periods of enslavement and the attendant two emancipations, Americans of African ancestry not only planted and harvested food but also cooked and served it to people who would never share a meal with them. Even after official enslavement ended, most of these practices continued. Whites then "helped" Black females by hiring them as maids.[85] The one common theme in virtually all interactions during and after official enslavement is that the enslaved and the nonenslaved were and are forbidden from eating together.

Many anthropologists, including Mary Douglas, have written extensively about the importance of food in social and cultural contexts.[86] In some instances, they have also explored the importance of whom one eats with. Claiming that food is a code that expresses how close or estranged we are in our relationship to another person or group, Douglas helps us understand how and why Black and White Americans eschew dining at the same table. We all remember that the driving force of the initial actions of the civil rights movement was the elimination of the barriers to eating in public spaces—the ubiquitous cafeterias and lunch counters. Interestingly, the issue was not the desire to eat *with* White people but simply to eat in the *same* public spaces.

Historically, opting to violate this rule could be fatal. In "Deciphering a Meal," Douglas insists that food is at its core a code conveying both social and biological messages: the "pattern of social relations being expressed [is] about different degrees of hierarchy, inclusion and exclusion, boundaries and transactions across the boundaries."[87] This challenges the widely accepted belief that Black children's practice of eating in a self-segregated space embraces the reproduction of racial categories and self-limiting social practices.

In her book *"Why Are All the Black Kids Sitting Together in the Cafeteria?,"* psychologist Beverly Tatum suggests that the Black Table is about identity formation and reinforcement.[88] Undoubtedly, this a factor. However, the book's title reinforces readers' belief that Black students have the option of whether or not to sit at the Black Table, and it shapes their perspective prior to engaging with the text. Anthropological research suggests an alternative definition embedded in the hierarchy (structural violence) and boundaries of inclusion and exclusion in the school, the immediate community, and American society.

The Black Table at UGRH conforms to Douglas's analysis that food is a code for social relationships. This is most clearly manifested in the fact that this small space in the school's cafeteria is the most highly valued public space for Black participants. Since the Black student population is under 10 percent and there are only two lunch periods, like a merry-go-round, the Black Table is most often fully occupied.[89] The Black Table affords Black students a coveted cultural space to have a daily reunion and reassure one another that they are not alone. For the anthropologist, this is surreal.

The first lunch period begins at 10:35 a.m., the second one forty-five minutes later. Who eats lunch at 10:30 in the morning?, the anthropologist wonders. Despite the safe space that the Black Table provides, it is also grounded in the "gated" nature of the school's curriculum and academic practices.[90] The table is segregated by gender, revealing that the females overvalue the potential for romantic connections. Viewed primarily as sisters, Black females are consigned to a buddy or some other vaunted nonincestuous role.[91]

Unlike the insular nature of other tables in the cafeteria, the boundaries of the Black Table are porous. For example, on most days, at least one White female (usually more) manages to sit behind the Black guy she is dating or trying to date. Moreover, one biracial girl, Sloane, who plays basketball and agreed to participate in the study but who does not typically associate with the other Black girls, is frequently in the second row of seats at the table because although she is madly in love with one of the Black guys who sits there, she does not want to be identified with the "unadulterated" Black girls. The fact that the various White girls opt not to sit in the seats at the table but in chairs that are pulled up behind "their men" is emblematic of what Kyla Tompkins describes as the violence affiliated with eating.[92] It also reveals how food and sexual desire cross and/or maintain established boundaries.

The code articulated in food and the attendant social relationships compel students to embrace the boundaries of the Black Table, making them extremely reluctant to forgo this valued space and time in order to talk with a researcher or anyone else. If the anthropologist were deliberately naive[93]—which she was at the beginning phase of the study—and made lunchtime appointments with the students who had agreed to participate in the study, they would promise to show up and then fail to appear. Most of the Black students, especially the females, would not think of forgoing their lunch-hour experience to spend time talking about the problems they confronted on a daily basis at the school, even though they clearly wanted an adult to know what they were undergoing and how it was affecting their academic and personal life.[94] This is quite different from their willingness to miss a designated study hall, which both the Black and White girls would do at the drop of a hat—not because they did not value studying but because they are isolated from their peers in study-hall settings. As Dorothy Holland and Margaret Eisenhart note about romantic relationships at the collegiate level, high school girls typically subordinate academic effort to "socializing, friendships, and romantic relationships."[95]

Romance in the Red-Light District

As in many high schools, at UGRH there are spaces that are privileged and spaces that are either much less or not at all privileged. In the privileged spaces, at the core of which are the numerous classrooms and labs given over to academic subject matter, only what is "nice" and gated is approved. In the stigmatized spaces, no one is considered elite or privileged, their existence denied by their compelled silence and underachievement. The Red-Light District—the space on the ground floor down the hall from the cafeteria and immediately across from the school's library—is one such nonprivileged space. Perhaps because this space is off the major thoroughfare, is darker than other areas, and is where many of the art classrooms and art projects are located, it has a different vibe than other spaces in the building.[96] Its avant-garde ambience is operationalized in response to the presence of a diverse mixture of racialized bodies.

One dark classroom, its blinds bolted to the windowsills and its door closed at all times, is a much-desired lunchtime social space. This northeast corner of the school is marked as the Black area (a euphemism for the ghetto) of the school. The Red-Light District is filled with not only Black bodies but a diversity of racialized bodies, hip-hop music, and potentially "cutting-edge" activities. The sexual attraction and tension between White girls and Black guys is tantamount to a blinking neon light in the space. The space is closely monitored by bulky White male "community aides" carrying walkie-talkies that are constantly in use. They are strategically placed every few feet in the hallway near clusters of lockers and hall intersections, enabling them to satisfy their voyeuristic interests by gazing at and craving young, nubile Black (and White) bodies— male and female—while ostensibly making sure that school rules are followed to a T. Students—male and female, Black, Brown, White, and everything in between—who desire a lunch break that is less subject to the unblinking gaze of the nonhip segment of the student body and to the intrusion of faculty congregate in this area. While school officials imagine what is happening in this dark corner of the school, they take a "See no evil, hear no evil" posture. As long as community aides keep everything under control, or at least make sure that nothing spills over into the rest of the school, the professionals are content to misrecognize what is going on.

Archaeological Data of a Nonmaterial Kind:
Digging and Digging and Digging

The research reported here was limited to four primary methods, only three of which are included in this book: (1) participant observation in nonclassroom spaces at the school; (2) formal and informal interviews with the students who had official permission to participate in the study; and (3) classroom observations of individual study participants.[97] Some ancillary methods included attending sports events, "hanging out" with individual girls during study blocks and at after-school activities, and several informal interviews with parents. Focus groups—a popular research strategy—were not utilized. The anthropologist was never with more than five Black girls at any one time, and the only time she was with more than one White girl was when she was with the cheerleaders—the female group that has the most power and prestige and that is typically designated to teach peers the appropriate route to womanhood.[98] The most dominant Black girl group was the step team, and since ReRe, the team captain, was such an effective leader, getting her cooperation was essential in order for the anthropologist to gain access to other girls in the group. The school's nearly twenty-five cheerleaders were a more fractious group even though it had no more than two Black female members. Of the two Black members, only one fit the stereotypical image of a cheerleader, compelling the anthropologist to constantly revisit Don Merten's claims regarding the inevitable congruency between an individual girl's perceived social status and the extracurricular activities she seeks to be a part of, on the one hand, and the activities that she is allowed to access, on the other.[99] The anthropologist also interviewed (both in person and on the phone) some of the parents of key informants. The following is a typical example of the stress she experienced:

It's Tuesday and I'm just returning from the research site. I am trying *not* to be discouraged by all the obstacles I am facing. This

is *such* unbelievably difficult work. Not because the task itself
is difficult, it's just the hidden resistance of the people who are
potential informants: the female students' inability or unwillingness to return the forms. Every day I see them and I ask, "Did you
bring the form[s]?"[100]

During the initial stages of the study, the anthropologist almost
quit several times. She was not prepared for either the number or
the persistence of problems she encountered—including obstacles
that seemed to be deliberately placed in her path. Her inability to
get forms signed for twenty students, as required in the approved
research plan, was the most debilitating. Walking was central to
this study because, in trying to find twenty appropriate students,
hundreds of female students had to be considered, eliminated, or
accepted. Some students indicated that they were interested in
participating in the study but were kept out by parents who refused
to sign approval forms. Others who expressed initial interest
subsequently changed their minds; their reasons included "I want
my friend to participate and she doesn't want to" and "My boyfriend
does not want me to do it." She was able to survive inspired by
hearing her mother's voice repeatedly reminding her that if it did
not kill her it would make her stronger, and she managed, somehow,
to complete the project.

This stage of the research was unmatched in terms of the dissonance the anthropologist experienced, reminding her constantly
of similar ethnographic issues reported by many other researchers,
anthropologists[101] and nonanthropologists alike.[102] Among these,
Kirby Moss's ethnographic descriptions of his attempts to study
"poor White [folks] and the paradox of privilege" are probably
the most telling in that they closely parallel the anthropologist's
dilemma at UGRH. Like him, she constantly struggled with the
irony embodied in the prevailing belief at the research site that
Whiteness is the only site of privilege. Even more important, according to Cheryl Harris, it is "whiteness as property" that makes "tres-

passing" and efforts aimed at de-privileging so daunting.[103] Consequently, her mere presence as a Black professional caused many potential participants and adults to be confused and uncertain about how to name her or respond to her. Their aversion to being labeled "racist," as well as their desire to promote UGRH as a site unstained by the legacy of Black enslavement and racial discrimination, compelled many of them to embrace a contorted stance manifestly evident in their body language and social interactions but never in face-to-face linguistic practices.

Phase One: Roaming and Foraging Endlessly for Student Participants

As the research protocol called for twenty female student participants, the anthropologist searched for ten Black girls and ten White girls—primarily in public, nonclassroom spaces like the main office and the counselors' offices, the basement gym, the cafeteria, and even around the pool, where Black girls were scarcer than rare birds.[104]

The following text from her field notes captures the counselors' willingness to help her avoid some potential faux pas, especially in dealing with the students' parents. The meeting referred to was arranged by the male head of the unit and took place approximately three months after the study began.

> Four males and four females, all White, attended the 10:00 a.m. lunch meeting in the counseling suite. They talked and I answered their research-related questions.[105] These counselors, social workers, and psychologists shared with me their specific duties and responsibilities at the various sites in the school district. I chronicled the specifics of my planned study and reassured them that any info they shared comes under the confidential clause of my research, that I would not reveal the name of the school or the participant, and that I am absolutely committed to confidentiality.[106]

During this meeting, they advised the anthropologist repeatedly that UGRH parents are extremely protective of their children. They also reminded her that they had limited contact with the school's "normal" kids and would be more likely to be able to help her if she were interested in "abnormal" kids, kids who were bipolar, depressed, or suffering from developmental disabilities. One member of the group suggested that they should call parents on behalf of the anthropologist. That idea died almost immediately. Instead, one of them offered the following genteel opening that the anthropologist could use to do the work herself: "Your child is tangled up in the social web of the school." This critical sentence, the counselor insisted, would soften the request, making it less threatening.[107] The anthropologist gave them her contact information, and they agreed to e-mail her with suggestions for a name for her study.

She left the meeting feeling hopeful that she would be able to move on to the second stage of the study. However, despite the success of the meeting, leads from this group were not overwhelming. For example, one member of the group, who clearly wanted to help, sent her an e-mail with the names of a couple of students who were ideal candidates. Fear was manifested in the note in an urgent sentence asking her to respond immediately and to assure this member that she would not tell these students or their parents who had recommended them. Like the anthropologist, this person realized the inordinate costs associated with being perceived as a violator of the extant rules.

For weeks, the anthropologist had no access to a private room in the building and had to wait until she returned to her office at the university or home to call parents, which was often too late. The prevalence of divorce in this community exacerbated the problem, as this excerpt from her field notes illuminates:[108]

> There is so much divorce and breakdown of family. When I call the *mother*, it's the *father* I have to talk to, in a separate household. I call the *father*, and it's the *mother* that I have to talk to. I feel like I have called everybody at this school.[109]

The anthropologist waded through this daily labyrinth of trying to recruit participants. The following example is a case in point:

> One of the teachers whom I trusted almost immediately
> identified an ideal White student whose "life is absolutely
> awful." She has three or four older brothers, most of whom are in
> prison. Her father is the last person I called today (all the other
> parents were either mothers or stepmothers). I'm preparing
> to give him the big spiel . . . , trying to soften it because I don't
> want him to think that I think his daughter is aggressive. He
> says, almost immediately, "Oh, of course you can talk to her." I'm
> flabbergasted. His almost immediate "yes" was [so] unexpected.[110]

His response was distinctly unlike that of most of the female parents, who interrogated the anthropologist about every detail of the study. Typically, she was on the phone with each female parent fifteen to thirty minutes, and often more. Seeing that parents did not appear to trust her as a professional, she softened her approach, focusing on the most difficult task for each participant: keeping a diary for ten weeks. For this, she offered to pay them movie money—ten dollars a week.

The anthropologist began to see a pattern of differential access. An overwhelming majority of the Black parents—regardless of gender—worked outside their homes, often at job sites that did not permit them to take phone calls when they were not at lunch or on designated breaks. She took into consideration the fact that for many of these parents, their jobs fit into the category that Ogbu identifies as "jobs below the job ceiling"—jobs that generally do not embrace the idea of autonomy.[111] Contacting the parents of White girls was far less problematic, and also more varied. The anthropologist spoke with about as many fathers as mothers, even though they often had spouses who were not the biological parents of the potential participants.[112] It was much easier to reach them at their jobs if they were working. She was able to reach many mothers at their home telephone numbers, even during the day.[113]

If parents did not object to their child participating in the study, the anthropologist assured them that their child would bring the appropriate form home and asked that they confirm their approval by signing it. Finally, she asked them to sign a second form agreeing to participate themselves.[114] Despite her objection, the Research Subject Review Board (RSRB) insisted she must get parental approval *prior* to talking to potential participants, even though the first person she met face-to-face was the student.[115] She feared that a phone call from a strange, disembodied, Black-identified female voice with a southern accent would not inspire either White or Black parents to allow their teenage daughters to participate in the study.[116]

Ideally, the anthropologist expected to get recommendations from school personnel identifying aggressive female students and then to call their parent(s) to ask for permission to talk to their children. If a child agreed to be involved in the study, the anthropologist would then ask the student to take the parental approval forms home and return them with the required signature(s). If the child forgot or failed to do so, the anthropologist was compelled to call parents to follow up. The following are a couple of typical cases:

> I want to talk to this student in part because she is of mixed heritage—mixed race. She's very anxious to be in the study, and obviously has a lot to tell me.[117] Early in our conversations she told me that she was going to be out of school for three weeks and hospitalized. I don't know what this means. She later told me she had changed her mind, and since she'd heard that I was out here yesterday passing out the journals, she was looking for me. The second student who I *think* is a White student, but who obviously has grown up in the Black community and says such things as, "Aah! I don't like that White boy!," seems very much identified with the African American community, and is also new to this school. According to the administration, she is already in trouble. I'm anxious to learn more about her. She is a very interesting student, but she hasn't had her parents sign the forms.

Today I asked her if she would please have her parent, or parents, sign the forms. I don't know if she'll [keep the weekly diaries for ten weeks] for me, that's the problem. She is the kind of girl that appears to be marginalized. Odd girl out.[118]

This roaming and foraging continued until October and beyond. It was the central issue in the anthropologist's research agenda, a blazing red light with a vivid warning: time is running out.

Phase Two: Observing, Journaling, and Interviewing for Insight—and Daylight

The mantra of ethnography that the anthropologist keeps on a hand-written note on the dashboard of her old car reads: "The ethnographer is the research instrument." During the more than two years of this study, there were many days when she absolutely loathed that message. There were days when she started or ended her field site visit so diminished that she had to cover the sign with her hand to keep from bawling. There were many days, especially during the winter months of the first year, that she involuntarily became an archaeologist, excavating not only cultural data but the energy and the will to survive below the surface.[119]

If the number of steps she took at the school throughout the study were indicators of success, this would be the most triumphant ethnography ever written. Regrettably, that is not how it works. On a daily basis, at least three times a week and sometimes more, she walked the full length of the W wing, which included stops in the main office and the cafeteria, on to the Red-Light District, the pool area, and the choral and arts section on the first level, then down to the lower level and the gym area and up the stairs to the first, second, and third floors leading to the remaining wings. She schlepped over this route a minimum of two times a day, often more.

Once she was at the site and saw the potential, she was thrown into crisis mode, challenged and unduly frustrated with the convoluted process. She dared not alter or modify the process because, as a former colleague assured her, the members of the university's RSRB were convinced that they knew more about how the study should be done than she did, even though they were not anthropologists and only one of them had done fieldwork. Furthermore, though she knew she was the only visible ethnographer from the university at the research site, she also recognized that the people at the research site were connected to the university via underground networks: networks of friends and neighbors who lived next door and down the street from each other, of people who knew people who worked at the university, of spouses, aunts, uncles, cousins, and other kith and kin of the adults employed at UGRH. Her dual consciousness compelled her to see them watching her with bemused contempt as she struggled to obtain the desired informants.[120]

The anthropologist's first source of information was the counselors, who provided a long list of names of Black girls regularly engaged in physical altercations. Since physical aggression was not what she was interested in studying, she tried to push back gently by telling them that while studying female physical aggression would be an interesting research project, it was not the focus of *this* study. Instead, she was interested in symbolic violence, the kind of violence that is the inevitable outcome of habituated practices that many researchers label "relational (or indirect) aggression"[121] and that are depicted in such popular-culture venues as the movie *Mean Girls,*[122] Rosalind Wiseman's book *Queen Bees and Wannabes,*[123] and Rachel Simmons's *Odd Girl Out.*[124] However, many of the counselors were unable to alter their long-held belief that the only girls capable of this kind of violence came dressed in Black bodies. Others understood immediately that there were many girls, including White girls, who fit this description perfectly. These professionals, primarily young White females, understood intuitively the nature of the research, having engaged in the practices themselves as high school students. In some instances, they continued to indulge in symbolic violence in their professional adult lives, in which they are rewarded with a paycheck for embracing the "drop dead sameness" ethos chronicled in Thomas Kochman and Jean Mavrelis's *Corporate Tribalism* and more recently in Sheryl Sandberg's *Lean In.*[125] The amount of information they shared regarding the personal and family lives of students both astounded and dismayed the anthropologist. She concluded that privacy did not exist.

In exchange for sharing this in-house information with the researcher, these professionals expected her to rapidly complete the study so that they could see what she, the combined nabob-anthropologist, concluded regarding these "mean girls" and their "abnormal" families. Marcel Mauss's notion of the paradox of gifting and giving was not just some remote theoretical claim, but a concrete expectation that in exchange for access to the school and the students, she would reciprocate with immediate access to her research findings.[126]

Once the anthropologist had finally obtained all the signed forms for the required student population, her observations became more focused on the specific girls who had received parental permission to participate in the study. In an effort to learn how female aggression, bullying, and competition are operationalized at this school—including how and why Black and White female students are rewarded for eschewing physical aggression—and to incentivize student participation, a critical subcomponent of this phase of the study was a ten-week payment offered to participants in return for keeping a daily diary detailing their interactions with other females.[127] As the following excerpt from her field notes documents, the "movie money" idea got out of control:

> When I got back from Minneapolis this weekend, I called parents and I looked at the list. One mother said that she expects a gift certificate from the biggest food chain in Rodman. I have not called this woman yet because I'm still trying to figure out how to respond to such an outlandish request. One of the other parents asked about compensation. . . . "Mercenary" is the word that comes to mind. I want to talk to these people and get their kids involved. I try not to emphasize the fact that I hope to be able to give these kids ten dollars a week for each week that they keep the

diary. I don't want people to be involved because they're getting compensation, but apparently compensation is important to a lot of parents.[128]

During this stage of the study the anthropologist was allowed to use a second conference room. She got the key from someone in the main counseling office on an ad hoc basis, and if one of the counselors was using the room or had a planned meeting, she had to find another location, even if she was in the middle of a formal interview with a student. This was extremely unsettling because it was so difficult for both parties—the anthropologist and the student—to find a mutually agreeable time (and space) to meet.

Phase Three: Classroom Visitation and Parental Engagement

One of the African American participants in the study gave the anthropologist the following information:

> I'm in the tenth grade, and I have been at this school for one year. I don't like it here. It's boring, and there's too much drama. The classes are boring and the way the teachers teach is boring. The work is too easy. I don't know. I just—I get all my work done, and it's just—I have nothing to do. So I just wander around the school, 'cause I have nothing to do.[129]

The anthropologist remembers how surprised she was during her first classroom observations to see how many female adults were available in many of the classrooms.[130] For example, the first time she observed McKayla, a tenth-grader and one of the ten Black girls who agreed to participate in the study, there were four adults with her biology class of twelve students: the teacher of record who presented the lecture, a volunteer aide who wrote the lecture on the blackboard in the classroom/lab, another unpaid aide who used an overhead projector to summarize points for the students,[131] and a paid community worker who stood in the rear of the classroom/lab, presumably to deter inappropriate behavior and to run errands or warn of pending danger.[132] The anthropologist looked around the room repeatedly, searching for signs of interest or excitement on the faces of the students. These emotions may have been present, but she did not see evidence of them. Most of the students were dutifully copying the carefully crafted information offered to them, while propping up their bored chins and faces with their free hand. Apparently, the greatest intellectual challenge the students in this classroom (and many others) faced on a daily basis was copying in their notebooks, either from the board or from the overhead projector, the information from one of the two mediums that aides used to summarize the teacher's lecture. Thus, they were freed from the task of trying to discern what to include in their note taking and what to leave out.

The activities in a science classroom offer another example of the nature of the academic work. The enrollment in this class was much larger (twenty-three students), and there was only one adult in addition to the teacher. In this case, it was the rampant inefficiency that got the anthropologist's attention. After each correct response to a question, the teacher would throw a small white stuffed animal into one of the four student areas. The student who caught it was expected to bat it on to another student, and that student would bat it to another, and so on. This activity—and the subject matter of the class itself—was mind-numbing for the anthropologist. Nonetheless, there were virtually no discipline problems, except that the teacher asked them to keep their voices down as they giggled and scrambled to catch or bat the stuffed toy. The students were engaged, and there was lots of laughter and hand raising—and presumably, passing grades.

The anthropologist made several unsuccessful attempts to talk about Ally, one of the students she observed in this teacher's classroom. She finally concluded that this relatively young female teacher was not going to talk to her about her classroom practices or about the academic repertoire of the student in her study. The anthropologist silently admitted failure and moved on. This is typical of how the teachers responded to her requests following classroom observations. She concluded that they feared negative repercussions if they refused outright to allow her to observe their classrooms, but they were not willing to discuss what went on in class. They compromised by appearing to cooperate by allowing her to observe their classrooms but ending their support there.

The researcher's interactions with the students' parents were also fraught with conflict and misunderstandings, differentiated by race and gender, with gender being far more salient than race. She talked with only one Black male parent during the study and with approximately five White male parents; all other parental interactions were with female parents.

With the possible exception of the Black male parent, the male parents appeared far less fearful and more willing to trust that she was not going to hurt their daughters. In striking contrast, the mothers and other female guardians appeared far less sanguine about the goals of her study and about her as a researcher. The following examples from her field notes are typical of the distinctions between the male and female parents.

> I called another parent this morning. He was the only (White) male parent with whom I've spoken [today]. . . . He was very open to the idea, said he'd already talked with his daughter [and his wife, his daughter's mother] about the study. . . . And he said that she seemed predisposed to wanting to be in the study. He asked if I knew she had an eating disorder and wanted to know if that would negatively affect my study, and I said no. When I told him that I was going to be away for the holiday, he said that was fine, that as soon as I got the letter and forms to him, he would get them back to me.

> This mother identifies as . . . African-American. . . . She's concerned that her daughter is being asked to participate in the study and that school officials had not forewarned her of this.

My response: "Well, I don't think *they* know who I'm going to choose, and so it would be prohibitively expensive to send out a letter to everybody in the school system." But she kept asking me if I understood, and of course I do, and maybe I should have given these people the names and *they* should have called the parents.[133] But they didn't tell me that I had to do that, and I didn't want to burden them with what I think is my responsibility. She wanted to know if her daughter would get some academic credit or something like that, and I said, "Well, no, I don't think so." She seemed a little bit miffed, and I assured her that I would send a note to the human resources director and the principal.

At 10:00 a.m., I called another parent. She said her daughter is a terror . . . recently involved in a scheduled fight. She [asked rhetorically], "*What* is a scheduled fight?" The family moved to this suburban school district [where] her daughter was suspended three times in the first three months. . . . She talked to her [daughter] before I called and said that she seemed predisposed to being involved in the study. She adopted this daughter [when she was] four years old. . . . Her [daughter's biological] mother was a prostitute. She told me all of this on the phone. She said her [daughter] takes piano lessons, everything, so she's an ideal child at home, but just when she gets to school, she goes bonkers. . . . She has a seventeen-year-old biological child who is just the opposite . . . ; she would never even know the name of the principal if she were depending on her biological daughter. . . . The daughter that I'm interested in as a part of the study has an outgoing personality. She helps her [adopted mother] tremendously, she could help her raise *her* children. The mother thinks that this child is . . . good at mothering, apparently. She gets good grades, but in the meantime, she plays bad guy, or real rough guy. . . . [The family] go[es] to church, and they keep her in the prayer lines. She doesn't know what is going on with her daughter when she leaves the house. She's sneaky, she said.[134]

From the first day the anthropologist was at UGRH, she drooled at the thought of observing the participants in their classes, wanting desperately to know how these students' performance differed from the students she had observed in predominantly Black contexts and how the gendered practices that are so central to the study fueled the unacknowledged female-specific bullying at the school. In addition, she longed to empirically document why there are so few friendships and connections between Black and White girls at this school. But none of this was possible, at least not right away. She had to wait until she obtained permission from the students and their parents. This bureaucratic issue did not, however, diminish her desire for more than a year.

The anthropologist realized that, unlike many of the earlier components of this research, classroom observations would be drastically different from those reported in her earlier works, especially those chronicled in the Capital High study.[135] She was anxious to observe the classrooms in part because she had heard many competing narratives regarding the efficacy and difficulty of the approved curriculum, including repeated claims by African American students that they were not adequately challenged by the limited expectations and demands of the courses they were allowed or assigned to take.

At this particular research site, the classroom demographics were drastically different from those of her earlier research sites, both with respect to the relative scarcity of Black students and also with respect to the abundance of adult support—much of it unpaid. The anthropologist was anxious to see how this altered the classroom dynamics and the performance of students—not only of the girls who agreed to participate in the study but of others as well.

The approved research protocol allowed her to observe each of the twenty study participants in their classes, with their teachers' approval. None of the teachers she approached refused her request outright, but at the same time, none of them appeared overly enthusiastic. She looked for the disjunction between their perpetually smiling faces and the lifelessness and vaguely masked hostility in their eyes. She approached each of them gingerly, almost as an uninvited guest at a party. She tried not to appear threatening by assuring them that her goal was not to evaluate their teaching practices but to focus on the student(s) and to find answers to some of the following questions: Was the student regularly prepared for class? Did she routinely complete the required homework? Did she regularly appear engaged or unengaged with the subject matter? Did she actively participate in classroom projects and discussions? When called upon to participate in class, what was her typical response pattern? What was her relationship with the other students in the class, especially the other females? Did the teachers see evidence of female-specific, nonphysical bullying and aggression? If yes, what was this particular teacher's typical response to it? Finally, she asked classroom teachers if they would be willing to give her a written or oral evaluation of the student's performance beyond the days she observed.[136] A few did; most did not.

CHAPTER 3

Nadine

WORDS AS VIOLENCE AND MISRECOGNITION

Sticks and stones will break my bones. But words will never harm me.

—*The Christian Recorder,* March 1862

Words as Violence—Misrecognized

"Nigger bitch."[1] You hear these vile words and you cringe; your heart palpitates and you shiver, as though the temperature in the school cafeteria were five degrees below zero and not seventy-five above, on a beautiful spring day in a suburban community in upstate New York. Your body is suddenly very cold, yet your face burns with indignation and humiliation. You try to control your emotional state and, by extension, your body temperature.

You are intimately familiar with these words. They are like a first and last name; they define and convey an identity. The two nouns are interchangeable; you are never sure which name is first and which is last. "Nigger bitch" or "bitch nigger"? They couple Blackness and femaleness in a pulsating mass of unalterably negative energy. They scrape through your Black, female skin, piercing your psyche so completely that you stagger under the pain while you fight to maintain your balance and composure. The power and weight of these words compel you to engage in a kind of involuntary bipolar hemorrhaging: I am not a "nigger bitch"; I am a "nigger bitch"; I am not a "nigger bitch"; I am a "nigger bitch."

In fact, you are a seventeen-year-old, self-identified Black female student in a predominantly White suburban high school. In the last semester of your senior year, you are looking forward with ambivalent excitement and anxiety to graduation and your new life after high school. At just over five feet tall, weighing less than a hundred pounds soaking wet, and speaking in an exceedingly soft voice, you exude dominant femininity—except for your brown skin. Your shoulder-length hair, the primary visible marker of American femininity, is permed and carefully coiffed on a daily basis.

You have agreed to participate in a research study of female aggression and competition. Both you and your mother, the only parent intimately involved in your life, have signed the researcher's university-approved consent form. In her field notes, the anthropologist recalls her first encounter with you and the subsequent phone conversation with your mother:

> Another young woman, whom I had *not* been able to find, despite the fact that so many people told me that she would be an ideal participant, came into the main office and I just happened to be there. I asked her if she would consider participating in my study, and she said yes immediately. I gave her the formulaic spiel: have to call her parents first to see if they would permit me to talk to her. She said she thought her mother would, and she gave me her mother's work phone number. . . . I assured her that I would call her . . . immediately, and then I would get the forms and bring them to her in her . . . fourth-block class. . . . First I asked . . . her . . . if it would be okay to call her mother at work, and she said yes. . . . I called her mother. . . . She was very, very nice. And the first thing I said is, "There's nothing wrong, I'm at your daughter's school," and then I told her who I was; that I worked at ——— . . . that I was doing a study of female aggression and—everything about females to try to determine what factors impact their academic performance. . . . She said, "Sure." Since her daughter had said she thought she'd be interested, I then went back to her daughter and asked her—I told her that her mother said yes. . . . I told her I would have to duplicate forms I had with me. I was using the printing machine at the school. I feel guilty about doing

that, but it couldn't be avoided, because if I delay, I have found that it just never gets done . . . the students don't bring the forms back, it takes them forever to do anything. Oh, my God! . . . I gave the student the forms.[2]

You know the researcher teaches at one of the local universities. You don't quite know which one (she's told you but you've forgotten), but you know it is a prestigious college. You are impressed that she is called "Doctor," but at first she seems more like your White teachers than like you.

In addition to the fact that you like being invited to participate in a university study (Wow!), you really need someone to talk to about the angst you are experiencing over belonging and dating and over life after high school. Moreover, you've been accused by school administrators of engaging in (physically) violent behavior in the past. Indeed, your mother moved you and your brothers and sisters into this community and away from the urban center in order to enable you to change schools and start over. While all of your schooling has occurred in suburban systems, you—and all the other Black kids you know at your current school—are often treated as though you are "matter out of place,"[3] uninvited guests in your own school.

Guests. The word conjures up images of how you feel when you are compelled to spend time at your mother's only White girlfriend's apartment: you are very, very careful, and very, very silent. When you are in the classroom—especially English class, where discussing opinions matters—you virtually never speak, even when you know the answer or would like to ask a question. Your silence is deeper if the teacher is White. She (or, occasionally, he) may not verbally correct your grammar, but the teacher's body language and other nonverbal responses spell disapproval. You are sure you are not misreading their cues; you've had a lifetime of experience interpreting this language.

You want desperately to be involved in this study because the researcher has offered you a chance to talk about your interactions with other girls at school. You and your best girlfriend, Keyshia, who is also Black, have recently made an effort to repair your broken relationship. Last year you feared it had been ruptured beyond repair by her decision to go out with Kyle, the boy you were dating at that very time, and to keep it a secret from you. He was a big man around campus, rumored to be a "street pharmacist." Guys who have access to drugs, regardless of race, are hugely popular among the girls at all the schools you have attended. Kyle, who (secretly) dated your best friend Keyshia, was a senior and graduated last year. Now he is living in California, trying to become a hip-hop artist. Like you, your BFF Keyshia is a senior this year, and she is bringing him as her guest to the senior prom. What a downer! You have decided not to go to the prom this year, even though you have moved on and are dating a White boy who does not attend this school.[4]

The researcher, who describes herself as an anthropologist (you are not sure what that means), claims that not all violence is physical and that some forms of violence, especially the kind most often practiced by girls and women, involve the use of hurtful words. You know what violence is, but what does she mean by "symbolic violence"? Symbols, as your English teacher routinely explains, are words or images that stand for or point toward something else, so how can symbols inflict pain? You are really beginning to worry about this anthropology lady. There's nothing symbolic about the violence you know: shootings, murders, beatings. Yes, words can wound, hurt a person's feelings, but if you confuse them with violence, like that lady anthropologist seems to be doing, you are borderline cuckoo and can get into real trouble.

The anthropologist claims that even gossiping about another person can be defined as an act of violence and that verbal aggression is generally associated with females, while physical aggression is generally associated with males. You do not understand and are not sure if you can agree with her. How could people talking about you and hurting your feelings be equated with the violence that occurs when someone hits you? This claim violates what you have been taught and take for granted; it's not how the authorities at school see things, or what adults at home care about.

Moving from words to a more abstract example, the anthropologist explains that hunger is also a form of violence perpetrated by a society that refuses to provide parents with adequate pay for their labor so that they can feed and shelter their children. You look at her like, "Omigod!! This lady's credibility is really on the line."

Nevertheless, your uncertainty, ambivalence, and suspicion that the researcher might be on to something are fueled by the conflict that occurred last year. While you have not thought of violence in the way the anthropologist talks about it, you know that when Keyshia began dating your boyfriend Kyle, and did not even tell you, that experience was the most hellish and painful in your life, far worse than some physical fights of which you have been a part.

"The Fight"—Nadine's Version

On this beautiful May day, you and your former BFF Keyshia enter the cafeteria together and put your backpacks on the chairs at a table in the middle of the room, close to the two major serving lines on opposite ends of the room near the kitchen. You both decide to take a pass on the full, heavy-duty lunch (a choice of mashed potatoes with puddles of gray gravy, various forms of pasta swimming in tomato sauce, the obligatory greasy pizza from one of the national chains, rice, vegetables, bread, apple pie, and similar offerings) in favor of the shorter line selling packaged foods, including potato chips, pretzels, Doritos, soda, ice cream, and chocolate-chip cookies.[5] You purchase the popular snacks you both like and return to the table where you left your backpacks.

As you round the corner and see the table you have chosen, you become aware that a group of White girls is sitting there. It slowly dawns on you that the group is made up primarily of the school's cheerleaders, though they are not in uniform. Your BFF recognizes them before you do. They argue that they have prior claim to the seats at the table and all the other chairs there. Both you and Keyshia insist—you more strongly than she—that you had the seats first and that you are not going to move. The disagreement escalates.

The American hegemonic discourse practice of taking turns when speaking falls by the wayside as the larger group of White girls all chime in to say not only that the two of you—African American females—are out of place in seeking to occupy two of the chairs at this long table, but also that this entire table belongs to them because they sit here every day. In the more familiar female discourse style, everyone begins talking at the same time, words cascading like water, bumping into each other, creating an unfathomable flood of discourse, littered with the gender-specific racial and cultural debris these young women have absorbed in their sixteen, seventeen, and eighteen years of life.

You try to argue that no one can claim proprietary rights to a seat or a table in the school's cafeteria, that this is public, communal space. You doubt that anyone hears you because everyone is talking at the same time. Nevertheless, the moment Kirstin, a tall, willowy, blonde (a euphemism for White) girl, calls you the name—"nigger bitch"—everybody hears it. It is as if the speaker has thrown a stink bomb on the table and everyone is suddenly immobilized, holding her nose, waiting to see what happens next. The words echo amid a silence so profound that you swear you can hear individual heartbeats.

Your heart pounds. The blood rushes to your face, but because your skin is dark no one notices. You are suddenly, inexplicably chilled to the bone. Your sense of shame and humiliation is too much to bear. With your right hand, you reach up (the girl who uttered the slur is taller than you, about five foot seven), and with every ounce of strength you can muster, you slap her full across the face. Your hand stings, the force is so great. You notice your handprint on both sides of her face, interrupted only by her nose. Your antagonist's face turns from pink to beet red to splotchy purple. Tears well up in her eyes, and she begins to cry, silently at first; then she is convulsed by sobs. Her friends push you away with great force as they gather around her, forming a protective wall. Adults arrive, including an assistant principal who takes you immediately to his office, hurling your flimsy young body before him as he assumes command.

Just like that, you were disappeared. No one saw or acknowledged hearing from you from that moment until you returned to school five days later. The anthropologist called you several times on the phone, but you were so humiliated and embarrassed by what had happened that you refused to call her back. As she told you later, she kept looking for you. On the second or third day, she called you at your home number, and you answered. This is what she recorded in her field notes:

> I still haven't seen or heard from Nadine. As I waited in the
> office, talking to one of the secretaries, I decided to go back
> upstairs to call the Black girl who slapped the White girl, who
> was suspended from school. I finally got her on the phone; her
> voice sounded so tiny. So weak. I said to her, "Oh, I'd love to talk
> to you when you come back to school." And she said that she
> wouldn't be back until Thursday of next week. But she would
> talk to her grandmother to see if it was okay to talk to me at her
> apartment—after school might be a good time. So I said to her
> that I would be happy to do that. I'd stay after school to talk to
> her. I really want to know what happened, and why. I'm much
> more interested in *why* it happened. I know she was humiliated by
> the experience—the violence of this woman's decision to call her
> the n-word *and* the b-word combined [in the same sentence].[6]

The anthropologist met you at your maternal grandmother's very neat, very organized fourth-floor, garden style, two-bedroom, two-bath apartment, which is part of a huge apartment complex about midway between the school and the anthropologist's residence. You were currently staying with your grandmother because your mom was very unhappy with you in the wake of the fight with the cheerleader. You liked staying with your grandmother because she absolutely adores you, her oldest grandchild. In addition, the apartment is furnished in the traditional furniture that your grandmother loves, perched on standard-issue green wall-to-wall carpeting provided by the apartment complex; a traditional dining room with sliding glass doors opens onto a small patio. The anthropologist entered the apartment through the unit's only door, which opens directly into the galley kitchen. The kitchen is followed by the living room/dining room combination. For the next two and a half hours, the two of you sat on your grandmother's comfortable green sofa and talked, with the tape recorder catching every word and sound.

When the anthropologist asked you about the fight in the cafeteria, you acknowledged, in hindsight, that you behaved in a way that did not bring honor to your already questionable reputation as an angry Black woman, but the vileness of the terms the cheerleader had used hurt too much to let her get away without some hurt as well.

> I want to tell you about this fight. I never liked her. I don't know why. It was just the way her and her little group walked along, thinking they're all that. I don't like to see that. I just don't like people like that, and—I'll admit *I* was the aggressor. There was like four or five of them, and I was getting on their nerves. And— then I started going, and they jumped aside. . . . And then they told me to move out of their way so they can sit down. And I said, Hell no, oh no. This was before I hit the girl. And I went up to her face, and slapped her, and I said to myself again, "You will find yourself in trouble." . . . That girl really pissed me off, when she called me a "nigger bitch." No, no. No, that was a oh, no. So— huh-uh. I got up in her face, and I punched the shit out of her. That just ticked me off. And I, you know . . . I shouldn't have hit her. It was stupid to hit her. But I was mad.[7]

The assistant principal, a youngish-looking White American male, Mr. Kanker, knows you; students at the school are assigned to these officials by gender and/or grade level. He has reprimanded you in the past, including that one time when you were involved in a physical altercation at the school. He knows you are a senior, scheduled to graduate in less than a month. No matter. He immediately suspends you for a whole week and tells you that you're lucky he's not recommending you be expelled. You try to engage him in a conversation that will make him realize that slapping your antagonist was warranted; she called you two of the most vile names anyone can call a Black female. He refuses to listen, repeatedly reminding you that violence is not tolerated at this school.

Mr. Kanker called your mother at work and told her that you had just been just involved in a fight and that she must come immediately to take you away; you were no longer permitted to be on school grounds. Suspension denies you access to the library and all other academic resources. Your appeal for understanding, your plea to be allowed to continue to study for your impending senior exams, went unheeded. He reminded you that you had been in trouble before and that you knew the rules against engaging in violence. When you tried to argue that you were also a victim of violence (the anthropologist had told you about this kind of violence when she was recruiting you to participate in her study), that you were violated by the use of those vile terms, he ignored your feelings and concerns. He pointed out that there was no comparison between your response—hitting your antagonist—and the provocative names she called you. The message conveyed by the professional adults at the school, including Mr. Kanker, was that the only harm in this dispute was physical.

In striking contrast, your antagonist's emotional discomfort was recognized and validated along with her physical discomfort. She cried angry tears, her face a motley mixture ranging from pale pink to bright purple. There was no way to miss her anger. She was immediately escorted by her friends and several adults to the principal's office, both to inform school officials and to call her mother. She was followed by her younger sister and a posse of her friends who vowed to "sue her" (you, the Black girl).

The next day, in the wake of the fight between Nadine and Kirstin, the anthropologist's field notes reveal what she learned in the immediate aftermath:

I tried to get more information regarding why Nadine was suspended yesterday. I learned from her counselor that she was suspended for five days, and the assistant principal, Mr. Kanker, said that Nadine was lucky because they gave her a break. Because at this time of the year, school officials are reviewing everything, this is very important, and they let her off easy. . . . And the information that I got from multiple informants—not just one— was that [Kirstin] used the "n" word. And when she used the "n" word, added to the word "bitch," . . . [Nadine] slapped her back into yesterday. Her counselor said that this is something that's been building up since September.

. . . The first student . . . I interviewed the day after the fight the next morning said that she didn't know why there was a fight. All the students *know*, of course, that there was a fight yesterday, that Nadine hit the White cheerleader in the cafeteria. One student informant said that she didn't think that it was racial in nature, be- cause the White girl who called this Black girl a "NIGGER bitch," had a Black boyfriend, suggesting, in her response to the incident, that because the White girl had a Black lover, she could *not* have racist feelings, or be a racist. Because she was having sex with a Black man, she could not be labeled a racist.[8]

Interestingly, while in the hall of the Z wing one morning shortly after the fight, the anthropologist told you (Nadine) that she had run into Mr. Kanker, the assistant principal who had been intimately involved in your dismissal from school. This is what she told you she recorded in her field notes on that encounter.

I saw the assistant principal who was the authority figure involved in Nadine's dismissal from school. Someone suggested that I should talk to *him* about the student who was kicked out of school for fighting, or slapping, a White girl who called *her* the "n" word, which is unacceptable if you're a Black person, and the "b" word, [which] is unacceptable to a White person—a gendered female person. She was thrown out of school. So they said to me to talk to Mr. Kanker, the assistant principal. . . . He would have more information. I saw him in the hallway, and I said to him that I wanted to talk to him about this student. He said, well, he couldn't talk to me now, of course, because there was another life-threatening conflict that he was trying to resolve. I said okay, I'll try next week.[9]

Avoiding "Boys Are My (Only) Entertainment" Syndrome?

Your decision to date a White male student was widely known by the other students at the school, both Black and White. This may not only have subjected you to greater scrutiny by all segments of the school community, but it also was probably one of the factors that led to the confrontation with Kirstin, the White cheerleader in the cafeteria. This is how you describe the trigger fueling the physical altercation in the cafeteria:

This fighting started long before what happened the other day. . . . It started in February or March or March or April. I don't remember. I was dating this White boy. He's not a student at the school, but he is well known here at UGRH.[10]

You admit that at the time of the incident, you were not living at home with your mom. You tell the anthropologist, "I'd been—I was living [at a girlfriend's house]." You were not able to live at your dad's house (your parents do not live together) because both he and your mom disapproved of your dating a White guy. So you were staying at a friend's house, with occasional forays to your maternal grandmother's apartment.

When the anthropologist asked if your friend's parents approved of you dating this young man, you were not sure. Your doubts, you insist, were connected to the fact that you have managed to keep his racial identity hidden. This was not too difficult because of your prior experience with Keyshia's parents. Prior to the breach in your relationship, you and Keyshia had been inseparable. You were at

Keyshia's house constantly. Keyshia's parents saw themselves as doing what W. E. B. Du Bois admonished the "talented tenth" to do: reach back and help those members of the Black community who are less fortunate.[11]

You told the anthropologist that you were committed to having this White man in your life because, among other things, he is so "cute." Despite this, you acknowledged that he is also "mean": "Yeah. Sometimes. . . . and then I hate him and break up with him."

One of the major challenges facing you and virtually all girls at UGRH—and elsewhere—is to engage the widespread gender-specific dictum that rewards girls for seeing/approaching pubescence and early adulthood with the goal of having boys as their only entertainment. This leads you (and maybe them) to overload their lives with desiderata that are intended to make this goal achievable. Your feelings about one of your boyfriend's White girlfriends at UGRH embody this notion. You talk about jealousy, about being called names by this girl, and about wanting to fight her:

> But a lot of people likes to be involved in our relationship, and
> that's—I don't like that at all. . . . A lot of people likes to be
> involved in our relationship. For example, he has a best friend,
> she's a girl. And she doesn't think we should have a relationship
> with each other, and so she would go to him, and say, "Oh,
> Nadine's dating these other guys in school." And it'd make him
> mad, and jealous. You know. . . . She's jealous, she doesn't even
> know me, and why you (she) going to . . . him, calling me all types
> of names and—because they all know. Now I want to fight, all of
> this should not be going on. . . . I hate her. . . . Because she doesn't
> even know me, always talking about me and all this. . . . Now it's
> none o' . . . *your* business.[12]

Tales Growing out of School Innocence

In an effort to share with Nadine some of the ideas that I discuss when I have taught introductory cultural anthropology courses,[13]

I told her a story that was recounted at the Congressional Black Caucus dinner in Washington, D.C., by a Black psychology professor from Ohio who grew up in Birmingham, Alabama, during the mid-twentieth century. When she was twelve, she recounted, she got on a city bus and sat down next to a woman she thought was Black. The woman did not self-identify as Black and yelled at her over and over again, "Get away from me! Get up from here!" Paralyzed with fear and humiliation, the professor recounted that she had been unable to move. She had heard the woman, but it was as if her body were frozen to the bus seat. She wanted to move but could not. The bus driver heard the screams of the White woman and, in his protector role, he stopped the bus. He came back to where the two of them were sitting and ordered the young girl to move. If she did not move immediately, he told her, he was going to call the police.

Somehow, the professor recalled, she was finally able to unfreeze and make her body move. She remembered getting off the bus and running as if she were on fire, nonstop, all the way home. She could hear her heart beating in her chest, sounding like drumbeats: kaboom, kaboom, kaboom, kaboom, kaboom, kaboom, kaboom, kaboom, kaboom, kaboom . . . The professor remembered that by the time she got home, she knew she could not tell her dad about the incident. Protecting her was officially his job, but, she knew fearfully, if she told him, he would feel compelled to confront the bus driver who had "thrown" her off the bus. Most confrontations between men got physical. His efforts to protect her could not only have gotten him hurt but could potentially have put a lot of other people in real danger: herself, her immediate family, and the entire Black community in her home town. Yes, he was "da man," but his "patriarchal dividend" was computed within a stratified hierarchy, and Black men were not allowed to exercise power at White men's expense.

The professor's gender identity was immediately inverted. Ironically, she became an army of one compelled to protect herself, her dad, and the larger community in which she lived. Through her silence she shielded her family and everyone in the community.

No one had ever learned from her that she was threatened and humiliated on the bus that day. When others told the story, she denied it. What she could not deny to herself or anyone else was that she lost her childhood innocence that day. At the age of twelve, she involuntarily became an adult. Ann Ferguson calls this premature end to childhood "adultification."[14] That day, the professor became a Black woman and someone whose need for protection was rarely acknowledged, let alone assigned to others.

In John Langston Gwaltney's *Drylongso: A Self-Portrait of Black America,* a blind anthropologist's stunning collection of oral histories, a Black girl growing up in the 1940s South tells of seeing the White owner of the land her parents sharecropped come to the house every week, take his penis out of his pants at the front door, and, while her father was plowing the fields, force her mother to have intercourse with him in her presence. She was four at the time. Her mother did not have to tell her not to tell her father.[15]

Fast Forward to the Days after the Fight

Nadine, Nadine, Nadine. Look in the mirror. What makes your big head so hard? Don't you know you are not supposed to fight? Protecting yourself is not your job. You are a girl, and since time immemorial, girls' protection has been outsourced, assigned to others who exercise officially recognized power. All these protectors are gendered masculine, except for your mother, who is responsible for your welfare even though she is not always entitled or empowered to protect you. Depending upon your life stage, these outsourced protectors are likely to be the school principal, assistant principal(s), school counselors, and Officer Friendly (who is officially at the school everyday). Out of school, on the streets, they are your father, brothers, and male cousins, not to mention your clergyman, the fireman, or a soldier boy—anybody but you. When you are older, you are supposed to rely on your husband.

What is more, you have been religiously socialized to be nice ("Be nice, Dee Dee, be nice"), to avoid doing anything that looks like you are not dependent on those around you for protection and approval. Being perceived as dependent by the right people both at school and in the community makes you eligible for this protection. So why in the world would you choose to fight for yourself?

Yes, I know. Your situation is complicated by the fact that you are socially and culturally identified as a Black girl, born and reared in America where Blackness is a cultural symbol most often associated with embodied power, masculinity, and evil. Concurrently lured and loathed, your Black skin forces you, Nadine, to twist in the wind, valued only for your ability to give in order to enhance the life of others.

You are keenly aware of the mismatch between the culture of the dominant White society, which prevails within your school, and the culture of the Black community. It is the almost unanimous denial of the presence and dominance of this mismatch that has unraveled and continues to unravel your academic effort. Most of the time you feel like a fly in buttermilk. Admittedly, both Black and White culture have unacknowledged gender dimensions for girls and young women, but you hear contradictory messages. School requires niceness and conformity, while affirming masculine achievement and treating you like a body out of place. Home demands responsibility and independence, relying on you to act for yourself but to put others first. Navigating each milieu is difficult; meeting the demands of both at once seems impossible. You are well aware of the relative academic success of Black females in the school context, just as you are aware of the heavy reliance on women's work and sense of balance in your home community. But you are supposed to appear deferential and dependent. The contradictory demands are enough to make your head spin.

Okay, Nadine, look in the mirror. The mirror, Nadine. Look in the mirror. What do you see? Is it pain or fear, or a combination of the two? Do you know the declaration by the famous French sociologist (you have heard the academic term "sociology" more frequently than "anthropology") Pierre Bourdieu, who insists that not all violence is physical?[16] According to the one anthropologist you know, the vile terms that the White girl called you are a form of (what did she call it?) sim——, simulated—no, symbolic violence. You do not know what that means, but her definition seemed so clear. She said there are other anthropologists, like Paul Farmer, a Harvard anthropologist and doctor who works among the very poor in Haiti, who insist that these everyday forms of violence, like what you experienced, Nadine, are not always recognized by the people upon whom they are inflicted.[17]

To be fair, you realized that what you experienced was hurtful. (You have been called the n-word many times, and each time the pain is the same: profound humiliation and shame.) But you did not identify it as violence. It isn't sensible to call the White girl's words "violence" when she got off without any punishment. As you noted in your first interview with the anthropologist, the adults responsible for your protection were not even willing to admit that you had been hurt by the vile names your antagonist called you; they "misrecognized" what happened to you and were certainly not willing to label it violence. You felt that it was extremely humiliating and demoralizing, but you had no name for it. Although your pain was so raw and so unfiltered that you felt naked, fully exposed, you would have agreed that what happened to you could not appropriately be labeled violence. And you would be the first person in the group to call what you did to the White girl violence. You are still having trouble with what this anthropology woman keeps spouting, pointing out how the everyday practices you have engaged in all your life—things that you choose to do as well as things that you are expected to do—are examples of symbolic violence. Again, you are not sure you know exactly what this term means. In addition, she keeps talking about female subordination as a form of agency or power. Help!! Would someone please make her speak English?

An Anthropological Postscript

The "nigger bitch" incident is forever etched in my memory, recorded in my field notes and in my formal and informal interviews with Nadine, who admitted slapping Kirstin, the White female student, but only after Kirstin bullied her, calling her the vile name. Casting Nadine as the *bully* rather than the *bullied,* school officials did what is usually done in such situations: they punished the person who was actually bullied (Nadine) rather than the person who was actually the bully (Kirstin). In *The Anti-Bullying Handbook,* Keith Sullivan describes a racial example with a similar outcome, involving a Maori boy in a school in New Zealand:[18]

> Rangi is working by himself in the classroom. The door opens. What are you doing, Maori boy, taunts David. "Did ya fall in the shit, black boy?" He struts closer. "Are you reading something? I didn't know you could read." "Hey, nigger," the other boys say as they start to filter in and see Rangi on his own. Instead of ignoring these taunts and provocations (as he has done four or five times over the last month), Rangi loses his temper. He turns on David. The two boys fight and Rangi is clearly the better fighter and is winning. David's friend Jim steps in, grabs Rangi around the neck, and pulls him away from David, throwing him on the ground. He helps David up. The duty [supervising] teacher arrives, and David and Rangi are taken to the deputy principal's office. David has been crying and says that he was just having fun and that Rangi went "psycho" and really hurt him. When questioned, Rangi is surly and insolent and is suspended from school for a week for fighting and being rude to the deputy principal. David's friends back him up and say that Rangi went "psycho" for no apparent reason. David is given a warning about fighting but is largely seen as the innocent party.
>
> Rangi is identified by those in authority as the aggressor. He is not listened to. Instead, the boy with more credibility in the school is believed.[19]

I was especially interested in the outcome of the case of Nadine versus Kirstin for two reasons: (1) It was the quintessential exemplar of female-specific, cross-racial physical and emotional violence.

(2) I had tried, unsuccessfully, to get Kirstin and her younger sister Katlin, both of whom were cheerleaders, to become two of the twenty female students who would form the core group of my ethnographic study on female aggression. Ironically, their parents gave me enthusiastic permission to talk with both the "victim" and with Katlin. The parents wanted their daughters, but especially Kirstin, whom Nadine had slapped, to participate in the study. However, both Kirstin and Katlin declined my invitation. At the time, I was flattered by the parents' obvious desire to have their daughters participate, and I was perplexed by the sisters' refusal. I did not have the entire story at that time. It was not until I learned, much later in the study, that this young White woman was dating a Black guy at the school that I fully understood why her parents appeared so anxious to have her involved in my study, and why she was so reluctant to participate.[20]

At the time this fight occurred, I had been observing bullying and female aggression among Black and White girls in this suburban high school for just under two years. Because I was sitting in the office as they marched in (I heard the details from the Black girls—Nadine and Keyshia—later), I observed firsthand the White girl's flushed face, her tears, and her obligatory sobs. The "victim" came immediately into the principal's office and closed the door.[21] I listened intently as her sister called their mother on the dedicated student phone in the office—near where I was sitting—telling their mother that Kirstin had been physically attacked by a Black girl. Apparently, their mother agreed to come immediately to get them out of harm's way.

Being labeled by the vile name "nigger bitch" is a form of violence that school officials, like most Americans, do not identify as such. Most people misrecognize violence that does not take physical form as essentially harmless; after all, these are only words, not "sticks and stones."[22] At UGRH, the Black girl's physical response was the only action deemed worthy of punishment. Moreover, because physical aggression is associated with males and not females, this and similar incidents raise powerful questions: Are Black girls overly racialized and insufficiently feminized? Does their racial identity neutralize their gender identity? And, more critically, what are the consequences of being racially Black and gendered female?

Now that I have completed the study, I realize how what I had read and experienced in life and what I was teaching in my seminars at the university influenced my thinking and interactions with the study participants. Virtually none of them had ever thought about female aggression in the ways described by such authors as Rachel Simmons (in *Odd Girl Out*), Barbara Coloroso (in *The Bully, the Bullied, and the Bystander*), Lyn Mikel Brown (in *Raising Their Voices* and *Girlfighting*), Mary Pipher and Ruth Ross (in *Reviving Ophelia*), and Sharon Lamb (in *The Secret Lives of Girls*)—all popular books with detailed descriptions of female-specific exclusion and other seemingly nonviolent forms of domination.[23]

The widely held view of what is appropriately regarded as violence subverts or at least negatively affects the academic performance of all females, but especially of Black females. Indeed, recent efforts to broaden the definition of the concept are often viewed as an overcorrection and are considered "politically correct" (PC), a synonym for revisionism that erodes standards and norms.

Systematic study of this phenomenon is urgently needed. Competition and aggression between girls is widely thought to be either harmless or only a minor problem, but it is both harmful and widespread. The female-specific goal of girls' competition—loss—is not fully understood as female agency, and if we desire to understand and change these female-specific practices, we have to transform the extant reward system that incentivizes loss and analyze how and why it works. The unique and formidable competition between and among Black and White girls is one of the best examples of the "presence of an absence" in the culture, but perhaps the most important in understanding how women compete and how to both understand and alchemize that competition.[24]

CHAPTER 4

Brittany

SHE TALKS LIKE A BLACK GIRL

"That White boy hit me. That White boy hit me. I hate that White boy. Make that White boy stop hitting me."

The anthropologist stands stripped down to her cultural underwear, confused by the rules of her racial socialization. She is trying, at the same time, to figure out why a White girl would use this language when talking about another member of her "native" group. The anthropologist is also confused because the power of Whiteness is generally encased in invisibility; its normality is constructed as absence, fueling, perhaps unintentionally, its power. That is, in practice, when talking about other Whites, Whites never modify gender by referencing the race of their subject. If, for example, a White girl were talking about a White boy, she would not identify him as White and would be more likely to say, "That boy hit me. That boy hit me. I hate that boy. Make that boy stop hitting me."

Just as the anthropologist begins to analyze this strange construction, Ms. Lorraine, a White teacher who also heard the young woman's statement, offers a racial characterization of the speaker's usage: "She talks like a Black girl." Several other adult White females who are present, including a sentry, smile knowingly, confirming Ms. Lorraine's assessment: "She talks like a Black girl."

The anthropologist's mind wanders, meandering back and forth, to the adults' assessment of the girl's statement and their confirmation of what it means. The anthropologist asks, of no one in particular, "Is she a Black girl?" Silence and then more silence. The other adults look at the researcher as if she had suddenly grown two heads, and they walk away. Translation: The anthropologist is dumber than we initially thought. The sentry tells the anthropologist that the student is White.

However, the anthropologist does not accept this claim regarding the girl's racial identity. She is seeing this student for the first time. Given the wide range of colors and hair textures in "the Black community," assumptions about who is and who is not Black are, at the very least, risky. Admittedly, the girl has the light-colored skin that is frequently associated with the essentialized racial category "White," but for an anthropologist, the important question is, How does the student *self*-identify?

What does it mean to her to "talk like a Black girl," specifically at this school, the anthropologist wonders? What does it mean to be a Black girl, and who makes that determination? The anthropologist feels like Alice in Wonderland, she feels like she is in a world that is upside down. She struggles to regain contact with the realities of the world as she has long known them.

Indeed, this is what the anthropologist records about this student in her field notes, about a month into the study:

> I was at UGRH earlier today, and I—saw this particular White
> student who obviously has grown up in the Black community. . . .
> She says such things as, "Aah! I don't like that White boy!" I
> think she's very much identified with the African American com-
> munity. She is also new to this school, and is always, according to
> [some members of] the administration, in trouble. I don't know
> the nature of the problem (yet); I am just beginning to get to
> know her. I'm anxious to find out more about her. I desperately
> want her to be in the study. I think she is just absolutely ideal for
> my study. I don't know if she'll write [the diary entries] for me,
> that's the problem. But I know that she is the kind of girl that
> appears to be marginalized. Odd girl out . . . In following Rachel
> Simmons's argument in her book *Odd Girl Out.* This girl appears
> to be an odd girl.[1]

Performing Blackness in White Face

In striking contrast, *you*, Brittany, do not share the anthropologist's uncertainty or estrangement. You are secretly pleased ("I nailed it!") when someone, especially an adult, accuses you of accurately performing Blackness, aka "acting Black."[2] The adult females at the school who view themselves as White are aghast at your *inappropriate* racial performance. They attempt to restrain your behavior and your discourse practices. They tell this stranger (whom they see as a Black, then as a female, and then, finally, as an anthropologist) that you, Brittany, are guilty of appropriating a Black female discourse style—and maybe even a Black female identity. The anthropologist, as she sees you for the first time, cannot judge how you self-identify. Therefore, she cannot judge the accuracy or the adequacy of your racial performance or the adults' assessments of it.

As your statement ("That White boy hit me. . . .") suggests, in your constructed social world, the White boy is as strange to you as he would be to most Black girls at this school. You grew up in the core of the city that spawned this suburban community where you are now forced to reside. From the time you were two years old until last year, you lived in the city with your mom, a single parent, and thought of yourself as a Black girl with very light skin and dark, flaccid, pseudo-curly hair. You know that the adults in your life, including your mom, dad, and your grandmother, Granny, self-identify as White (with an Italian-German ethnicity). To please your family, you also try to identify as White when you are in their presence.

When you were with your friends and peers in your predominantly Black school and neighborhood, you talked, acted, and behaved as you imagined a Black girl would. You tested your racial performance against the backdrop of your Black female peers' approval. In this Black, gender-specific performance, the costume did not appear to constrict you; you were able to breathe freely, rather than feeling suffocated, as you do at your new school. You were able to stand upright, and you spoke powerfully and directly rather than softly and uncertainly.

When you were very young, prior to your parents' divorce, you lived with them as their only child in a sundown town. Your BFF Asha's family members tell you about many of the suburban communities in this area that excluded American citizens of African ancestry (or who looked as if they were) as homeowners and renters. These communities embraced African Americans as workers but required them to get out of town by sundown (hence the term "sundown town").[3]

When you are at Asha's house, as you often are, you listen keenly to her family's oral histories of their experiences. You understand that the community you were born in is one that actively, albeit often informally, kept Black Americans from becoming permanent residents. Indeed, Loewen describes these spaces as excluding people of African ancestry by "kinder, gentler means" than the practices evident in the Jim Crow South.[4]

Semirural areas like the one you grew up in proudly self-identified as "villages" to connote a nostalgic return to the days of premodernity, might also be accurately referred to as White spaces.[5] They were both precursors and embodiment of gated communities, occupied solely by Whites whose norms and values were reflected in all aspects of that geographical space.[6]

In these communities, Asha's family asserts, African Americans were allowed to seek and obtain full-time employment, but they were forced to leave every day before sunset. You never like thinking about this. Now that you are older and understand more, you fully appreciate how dehumanizing this practice was. Could it still exist on some level today? What about the rights denied Latinos, who are widely known as illegal aliens? It's all a bit much to think about, and moreover, it angers you.

OMG!! OMG!! Is My Mom a Racist?

You sense that your mom, Granny, and other family members see you as an old soul, too sagacious for your age, and too idealistic.

They are your greatest admirers and supporters, yet they fear you the most because you choose to perform Blackness, not Whiteness. Neither your family nor your teachers have been impressed with your grades lately. Your teachers repeatedly assure your mom that you are capable academically and attribute your poor grades to "running with the wrong crowd."

In "the wrong crowd" what your mom hears is *those loud Black girls,* who are having a bad influence on her sweet, innocent Brittany.[7] Unlike your mom and many of your maternal family members, you see your Black friends as being no different from *you*—and you refuse to give up your BFFs just because they are Black. After all, that is how you see yourself.

You face a very difficult decision, partly because you became the sole focus of your mom's life after your parents' marriage ended. She concentrated on teaching you to master the appropriate social rules, essentially how to be a people pleaser who makes others comfortable. In many ways, she also treated you as her social equal. She often told you stories about her life that, you realize as you look back on it, were probably age-inappropriate. She also wanted you to choose sides in the marital issues she had with your dad, which you felt was unfair, and you resented hearing negative information about him. Your dad could do no wrong in your eyes. You still feel that way, though to a lesser extent.

When your mom and dad divorced, she was granted sole custody and your dad had visitation rights. She moved from their rented apartment in the sundown town back to the city in the Italian community where she was born and raised. She had attended a Catholic school in that community. Initially, the two of you moved in with Granny (your babysitter), until your mom could afford a small apartment nearby.

When you were old enough, your mom wanted to send you to the same school she had attended, but she was financially unable to do so, and your dad's salary and contribution to child support made you ineligible for a scholarship. She reluctantly enrolled you in the nearest public elementary school, which primarily served Black students and other students of color, making you what Edward Morris called "an unexpected minority."[8]

Since the beginning, your mom and her family were unhappy with the idea of sending you to the public school. They were terrified that something bad might happen to you, not to mention fearful that you would get a substandard education. Their financial position gave them no other options. You are convinced that that was the only reason you were allowed to remain in that school. You noticed that virtually all the White parents with school-aged children in the neighborhood sent them to either Catholic or private school, especially for junior high and high school.

Truth be told, you think of your mom as a racist. She, of course, does not think of herself that way. She hides her feelings within the family home, but you see them surface when she is among family and friends. You are smart enough to know that this is not unique to your mom. When you tell her she is a racist, she gets extremely angry and says that you are "young" and "foolish" and do not understand the social issues in American public life. Despite your mom's denial, you conclude that she is certainly anything *but* an advocate of equal opportunity. She doesn't believe that Black Americans have or should have the same rights and privileges as White Americans.

Granny knows your mom's views, too, and she constantly laments that she gave birth to someone who does not believe in or promote social justice for all Americans. You know this makes Granny incredibly sad. To be honest, Granny has never been a flaming liberal or anything like that, but she at least gives lip service to the ideals espoused in the Constitution. She goes to a soup kitchen to prepare meals for the disadvantaged once or twice a year. Moreover, she even writes a check for one hundred dollars each and every Christmas to the United Negro College Fund because she, too, believes that "a mind is a terrible thing to waste." She tells you that if more people would help the disadvantaged, we could end poverty and racism in America. You think this is extremely naive, but she's your grandmother, and grandmothers always deserve a pass.

Your mom doesn't appear to notice Granny's anguish, or else she deliberately ignores it. After all, her mother will love her regardless of how she behaves or what she believes. Your mom has a major preoccupation with not wanting anyone to know or believe negative things about her. That is not unusual, you conclude, especially for females of her generation. All her socialization has been acquired with the following mantra in mind: Be nice, be caring, and be considerate—even if you have to fake it. The anthropologist has told you that there is ongoing research suggesting that girls, especially White girls, are repeatedly socialized to be "people pleasers."[9] This means that women like your mom equate competing head-on with other women with a lack of caring. Since caring is the most important female virtue, competition is masked beneath a veneer of civility and politeness.

Like all humans, White women desire to achieve individual goals in and out of the workplace, but they are compelled to hide their competitiveness because an ethic of caring trumps winning and direct competition. (The anthropologist frames it as "competing to lose.")[10]

You pretend not to believe what the anthropologist says, but you are amazed at how this captures what you see happening all the time between your mom and the women at her job. She calls them her coworkers. They are so supportive of each other, so nice in face-to-face interactions, laughing and sharing secrets and gossip about the people for whom they work, asking about each other's children and grandchildren. They tell each other about their weekend activities, vacation plans, marriage and family problems, and other intimacies. The claws don't come out until one of the women does something that makes her stand out from the others.

Two recent examples are indelibly imprinted in your mind. The first one involved another White woman, Molly, who had worked with your mom since before you were born. Molly told her coworkers that she was bored with her current job, saw no chance for mobility, and needed more money because of her family situation. She had two children with a man she had lived with but never

married. He had recently moved out, telling her he no longer
wanted to be in the relationship, and then immediately moved in
with another woman. Molly was devastated. She was seeking child
support, but she needed help immediately.

She applied for a higher-status job in another department
without telling your mom or any of her coworkers, and she landed
it. Your mom and the other members of the group never forgave her.
They had also known about the job opening, one they all coveted,
but they had either been too afraid to apply for it or had simply
chosen not to. Molly was ostracized immediately and permanently
from the group. You remember the ferocity of your mom's phone
conversations with her remaining coworkers at home every night
(for weeks) after this, with constant use of the b-word. The group
hated Molly for getting a promotion. They considered her selfish
and mean for seeking more money and higher status. They viewed
her as a traitor to the "group think" that fueled the office's cohesion.
They had been adhering to the rules of noncompetition with one
another, which is considered female-appropriate in the postmodern
corporate workspace.[11]

You also remember when your mom's bosses hired a young Black
woman, Jolene, to replace the secretary in your mom's department.
Your mom had a hissy fit that exceeded all her prior ones. Day after
day, she came from work complaining furiously that her world was
coming apart at the seams. She could not believe that the powers
that be had hired a Black applicant over her strong objections,
which she pretended were not rooted in any animus toward Black
people. She just decided that Jolene did not have the necessary
skills or experience to do the work. The most aggravating thing for
you was that she had yet to work a single day with the woman. She
was already certain (stereotyping as usual) that, because Jolene was
Black, she would be inept and would be a burden.[12]

Your mom screamed at you and Granny that this was nothing
but an "affirmative action hire." One night, Granny suggested that
perhaps Jolene's lack of knowledge was due more to her position as
a rookie than to her identity as an African American. Your mother

could not believe her mother's response, and told her so in no uncertain terms.

"Why do you always disagree with me?" she yelled. "I am the person working with this incompetent woman. I am the person that the department expects to get the work done, and if I fail because she is not doing her share of the assigned work, it will reflect negatively on me. Of that I am sure."[13]

Granny thought better of responding and left the kitchen. You felt your soul shrink at the venom in your mom's voice. You knew that Jolene was in for a very difficult time, even though she had done nothing to warrant your mom's wrath. This made you think about a play performed by the seniors at Feeder High School the previous year. You went to the performance because Asha's older brother, Rodney, was playing the lead role of a crazy, murderous barber. He was *really* good. You remember most vividly the revenge the main character inflicted upon innocent people because his wife cheated on him with that stupid judge.

When you heard your mom criticizing Jolene, a central theme in the play came immediately to mind: those poor innocent people lost their lives in the barber's chair as he butchered them, one by one. You imagine a similar scenario happening at your mom's worksite. She was angry with the people who hired the Black secretary, but they are more powerful than she, and she needs their support to retain her job. She cannot retaliate against them, so what option does she choose? Misplaced revenge. She will make mincemeat of that young Black secretary. You just know it.

Embracing a Black Cultural World

Until you were in fifth grade, your mom was very protective of you and insisted that she or Granny walk or drive you to school. Every day they did this, until you had a hissy fit one night and insisted she stop treating you like a baby. You were ten years old, for Pete's sake, and your school was only two blocks from home. She backed off—a little—allowing you to walk to school without her at your side.

All the kids at school, especially your friends, knew of your torturous relationship with her and of her tendency to have age-inappropriate expectations of you. They found it amusing. You're sure they thought of your mom the same way you did: a wet blanket, suffocating you, and too heavy to lift off.

Unlike your family, you loved your school and your friends, and you felt respected and loved by them in return. Your teachers, about 90 percent of whom were White (the anthropologist told you that even today the official statistics for your former school district are that 85 percent of the students are minority and 85 percent of the teachers are White, a virtual flip), were unbelievably supportive and encouraging. Yet they were constantly attempting to curtail and correct your attempts to perform Blackness instead of Whiteness. You had several Black girlfriends at school, but your family and most of your teachers disapproved of these friendships. Your mom kept trying to connect you with your cousins and extended family. She also tried to promote friendships with her friends' and coworkers' children.

"You and Emily were such good friends before you started school," she would tell you, referring to a friend's daughter. You don't recall this, but she has pictures, so it must be true. *Your* first memories of a special girlfriend are from first grade, and that friend had much darker skin than yours. Asha and you, chocolate and vanilla, you were virtually inseparable.

Your friendship grew, and your circle expanded to include other Black girls as you went from elementary school to junior high. These girls thought of you as one of their own, and they embraced you in ways that they never, ever contemplated doing with the other two White girls who were now in your classes. Among the adults at school, this was not a good thing. You noticed that your teachers began to be less supportive of you, which you attributed to the fact that your primary friends were Black girls.

Teachers would ask you to see them after class or school. You struggle to remember the actual number of times, but they would say things like, "You're such a great kid" and "You're so smart." Next, they would explain how your relationships with unsavory characters (your Black friends) were threats to your academic future. You were always puzzled and bothered by the idea that your relationships had any bearing on your education.

When you were in elementary school, your teachers often called your mom at work or talked with her at PTA meetings. (One teacher came to your house multiple times.) They told her how academically gifted you were. Then they warned that hanging around with the wrong crowd was not only undermining your current school performance but jeopardizing your academic future as well. They repeatedly told her that you were dumbing down your academic performance, as they perceived it, so you would not outsmart your Black and Brown peers. Most critically, you remember them disproportionately rewarding you for your academic efforts, in ways they did not reward your Black girlfriends. (The anthropologist tells you about a study suggesting that teachers reward Black girls more for the performance of race-appropriate social roles than they do for academic performance.)[14]

As you view it, traditions affiliated with the idea of being a White girl are too oppressive, too constraining. Your sense of constraint and limitation is not to be equated with ordinary forms of oppression and subordination. No, the kind of oppression you experience when you try to be a White girl, when you try to perform Whiteness, is one of unconditional restraint. You feel as if you're trapped in a vise. You wonder if you can continue breathing. The breathing difficulties you experience while trying to embody this White female role propels your efforts to run from it, much to the chagrin of your mom, your grandmother, and all your extended maternal family.

When you think of it, if you were in control of the language used to describe your experience as a White girl, you would use the word "compression" rather than "oppression." Why? "Compression" implies decreasing in volume in response to applied stress. (There's that suffocation thing, again.) It more accurately captures how you feel when you have to perform female Whiteness.[15]

You think about the two other White girls who were in your

class at your previous school (fewer than one hundred out of two thousand enrolled students were defined as White), and you realize that the other White girls were virtually invisible in so many ways. They were both petite, both had blond hair (yours is dark brown), and neither said much, in or out of class. (Did their silence give them power, you wonder?)

Unlike you, the other two White girls were known as "good girls" by their peers, but they were regarded more ambivalently by the predominantly White teaching force. Most of the teachers identified them (and you to some degree) as "trailer trash"—probably because they attended a city school.[16] Teachers did not consider the other White girls academically gifted, and thus they were not eligible for consideration at schools like Harvard or Princeton. This opinion is also interesting and is probably rooted in the teachers' belief that if the girls were really smart, their parents would sacrifice to enroll them in a more prestigious school.

You think it fair to say that, like you, White kids (especially females) who attend predominantly Black schools are blackened not only by their peers but also, more critically, by school officials. To use a phrase you saw in one of the books the anthropologist had, White kids in these contexts are compelled to stretch the understanding of what it means to be White. They create a new form of Whiteness that might best be summed up as "White chocolate."[17]

Candy, a White girl at your old school, is anorexic. She told you so last year, at your old school, when you said that your mom constantly policed what you ate. Were it not for your grandmother, you would have been starving most of the time. Your mother was not so much concerned about your health as worried that with puberty you would become fat. You would be a fat girl, and none of the boys would date you—not that she wants you to date the boys who attend your school anyway.

She worries that you will become unattractive to the most important boys in your age range (the boys at church and outside the immediate community, of course). You are smart enough to know that your mom attributes the failure of her marriage to her own weight issues. She thought that she became sexually undesirable to your dad because, after she gave birth to you, she wasn't the young, sexually provocative girl he married. (When they got married, he always teased her that his two hands could completely encircle her waist.) Were you to blame for the dissolution of their marriage, you wonder?

You also wonder what is indicated by the rampant incidence of anorexia among young White girls but not among the same demographic of Black girls. Does it suggest how powerful the expectation is that you—a White female—should be seen (like a potted plant) but not heard?

Even today, your mom constantly tries to keep you on track, celebrating what she sees as the proper White-girl role. She views "fat" as the arena where Black girls play, and she constantly emphasizes that you are not a Black girl.

As your mom sees it, sexually attractive females, especially White females, are not fat. "Fat" is an image she assigns to lower-class women, particularly Black women. Your mom's take-no-prisoners approach to what it means to be fat compels you to revisit an article the anthropologist gave you that chronicles how Black girls, and women in general, are demonized in what the author identifies as a "fat-hating culture."[18]

Your mom does not even like you to eat at your BFFs' houses, especially Asha's. She fears that you are consuming too much high-calorie, unhealthy food there, and you are.

The Cost of Eschewing a Gender-Appropriate White World

As a socially defined White girl, you are expected to mirror the dominant, culturally appropriate, idealized image of femaleness—small—and are denigrated if you do not. You are also expected to be nearly silent in voice (does this mean no public or even private opinions?), to demonstrate selflessness manifested as caring (self-sacrifice or suffering in the service of others?), and to exhibit a general patina or veneer of loss as a virtue.

"Be nice." You are subjected to this aphorism morning, noon, and night. Is this the central trope, the gagging one must engage, to embody White femaleness? Must you abdicate your desire to chart your own life course to be seen as acceptable and eligible for the status of "White girl"?

Outsourcing (this seems be an appropriate description) your power allows others to protect and take care of you and to fight for you so you can maintain the image of the bystander.[19] However, like the Black girls at your former school, you don't see anyone running either to protect or take care of you.

Like most of those girls, you listen nonstop to rap music. You mimic the way they talk and interact. One time, you even had braided extensions put in your hair. When your mom and especially Granny go ballistic and insist that you take them out *immediately,* you do. The right to be the actor in your own life is driven underground, requiring you to mask your anger and embrace the role of the proverbial bystander.

You observe that whenever a physical fight breaks out at school, the good, nice, White girls observe from the sideline.

Your family tells you repeatedly to maintain your individuality, to just do your work and forget the other kids. They insist that your Black girlfriends are not going to determine what college you attend, what job you get, or how much money you make—that is, unless you become enmeshed with them, identified as one of them. You always ask, incredulously, "What's wrong with that?" You want to believe that your family has your best interests at heart and want only what is best for you, but when you try to stand alone, you feel so weak, so isolated, and so vulnerable, like a single, infant tree in the path of an oncoming tsunami.

You consistently fight to bypass this living-your-life-in-compression role. When you entered the public school in the city, you found the cultural and racial diversity of your classmates and their varied experiences stimulating and invigorating. You loved their way of dressing, their freedom of movement, and their way of talking and interacting. Again, much to the chagrin of your family, you especially liked the Black girls' direct discourse styles (the culturally and gender-approved practice of speaking for themselves), particularly their ability to have a voice about what was happening in their lives.

Your mom repeatedly chided you for following their example. Your family couldn't stand the idea of you acting on your own behalf and talking in a way that was, to their way of thinking, inappropriate for a proper young lady. You were made keenly aware of this every day after school when your mom and Granny would tell you over and over again, in no uncertain terms, "Brittany, use your inside voice." "Brittany, don't act like those Black girls at your school."

Good girls do not fight the war themselves, your mom says. They get others to fight it for them. (Tell the teacher or principal if someone does something unacceptable to you, she advises, so that an adult will take care of it for you.) Not only do you ignore their advice to disengage with your Black friends, even worse, you sneak out of the house to "date" Black males exclusively, making out and messing around with them. This behavior precipitates a crisis. You are not supposed to date at all because you are too young, your family says. Dating Black boys takes it to a whole new level of "not allowed." This pattern of sneaking around was the straw that broke the camel's back just before the end of your ninth-grade school year.

Your mom went ballistic when she came into your room early one morning and you weren't there. A family meeting was called at Granny's house one Sunday afternoon. Your dad was even summoned for it.

Even though your dad lives in the area, in elementary and junior high school he wasn't that involved in your life. (Your mom said he was too busy making money.) Your mom said that when she complained to him that your behavior seemed to be spiraling out of control, he would shrug and make some "idiotic comment" that this was a phase you would outgrow. For the family meeting, the first he had been to in a long time, your dad brought his new, young wife. She appeared both to view this situation with total disdain and to be extremely uncomfortable. The new wife's presence made your mom even angrier than she already was about your little misadventure.

The meeting was a veritable blood-bath, with each of your parents blaming the other for your out-of-control behavior. Your mom argued that your dad had abdicated his responsibilities as a father (which leads to the question, Why was he invited in the first place?) She complained that he failed to pay the mandated child support when they separated, forcing her to haul him into court to have his salary garnished. She complained that he often didn't show up to take you on those weekends he had custody. And she accused him of being more concerned about his career than about your health, safety, and well-being.

As your dad turned beet red with anger and indignation, your mom argued that she wasn't strong enough to keep you focused and out of the clutches of the ghetto in which the two of you were forced to live. Granny took umbrage at that, repeatedly pointing out that your mom grew up in the same community and turned out just fine.

Your mom countered that the community and the people who lived there now were not the same as they had been when she was young. She also reminded everybody that she went to Catholic school, not public school, as you were doing.

For all these reasons, your mom said, your dad's involvement in your life was more critical. Times were different, she argued, and a White girl coming of age in a predominantly Black high school was too vulnerable. She told your dad, for the 150-millionth time (you knew exactly what she was going to say before she opened her mouth), that you and the other White girls at that school were especially vulnerable because the Black guys found you more beautiful than they found the Black girls. She said that made them—the Black guys and the Black girls (for different reasons)—more aggressive toward you and the other White girls. You see on the television every day that White girls are so much more desirable than any other females in America, she said, which makes them marked targets for rape and other sexual violence.

You told them in a very loud voice that you were *sick* of their preoccupation with race. "Race does not matter," you asserted. "People are just people!" you screamed. You couldn't stop yourself.

Was this really even about you, or was it just another opportunity for them to scream at each other?

(When you tell the anthropologist this part of your life story, she urges you to read a section of her book *Blacked Out* in which Ms. Mentor, a social studies teacher, asks the students in her U.S. history classes to share the most important physical characteristic they desire in a potential mate. Ms. Mentor claims that she was surprised at the gender-specific pattern that emerged in the classes she observed: male students showed a strong preference for women with light skin, but the female students' responses did not reflect this same sensibility. You roll your eyes and sneer at this crazy take on your life at school. Like many of the other White kids at your school, you hate the idea of being thought of as White.)

After your outburst in the family meeting, your dad gave you "the look" and you knew to cool it. Your mom, despite her snot and tears, saw this exchange and it recharged her batteries straight away!

She told your dad, in great detail, about your growing involvement with the Black girls at school. "Your daughter," she screamed, "is acting like a whore!" She was also alarmed and quite concerned by how much you seemed to be mimicking the Black rather than the White kids at school and church. She told him that you were a cheerleader in your predominantly Black public high school and a member of the gospel choir and the glee club, both predominantly Black. (Her voice rose even more. Apparently she forgot to model using her "inside voice.") You didn't point out that you were the *only* White girl in those activities. Now, you were the only White girl accepted for the school's step team, she told him. His response was anticipated. "Step team?" he asked. "What the hell is that?"

Then came the coup de grace. "Your daughter is running around with Black boys," she said. She suddenly stopped and looked at him, as if she had unexpectedly run out of gas. You winced. There was only one boy, and, yes, he was Black.

Now will you wind for me, slow wind for me
Oh, you wind for me, slow wind for me.[20]

Lamont. Lamont. Lamont. Just saying his name made you feel special, as if the nerve endings in every crevice of your body were exposed and tingling at the pronunciation of his name. Funnily enough, in the beginning you had sought both to avoid being in his presence and to find any way possible to be near him. Because you so loved being with your Black girlfriends, avoiding him was not possible.

It seemed that he was everywhere. He would walk up behind you, grab your arms, hold them gently behind your back, and, while breathing in your ear, say something as innocuous as "Hey, boob, aren't you out past your bedtime?" His voice sent chills down your spine, causing your knees to buckle as you imagined his big hands and luscious lips on various parts of your body. His skin reminded you of your insatiable desire for dark chocolate just before you went to bed at night. Your tendency to blush to a bright tomato red fueled his tendency to flirt with you and toy with your emotions. This made you very uncomfortable, but very excited at the same time.

At other times, he would wink at you across the room, and when he was closer to you, put his hand under your chin, lift your head ever so gently, and with the broadest smile this side of heaven, promise, "Boob, the next time I decide to highjack my ride, I promise first to borrow your dazzling, super brown eyes." *Lordie, Lordie, Lordie.* Your knees buckled, your legs, indeed your entire body, turned to Jell-O. Around him, you had trouble speaking—even breathing.

Lamont's powerful effect on you became crystal clear one night when you were at a party together (after midnight, of course, as you had slipped out of the apartment after your mom went to sleep). He sort of asked you, you guess, to dance. You were unable to control your trembling body as he slid his arms around your waist. He pulled you so close to him that to anyone looking at your silhouettes you looked like one person. Your face was pressed against his powerfully firm, muscular chest, and you couldn't escape the new smell of his super white T-shirt.

You recalled the rumor around school that Black guys who could afford to would only wear a T-shirt once. (Those who couldn't probably felt terribly inadequate, maybe even less manly.) Most guys knew where to find the street vendors who sold the popular T-shirts, and every day they forked over five dollars, in cash, to get a new one. In order to be seen as a big man on campus, guys like Lamont did it to set the standard. Their ability to purchase and wear new clothes on a daily basis conveyed a lot about the social hierarchy in the school and in the community: money first, then status, then respect.

As you danced with him that night, he suddenly twirled you around, forcing you backward as he took control of your dance routine. Unable to relax, you didn't enjoy the commotion your dance moves created. Your body, drenched in sweat (your mom would have said that that was *so* unfeminine), was on display for everyone to sneer at. You worried about a "stereotype threat," the claim that White girls can't dance, at least not as well as everyone else in the room. You knew this thinking was rampant in this predominantly Black setting. When the song finally ended, you were able to get your unsteady feet to carry you back to where your BFFs were sitting.

Asha wasn't there. She typically did not slip out of the house to join the rest of you. Her mom left for work too early in the morning and would have been sure to notice her absence—but you told her everything about that night. You confided in her about the way Lamont made you feel and that you really wished you could have been alone with him.

At the same time, you swore to her that you were never going to sneak out of the house again because you knew you didn't have the strength or the willpower to control your sexual urges. Your nights away from home were over. Asha smiled knowingly and summarily dismissed your assertion. "You *know* you like Lamont," she said. "You'll keep going after him."

Although you were only fifteen, you were wise enough to know that he was a shark (not in the bad sense, but just in the way of winning a score) and that if you had drunk even a little alcohol in his presence, your chances of surviving his "attack" would have been a negative zero. You looked at your friend Asha and thought, I'll just have to show you I can do it; then you'll see.

> So Lamont called me last night. He's this kid I used to talk to in the City. I was in love with him at one point. . . . I was like wow, I can't believe you're calling. I really used to like him, even love him. I was thinking about that last night. I don't know, I could mess with him all over again. I don't mean mess with him, like fool around with him, I mean talk to him. And he's hot. . . . [Later that evening] I was talking to his friend and his friend was like let me get your digits [phone number]. . . . I was like ask Lamont about that. I mean, me and Lamont used to talk and we loved each other and I wouldn't want him feeling uncomfortable about me talking to his friend. I mean I lost my virginity to [him]. . . . I guess I just need to be a pimp for a while. . . . I feel crappy. I talked to Asha earlier. I told her how Lamont called me. She was like I don't know if I would talk to him if I were you. And I know. I shouldn't. But he looks the best of everyone I talk to. He's freakin' hot man. Guys who look good get me crazy. . . . I told Lamont about this survey [the anthropologist's study] and he was like, but you don't even talk to girls. I was like yea, they suck, for the most part.[21]

Kumbaya: A Tribal Conflict

At the family meeting, your mind slowly reengaged with their conversation. Using an elevated version of his male "inside voice," your dad accused your mom of not being a good mother. While his new wife sat silent and stone-faced, he told your mom she was being too uptight about what you were doing at school and, most insidiously, accused her of taking her anger toward him out on you. "You have always blamed our daughter for what happened between the two of us. That is unfair," he insisted.

You sat there in disbelief as your dad claimed not to know about your school activities, even though you told him about them, repeatedly, on the phone or in person every weekend you spent with him. He insisted he certainly didn't know that you were singing gospel music (which appeared to have really grabbed his attention). You tried to remind him that you had told him about all of that, but Granny put her finger over her lips, signaling to you that you shouldn't interrupt. She took her carefully folded handkerchief out of her apron pocket and started crying silently into it. Her short, carefully groomed, snow-white hair glistened in the light from the window near her. You alone seemed to notice her discomfort, her sadness.

Your mom appeared horrified at your dad's accusations and reiterated that you were routinely leaving the house late at night and running around with Black boys. This gave her the chills, she said, and she feared that if this continued, you would probably end up pregnant (no, she had *not* given permission for birth control pills), if you weren't killed first. Something had to be done. (You were pissed off that they talked as if you weren't in the room.)

The decision was swift and clear to everyone in the room except you. You were going to have to go live in that lily-White community with your dad and his gold-digger wife. As you sat glued to your favorite chair in Granny's old-fashioned living room, you could not believe what you heard next. "Since you don't think that what she is doing is dangerous, and possibly life threatening, I am hereby giving you an opportunity to see how you feel when you wake up in the morning and she is not in her bed. I relinquish custody. I hereby grant you the chance to raise your daughter and see how good you are at it."

With just the right mix of a father's love and male bravado, your dad jumped up from the sofa and, looking directly into her eyes, assured her that he could do a better job than she was and that he was ready and willing to take on the challenge.

Perhaps your mom saw it as saving your life. You saw it as anything but. The thought of it is too painful to contemplate.

Hello! Would anyone like my opinion?

Your heart sank. You loved your dad, and—before he married

that young woman on your grandmother's sofa, who was judging you when she couldn't be more than a few years older than you—you enjoyed his infrequent phone calls during the week and your twice-monthly weekend visits with him in his large, suburban house.

The thought of living with him full-time in that strange community, not to mention attending that super-White, suburban high school, filled you with an unfamiliar dread. Add the potential loss of your friends, especially Asha and the members of the cheerleading squad and the step team, and you were sure that the world was coming to an end. For the first time, you realized how scared you were. You were not only leaving the only family and community you had ever known, but you would be alone in a way that you had never been before.

Living 'Nilla in a Black Family

In the past, when things got really bad at home, you could put your toothbrush and a nightgown in a bag and walk over to Granny's house. If you were really stressed out or depressed and couldn't talk with your mom, Granny would call her and tell her that you were safe at her house. She would then prepare you a wonderful meal, maybe a bowl of her yummy Italian wedding soup. She would give you hot chocolate and tuck you into bed in her quaint little guest room.

Sometimes you would go to Asha's house and eat dinner there, then go to Granny's house later. Your mom wouldn't permit you to sleep over at your Black friends' houses. "Too dangerous," she insisted. Before leaving Asha's house after dinner, you had to call your mom or Granny to let one of them know you were on the way to Granny's house.

Asha's mom worked as the manager of a public school's lunch program and could cook rings around most people you knew, including Granny. You tried to eat at their house at least twice a week, more if you could.

You loved joining your friend's large, garrulous family—five brothers and sisters along with the mom and dad—for an unbelievably good, soul-food dinner. For some reason, when you were stressed or depressed, all the noise and animated conversation restored your battered soul and rewired your brain. You felt better every time. You were never sure that it was the food alone. The acceptance and love you experienced in their presence added a lot to the experience.

Because you and Asha had been friends even before elementary school, her family always called you by the nickname they had given you: 'Nilla (as in "Vanilla"). You had no way of knowing that nicknaming is critically important in the Black community, and that it suggests two things: (1) You are unconditionally accepted. (2) Ideally, the nickname embodies what is perceived to be the essence of the person. They treated you as if you were a vital member of their family, which included having to help get the table ready for dinner and helping your friend and her younger sister clean the kitchen after dinner. (Of course, the boys got to leave the table to go watch TV or play video games.)

Because Asha's mom had to get to work so early in the morning, she always went to bed very early. The other female family members made sure that the kitchen was spotless so that when she came home the following afternoon, she could begin dinner without having to first clean or organize. You were always happy to do more than your share in this effort, but you had to be conscious of the time, because you had to get home or to Granny's house before the streetlights came on.

Your mom thought of Asha's family as decent (as far as Negro families go), but she tried to curtail your visits. There were lots of reasons. You already know that she feared you would eat too much at Asha's and become fat and unattractive, but primarily, she refused to reciprocate. She would never invite Asha (your best friend, for Pete's sake) or her family for dinner, or even a cup of tea. Such an invitation would suggest social and racial equality, something she could never sanction.

Praying for Deliverance—and Failing

Listening to your parents' conversation that fateful Sunday after-noon was unbearable. Your thoughts were always roaming to other issues. You'd miss Asha, there was no doubt. You thought about the loss of all of your wonderful friends, and that plus the thought of the coming family displacement made you totally lose it. You felt al-most unable to breathe; you wanted to yell and let them know in no uncertain terms that you could not live with this disruption in your life. Ironically, when you tried to speak, you could barely muster a whisper. You aren't sure whether they chose to ignore you or really didn't hear you. But, whatever the case, you were forced to honor the role assigned to White girls: the proverbial bystander.

Your mom's fears about your interest in only Black boys and your limiting of social interactions primarily to Black female peers, suggesting that you weren't White, had all become too much for her to handle. You were devastated. You cried nonstop for what seemed like days; your tears felt like acid running down your cheeks. Your eyes were so swollen, so bloated by your tears, that they looked like spotlights on your face. Granny washed them with warm water saturated with Epsom salts; "a time-honored remedy," she said. She used a white face towel and gently, gently, rinsed your painful eyes. It felt so good to have both your grandmother's love and attention and the soothing feel of the washcloth on your face; you appreciated it immensely (even though it certainly didn't make the swelling go away—at least not right away).

You tried unsuccessfully to get your mom to rescind her decision, vacillating between pleading and demanding; she would not budge. Surprisingly, your appeals to Granny were ignored. She was sympathetic but your mom, her baby, had assured her that this was the best thing for you. She told you that she loved you and would miss you badly, but she was not allowed to interfere in this fight. You couldn't believe that she wouldn't intervene to get your mom to change her mind; she had *always* sided with you when your mom made unreasonable demands of you in the past. She just kept saying that your mom was unbelievably angry and nothing was going to deter her from what she saw as an effort not only to save your life but also to save you from yourself. It was pure crazy-talk and you wanted nothing to do with it.

Reborn: At UGRH and in Your Father's House

That fall you enrolled at UGRH. You are living with your dad and his wife, Stephanie. She is only twenty-seven years old, eleven years older than you are. Your dad is fifty-three; your mom is forty-eight. Your dad owns a big house on a corner lot with a swimming pool. (OK, a swimming pool in upstate New York is a little over the top, but it suggests to your dad's neighbors, family, and friends that he has more money and status than they do.) You have your own room. Your dad owns a small but rapidly growing software company in one of the major malls in the area. He is doing extremely well financially. He has ten employees and has ideas about setting up a branch office in a neighboring state.

In striking contrast, your mom rents an apartment down the street from her mother in the city. When she met your dad, he had just completed his undergraduate education and was pursuing an MBA. She was a secretary in the business department at the university where he was a student. He swept her off her feet, and they were married. She moved into his apartment, and shortly after their marriage she became pregnant with you. Her salary was essential to their survival, and she worked almost up till you were born. After six weeks of maternity leave, she returned to work because the family desperately needed her salary to make ends meet.

After you were born, your mom appeared to be unable to regain her strength and vitality. She had gained a hundred pounds during the pregnancy and couldn't find the stamina or discipline to lose it afterward. Your dad was frustrated and disappointed. He had married a girl who could often squeeze into a size zero, and he was now looking at a woman whose body he didn't recognize. Sleep deprivation from having a new baby around was affecting both of them.

Plus he was swamped with his assigned course work. This only exacerbated the stress they were both experiencing. Marital meltdown was impending, and they were far less forgiving than they had been of the minor gaffes they made when interacting with each other. The bickering and fighting was never-ending. Shortly after your second birthday, your dad finally earned his MBA. Not long after that, he asked your mom for a divorce. She was devastated, having worked so hard to provide for the family financially on her secretarial salary while he was in school.

Now, when you are in tenth grade at this school, she still attributes her weight gain, the stress, the fighting, and the divorce to your birth almost sixteen years ago. These issues have compressed your life since birth and contributed to the pattern of behavior that has repeatedly brought you to the main office in this suburban high school, where members of the staff often remark to the anthropologist—sometimes in your presence—that you "talk like a Black girl."

As much as you hate living with your dad and your stepmother, Stephanie, you hate your school situation even more, so much that even though you are still very, very angry with your mom (and with Granny), you still call them both every night with the same first question: "Can I come home?"

Your mom's response never varies: "I love you, Brittany, but you have to stay with your father." Granny usually tells you that you have to ask your mom. Translation: No. The one bright spot in your life is that you get to visit your mom and Granny one weekend each month. It has become what you live for on a day-to-day basis.

Invisibility in a Spotlight Life

At your new school you are a total stranger; no one knows or appears to care about you, including the adults. Your dad took you to the school to register early, before classes began. You liked that idea. You were terrified by the thought of going to a school so different from the one you previously attended. The population was overwhelmingly White; the population at your school in the city was overwhelmingly Black. Unlike your old junior high school, this huge building (four contiguous wings, a swimming pool, and a music center) has only about fifteen hundred students, about 5 percent of them African American.

You are assigned to a counselor, Ms. Jordan, who is a fairly young woman, just three years out of college. When she looks at your transcript, she asks you, as if it were not on the transcript, if you had attended a city school. You fight back your desire to ask, "Can't you read, Bitch?" What you said, instead, was both gender and age appropriate: "Yes, ma'am."

"Yes, ma'am?" she giggled nervously. "Yes, ma'am," you said again. "Please," she said smiling, "do not call me 'ma'am.' Just call me 'Ann.'" This was a new experience for you because, at your former school, adults were addressed as "Mr." or "Mrs." and referred to by their last name only, even when everyone knew their first name. Was she granting you the right to treat her as your social equal or, at the very least, your peer?

You are a tenth-grader and a first-year student. Many of the others in your class attended elementary and junior high school together. You know no one. When you go home and tell your dad about how difficult it is to be so alone at this school, he tells you that you must learn to "sail solo." When you complain about not having any friends, especially female friends, he tells you that you don't need friends—boys or girls.

"That is not why you go to school," he sputters. "You go to school in order to obtain the skills that are being taught in the classes you are taking. You do not need friends. You need skills. You can get friends later." You don't believe him.

That you have to make it on your own is your dad's favorite aphorism. He promotes it at work even though he has a team of employees working together. He pretends to live it at home, even though he and Stephanie are inseparable. They're constantly hanging all over each other—making you sick to your stomach. He tells you repeatedly that you must learn to swim alone, to find a way to get the assigned course work done, and to observe and be in sync with the prevailing norms at school and in society at large. When you tell him that you need friends to help you do this, he discounts your desire to be connected to people at school and dismisses your feelings of isolation.

You concluded a long time ago that your dad is less concerned about your relationships with Black kids than your mom is. Although neither he nor your mom has any Black friends, he knows some Black people, both at work and off the job. He recently hired a clerical worker who is Black. She has an undergraduate degree, which is not the case for most of his workers (especially the White males), but she is still the lowest-paid office person.

The custodial work is outsourced to a big janitorial service in the area, and its staff is mostly Black or Latino. You hate that. When you were younger, you would ask your dad repeatedly about the color differences that you observed between his office staff during the day and his cleaning service staff at night. He always waffled. Your dad has virtually no contact with the night-side cleaning operation.

You don't know any of the people at your dad's office very well. You know the Black woman even less because she is new. You don't know this for sure, but you think your dad hired her to alleviate his young wife's fear of competition, which would surface if he hired a young White woman. She seems to feel a little more secure knowing that the woman is Black. (Too bad she doesn't know about your dad's penchant for equal-opportunity lovers, something you would never reveal to her—or to your mom). Policing your dad's sexuality is one of his young wife's major preoccupations. One day when you were both home, she called him almost every hour of the day.

You feel that you have to be more mature than the adults around you are. For example, when your dad again tells you that you don't need friends at school, you bite your lower lip to keep from calling him a fool or saying something equally offensive. Doesn't he know that humans are *social* animals who will do anything to avoid isolation? You learned that in your psychology course at your former school.

You are so very angry. You run to your room, slam the door, lie spread-eagled across your bed, and cry, stuffing the pillow against your mouth to keep your dad and his stupid gold-digger wife from hearing your sobs. (You have resorted to calling her this, rather than your preferred b-word, out of respect for the anthropologist, who says she finds it offensive and insulting to hear any woman referred to by that denigrating term.) To add insult to injury, in about five minutes Stephanie knocks on your bedroom door and tells you that you have to clean up the mess you left in the bathroom. You decide that you hate her and ignore her knocking and her ridiculous instructions. Later you hear your dad's muted voice in the bathroom as he tries to soothe her anxieties about your refusal to acknowledge and comply with her authority.

You challenge her right to discipline you. She is not your mother. Indeed, she's barely even an adult. You keep asking yourself why your dad married her. The thought of her having authority over you makes your face break out. Your dad is, in your mind, the only person in this house who can tell you what to do and what not to do. Feeling utterly powerless in your dad's house, you suddenly begin grinding your teeth at night. It has gotten so bad that your dad has to take you to the dentist. When the dentist asks if something in your life might be causing new stress, you tell a pseudo lie and mention only the fact that you hate your new school. That is true, but it is no way near the whole story.

You are angry with your parents, especially your mom and your new stepmom. This is both so deep and so masked, however, that when the anthropologist asks why you repeatedly direct anger at your mom and stepmom, but not at your dad, you don't know how to answer. You really don't know why you are not as angry with your dad. After all, he is the parent who asked for the divorce. He is the parent who often missed his weekends to have custody. He is the parent who married Stephanie—even *after* you told him you did not like her. You remember how angry you got when your report card came in last semester, and your stepmom opened the mail from the school simply because it said "Mr. and Mrs." She knew it was about you. You're the only person in the house with connections to the school. Your grades were not good, but without even waiting to consult your dad, Stephanie told you that you were grounded for three weeks. *Three weeks!* Then she called your dad at his office to tell him about your report card and the disciplinary action she had taken.

When you appealed to your dad to override her decision, he ignored your pleas and told you they were a team and that as long as you lived under their roof, she had as much authority in your life as he. Anger oozes from every crevice on your body but, regrettably, has no place to go.

When the anthropologist sought your parents' approval for you to participate in her female aggression and competition study, she was surprised at how quickly your stepmother said no. Her reasoning was that you needed to devote all your time to improving your grades this semester. The anthropologist didn't know of the family drama or about the history of your relationship with your dad's new wife. In fact, she didn't even know the woman who answered *was* a new wife. The anthropologist had just called the number of the person listed as "mother" on the data sheet school officials gave her.

The school had established a rule requiring the anthropologist to call the parents and obtain their approval before asking each student if she was interested in participating. She attributed this convoluted requirement to administrators' fear of and deference to parents.

The anthropologist tells you that she decided to call your father too. You think she recognized the childlike qualities in your stepmother's voice and wisely inferred that she was probably a member of the "second wives club," with all that that implied. Guessing that there might be conflict between a young stepmother and a teenage stepdaughter described as someone who "talks like a Black girl," the anthropologist decided to take a chance and call the father. She heard his voice as much more mature (shall we say older?) than his wife's. After a very long conversation about what the subject of the study was, its goals, where the anthropologist worked, and so on, he agreed to let you participate.

You are so grateful because it gives you a safe place to vent and get some relief from the compression that makes it hard for you to breathe. At the same time, it might help you gain access to and legitimacy with the Black students at the school. You keep trying to gain admittance to the group, but because of your skin color and hair texture, you think most of the Black kids, especially the girls, see you as White. They avoid all but the most polite kind of interactions with you.

Your fortunes may be about to change. You have just learned today that you have earned a spot as a member of the step team, the most visibly Black female activity at the school. Not only are the team members great performers of the cultural dance steps, but they are also among the greatest activists for Black social justice at the school. The young, first-year, White female adviser for the group thinks of you as the only White girl on the step team. (She is probably the only adult at this school who thinks that you are White, but that does not help you in the setting of step team practices.)

You hate her description of you as "the only White girl on the step team," but you decide not to try to correct her perception. You are well aware that most of the adults, especially the female teachers, dismiss you academically because they have judged your discourse style as "ghetto." You noticed that dismissive attitude in your science teacher when she initially called on you to answer a simple question. She suddenly changed her mind and said out loud, "Sorry, Brittany. I think I should call on someone else."

Your classmates, males and females, giggled nervously. The other two adult women in the classroom (teacher's aides) looked at you knowingly. You felt the blush start at the base of your neck and spread across your face, like fire fueled by a gushing wind. You hoped no one noticed. Given (White) women's general socialization always to be nice, especially to each other, you concluded that this teacher was outraged that your behavior is inconsistent with her perception of how young White girls should behave. (She is one of the many members of the community who has told the anthropologist that you "talk like a Black girl.")

At the first step team practice, however, everybody, including the team's captain, designates you the "White girl stepper." (The captain is really in charge because the teacher adviser knows absolutely nothing about step routines.) You understand the captain's comment to imply that she believes you are an incompetent performer.

Consequently, both the captain and your Black female peers are really, really blown away when they discover that you can perform the intricate steps as well as or better than the other twelve girls on the team. After practice, the team captain, ReRe, asks you how you know the routines so well. You tell her that you had been a member of the step team at your former school in the city and that you had loved it. You also tell her you were on the girls' basketball team and the cheerleading squad. She seems reasonably impressed and asks if you are involved in those same activities at this school. You are reluctant to tell her that your efforts to join both teams had failed.

Surviving a White Bantustan

You have been trying to find your way in this awful place (which you describe as the American version of a White Bantustan) since September.[22] Now that the second semester has started and all your schedules are different, you are right back in the middle of this hidden terror—starting fresh. The girls who are socially defined as White do not accept you. Either they avoid interacting with you or they attack you. When you smile at them or ask a question in class, they look at you with disgust. Some even silently mock the way you talk. More than once one of them has walked up to you and whispered the vile words "bitch" or "slut." The most overtly vicious girls call you a "nigger lover." They never do it publicly of course, never in the classrooms where everyone could witness your humiliation and their meanness. This would violate the White girls' inviolable dictum, "Be nice."

These "un-nice" practices are carefully choreographed to avoid witnesses, to be hidden from the prying eyes of adults and of most of your peers. The aggressions take place on the school bus, in hallways, the gym, the cafeteria, and other public spaces, but never within earshot of anyone who could discipline the girls. In these settings, no one would dare tell on the girls, who are often leaders or aspiring members of cliques. The meanness of these girls is so rampant that you try to always be in places policed by adults who can enforce the rules, hoping at least to lessen the frequency of incidents. This forces you to make changes in your routine, such as avoiding going to your locker unless it is absolutely essential. Last semester, you often asked your teachers if you could be let out just a few minutes early to get something from your locker. This plea failed because no students are allowed in the halls before or after the bell rings. This means that you carry more of your books and other supplies around with you during the day than most of your peers. You visit your locker when you think the girls (especially the girl whose locker is next to yours) are less likely to be going to theirs. Initially, you didn't know their locker routines, so you were often caught in the cross fire.

If your locker was the only site where humanity was detached, where you were called a "slut," a "ho," and a "nigger lover," that would be one thing, but this kind of violence is manifested in nearly every aspect of your school experience. Your decision to remain the person you were when you came to this place makes you a moving target.

Responses to you from the boys—Black and White—are very different from the girls' at this school. The male students are very friendly and welcoming, inviting you to parties, dances, and sports activities. You refuse all of these invitations because you still socialize with your friends in the city, especially on the weekends you visit your mom, not to mention that you are still carrying that crazy torch for Lamont. What is wrong with you? You know that Lamont has been seen "sniffing" another White girl. It would probably be good for you to accept some of these new invitations. The more interest the boys in this new school show you, however, the more the girls seem to isolate and harass you.

You limit these girls' relational or gender-specific aggression somewhat in the hallway by helping a Black girl who is in three of your classes and has a mild case of spina bifida. When you are helping a student who is perceived to be handicapped and or disabled, no one insults you or does anything that remotely resembles unkindness. Black and White, male and female, they see you as helping a poor handicapped Black girl and do nothing to prevent you from this task.

You have even started to develop a slight friendship with her. She, at least, does not turn away when you smile at her. You always tell her that you are more than willing to help her through the crowded hallways, but she often rejects the offer of help, telling you that she does not need it. Then you are forced to endure the injustices plaguing you in the hallways.

The disabled Black girl's rejection hurts your feelings. You tell her, "I just want to help you," and she responds by telling you that *she* decides what is helpful or not. When she does that, you curl up around your hurt feelings and think of her as being mean. When you call or text Asha or one of your other BFFs from your former school to tell them about this, they invariably tell you that she is right. You cannot decide for this girl, even though she is mildly handicapped, what is helpful and what is not.

When you are in the hall alone, the White girls are, to put it mildly, vicious. You have tried to join one of their cliques, but to no avail.

You don't get why they reject you. You know you dress appropriately because your dad makes good money and he hired a wardrobe consultant and gave you your own credit card to buy the appropriate clothing. You bought five pairs of jeans—the absolute must-have basic—many cute and sexy tops, and sneaks, flip-flops, and other shoes. So, you conclude, it can't be the way you dress. And it can't be that there is something wrong with your hair; you get your hair cut and styled at one of the most upscale beauty salons in your area (you even have minimal highlights). In addition, every other week—on those weekends you do not get to spend with your mom and your BFFs in the city—you get a facial and a manicure (and you wish Asha could join you for these).

Given your new peers' total rejection, you conclude that your appearance is not blocking your acceptance by the White girls and their cliques. And although you wonder whether it's your academic skills that are making you unacceptable, you conclude that none of the kids in the classes you take (you are permitted to take only one AP class, English) are any better at their schoolwork than you. Your dad wanted you to take more AP courses, but the other kids got priority placement because they had come up through the local school system and teachers knew them. When you mention this to ReRe, she tells you that you are very lucky; most students who are not from this community do not get to take the more college-oriented courses.

This is so annoying. You want so badly for these stupid people just to get it through their thick skulls that you are smarter than they think. You can consume whole pages of text with very little effort. Why can't they see that? You and Asha used to have reading contests because she was capable of the same level of performance. As friends with active library cards, the two of you commonly spent your days reading and reading and reading. Admittedly, Asha's ability to analyze written text was a little better than yours, but you are both frightfully skilled in this area.

Perhaps your peers at UGRH can't see this because you are failing most of your classes at this new school. It certainly is not because you lack academic ability. It's just that, on top of your schoolwork, there are a lot of things going on that you didn't anticipate having to deal with: (1) Your teachers don't like the way you talk. (2) You associate and interact almost exclusively with the Black kids. (3) The way the teachers teach is different. They place less emphasis on memory and more on what it all means. (4) You come from the city school system, which is widely believed to be inferior to the suburban schools.

Witnessing Low Academic Expectations—In Plain Sight

The following excerpt from the anthropologist's field notes captures the torturous nature of your academic life at UGRH:

> Today was the first day I observed Brittany in what was perhaps her least challenging class, something called Math Exploration. It's a watered-down version of the traditional math curriculum, designed to make it appear that the kids who would otherwise drop out of school and take low-skilled jobs had accomplished the same skills sets as their peers in the Regents and/or AP courses. Moreover, because she came from the City school district, UGRH school officials did not believe she was intellectually gifted despite the fact that her high school transcript documented the fact that she had taken traditional math courses prior to matriculating at UGRH. She and many of the other overwhelmingly White students were [clearly] bored stiff.
>
> It was her birthday, February 16th,[23] and she had told me that she was going to get tattoos as her birthday gift to herself. I could not believe that she would really tattoo her body, but when I arrived at the school the following morning, I saw her as I was running to her assigned first-period classroom. She was leaving the classroom as I was entering it. She said, "Oh, hi! I didn't see you out here. And I'm running to the potty." And she then said, "See? Look!" She was wearing what I came to identify as one of her favorite outfits: a pair of navy blue sweat pants and a white, short-sleeved, scoop-neck tee shirt. Unexpectedly, she pulled up her short-sleeved tee shirt and showed me a tattoo at the base of her spine, just before her buttocks. I gasped, not because of the tattoo, but because I did not expect her to display that part of her anatomy in the hallway—and to show it to me. I don't remember what the tattoo depicted; I was just aghast that she would show me such a private part of her body! But she did. I said, "Oh, my goodness, Brittany," which was the most benign thing I could think to say. It was some kind of image that I did not recognize, interesting but not what I thought it would be. Later I learned it had cost $170.00. Wow!

And before I had not quite finished "admiring" this image near her buttocks, she said, "See? My nose as well." She had her nose pierced!! Yesterday she told me that she was going to have her tongue pierced. But I guess she changed her mind about that. Ooh! I mean, just talking about it as I write these words, I'm in pain. I then asked her if it were painful, and she said, "Oh, no—a little bit. It's not nearly as painful as I thought it would be." Oh, my goodness! And I didn't know. I mean, I just could not believe that this is what she did on her birthday.[24]

Your life at this school is an unrelenting series of adjustments and adaptations. You never tell on the girls who harass you—not ever. You used to wear your coat during your morning classes, almost as if it were a shield from them. That only reinforced the idea that you didn't belong and that the rumors that you lacked mental capacity were accurate. In one of your diary entries, you share the following information about your efforts to remain attached to former friends and about the challenges of your new life.

I was at school all day. I was going to skip last block cuz Asha, my [Black BFF] friend, is having her birthday party in the City tonight. It will be a lot of fun. Asha is just like me. She likes guys better than most girls, just like me. . . . Sometimes they annoy me cuz they are girls, but I can't chill with guys all the time. . . . Rick came to pick me up. This kid really likes me. A girl in one of my classes told me he talks about me all the time. Then I and Rick went to Asha's house. There were so many girls there. Some I had seen at school or when I went to school in the City. Yea, I already didn't like some of 'em. Then they were complaining. Then I smoked and just let them do their "little" thing while I did mine. Then that was over and it was time for the birthday cake (at 10:30 at night?). Then I went to go do that and I was smoking a bong and I went to go upstairs and I remembered I had my bong, so I accidentally exhaled towards some girl. Some girl bitch walked up and was like "Bitch." It was an accident. My bad. You don't gotta call me a bitch. So I heard her say that, and I was, "Did you just call me a bitch?" She . . . hasn't even tasted life. And she got the nerve. You don't walk up to a girl and *ever* disrespect her.[25]

You're so sick of it all! You have been at this school more than one semester now, and you don't yet have a close girlfriend, despite your efforts to make friends, especially with the Black girls. Now that you are on the step team and you have demonstrated your ability, you think you have started to see some acceptance, at least among *them.*

More important to your parents, of course, is that your grades are suffering. You get decent evaluations from the teachers on the written work you submit, especially in your math and science classes, but you're reluctant to talk in class and often fail to submit assigned homework. Misunderstanding your silence, teachers conclude that you don't know the answers to their questions, and this hurts your overall performance. Teachers don't understand your fear of being further ostracized. The way you talk has been so stigmatized that you no longer care to use your voice in public, even when teachers prod you to do so.

In your search for acceptance and a sense of belonging, you often go to the main office between classes to talk with Ms. Redding, the receptionist. She is so warm, so accepting and forgiving—toward everyone. Regardless of what you look like, what you have done or been accused of, who your parents are, or where you live, she looks at you as an individual and appears to love you. You stand there naked in your marginalization, your lack of fit and belonging. Her smile and body language embrace you. You want desperately to tell her that your life at this school is a living hell and that everybody here regards you as inappropriately passing for Black. They identify you as White and hold you to "White standards," but in your eyes, you're Black and want nothing to do with their expectations.

Ms. Redding reminds you of Asha's mother. You feel guilty about that. You don't want to do what the anthropologist told you is so common: framing Black women primarily according to their social roles, as mothers and caregivers, mediators or peacemakers. Still, you can't help but find solace in a visit with Ms. Redding. Your teachers don't see, or pretend not to see, the invisible harassment your peers inflict on you daily. Indeed, the anthropologist bears witness to the fact that many of the adults deliberately ignore what is happening to you. To you, this means they secretly think you deserve what is happening to you.

Ms. Redding doesn't think that. Not a day goes by that you don't come into the main office to get your "Ms. Redding fix." Indeed, this is where you first met the anthropologist, one day between classes, and where your involvement with the study of female competition and aggression began. Just before you walked in, you encountered the White boy who had hit you, in that silly way he always does in trying to get your attention. (You think of him as a stalker—almost.)

An Anthropological Postscript

Brittany sees herself as an army of one—pushing back against a culturally approved, gender-appropriate role (an exercise of individualism her dad would be proud of). The nonverbalized, unofficial goal of most of the adults in her life is to teach her, without using physical force, to obey the rules that maintain those dominant ideals of femininity. So, for example, if the girls who taunt her can make her so uncomfortable that she alters her behavior to act appropriately "White" and female, everyone can assert that she changed voluntarily.

Socially defined as White, Brittany performs Blackness in her widely identified White skin. She is drawn to the Black community because in her previous schools, she was an assimilated minority among a Black peer majority. Her decision to pass for Black—an identity inversion that is only partially achieved—compels school officials to interpret her identity construction as pathological, going beyond what is widely attributed to Black Americans who opt to pass for White.[26] School officials and her White peers identify her as White and, as Cheryl Harris notes, Whiteness is valuable property that is rarely discarded or forfeited.[27]

Moreover, because Brittany self-identifies as a Black female and does not engage in physical violence—merely "talking [and behaving] like a Black girl"—she unwittingly captures the essence of female competition: relational aggression. Intriguingly, language, in its broadest sense (which includes images and logic as well as speech), is the most widely used form of nonphysical violence in human interactions, and even though it is the most widespread form of symbolic violence, it is rarely recognized as violence at all.[28] "Symbolic violence is the kind of violence exercised upon a social agent with his or her complicity."[29]

This is certainly applicable to the language Brittany uses here to describe, chronicle, and/or outline female aggression and competition, not only at UGRH but among women more generally. In the popular imagination, at this school and elsewhere, African Americans, especially girls, are viewed as "aggressive" even when they do not engage in physical violence. (This is why it was extremely difficult for me to get school officials to go beyond the idea of physical violence as the central criterion when they offered possible study participants.)

Merely self-identifying as a Black girl makes Brittany guilty of what most adults and students at the school recognize as "aggression," that is, the desire to harm another. Her direct-discourse style does not embody what Lisa Delpit identifies as the "veiled use of power," the central criterion in hegemonic female "ways with words."[30] Instead, Brittany's perceived "aggression" is embodied in her raw, unvarnished language and not, ironically, in physical violence. As Veena Das acknowledges, language is the space where suffering is not only (mis)recognized but also socially appreciated.[31]

Thus, as Brittany (and most people) uses it, language includes images and logic as well as speech. In this way, language parallels female aggression when it tends toward the symbolic, which is seldom taken seriously. Male violence, on the other hand, is readily recognized because of its overt physicality. This difference is evidenced in language itself when we demote "violence" among women to "aggression," although it is clearly *so* much more.

CHAPTER 5

Keyshia

THE BLACK GIRL'S TWO-STEP

Revisiting What Is Never Dead: The Past

As your mom drives you to school in time for your 7:35 a.m. class, the dense fog comes suddenly and inexplicably, an unexpected and undesired visitor in the middle of spring. Its abrupt appearance is not unprecedented, but it isn't normal either. The conflict-laden conversation between you and your mom about your recently unacceptable behavior and grades ceases abruptly, as she lowers her driving speed, turns on the car's high-beam headlights, adjusts her glasses, tightens her seat belt (insisting that you do the same), and focuses her attention exclusively on the road. These actions add to the sense of abnormality unfurling before your hazel eyes, doubly striking juxtaposed against your milk-chocolate-brown skin. You are inevitably startled by strangers' reactions to the color of your eyes and your skin color. There is, however, no time to contemplate such frivolities this morning.

You try not to be influenced by the uninvited fog as you exit the car, your mom's half-heard words (something about it burning off shortly) elevating your spirit, an ephemeral feeling because you and your mom are engaged in an ongoing feud about your schoolwork and your unacceptable behavior. As you close her car door and walk the few steps to the front door of the school, you are self-consciously aware of how hard your heart is beating.

Today is one of the most exciting days of your life. You are going to have lunch with your erstwhile BFF Nadine (aka Dee Dee), someone whom you've been out of touch with for just under a year. Using friends and back channels, you have learned that she is willing to talk with you for the very first time since the public breakup that took place last year, and you are bursting with excitement. More than anything, you want to tell her how sorry you are and to assure her that you did not mean to hurt her. It just happened. You were unable to stop yourself, unable to either stifle or conceal your overheated desire for a relationship with Kyle, her boyfriend at that time. Before you engaged in this awful betrayal last year, you were so close that several students "asked if we were gay, because we were such good friends."[1]

All these unpleasant thoughts are competing for dominance as you go further into the building on this Monday after spring break. You are anxious to get back into school and into the routine of your academic life (not that you really value the academic stuff— it's a game you can play and are able to win with almost no effort; you also wonder why your school achievement is so unlike that of your Black peers, and whether you are a fluke). And you are also struggling both to accept the fact that the short break is over and to retain the memory of how much you enjoyed your spring vacation and the sense of freedom you had. You often feel loaded with guilt about feeling free when school is in session, primarily because you know you should be doing more to meet your parents' academic expectations.

All the adults at the school tell one consistent story about you, Keyshia: there has been a major change in your behavior since you and your BFF had the fight last year. Many of them insist that it is almost as if you have become a radically different person overnight, and they are totally unable to understand such a fundamental change, especially given your family's class pedigree.[2] For example, although you readily agreed to participate in the anthropologist's study, to complete all the study's requirements—including the interviews, both formal and informal, and the ten-week diary—and to endure classroom observations, you were one of the students who would not complete a single diary entry, an essential component of the study. The following entry from the anthropologist's field notes is typical:

> I finally found Keyshia in the library. Was she hiding from me, I wondered? First, I looked for her in the study area, which is where she and fellow students are supposed to go during this study block. The teacher aide, who does not *like* this Black girl—to put it mildly—told me that she was in the library. And then she told me in no uncertain terms, that she didn't want me to take her out of the library because she was not supposed to go anyplace if she were unescorted.[3] I assured her that I would not. I went into the library to find Keyshia, who as the (Black) secretary, Ms. Redding, keeps telling me, has just changed overnight, it seems, before everybody's very eyes. When I went to talk to her last week, I had to go to the detention center because, apparently, she'd cut class excessively and lots of other things and was being punished. But Ms. Redding says this is the new Keyshia (I know she has not completed a single diary entry [at this point]).... But, you know, every time I talk to her, she says, "Oh, I'll bring it to you tomorrow, I'll bring it to you tomorrow." That never happens. I find this really annoying.[4]

What was totally intriguing to you (and to the anthropologist) was that no one would contact your parents about your school behaviors and practices: none of your teachers, not your assigned counselor, none of the other school administrators. They watched you as they would a massive car wreck, rubbernecking, with you as the spectacle. All the adults and many of your classmates and friends readily acknowledge that you are in trouble emotionally and that this is most clearly manifested in the precipitous drop in your grades and your widely unpredictable behavior, yet no adult at the school is willing to confront your possible wrath or respond to your silent cry for help by calling in your parents and informing them of the massive mess you are making of your life. You don't understand why they think you are on the road to disaster.

There are so many changes that even with her short history at UGRH, the anthropologist notices. The following is an example:

Recently, when I see Keyshia she has a cap, or something on her head covering most of her hair. She never has her hair uncovered. She has two small piercings, like small earrings . . . above her left eye. Yikes, I don't know. I don't know what is happening to this child. But when I went into the library, she obviously saw me and didn't want to have to face me and tell me that she didn't have the promised weekly diary to give me—again. So she hid on the floor under one of the tables. I did not see her. I asked the librarians if they'd seen her. One library staff member said yes. "She was sitting right there." She called her by name: "Keyshia. Keyshia!" She slowly emerged from under the table and stood up. Then I saw her. I asked, "Oh, my goodness, were you hiding from me?" She was sitting under the table. Keyshia is a Black girl with pecan-tan skin and eyes that are unusual in color among African Americans. Not *light* light, by any means, but sort of pecan tan. She was sitting at this table but there were no other Black kids there. All of her friends at the table were White and male and female. Again she promised that she'd bring it tomorrow. And then she said to one of her unnamed White female friends, "Would you remind me?"[5] She assured her that she would. The only thing I know to do if she doesn't have it when I go out there on Thursday, is simply to call her house and ask her parents for their help.[6]

Unlike the anthropologist, you see your problems as being inextricably connected to the way the school rules infantilize even the students they identify as seniors. You think it might have something to do with a widely held perception among both the adults and the students at the school, including you, that achievement is its own reward. That kind of thinking is no longer a way to motivate you.

It takes more to motivate me than that: getting my name among a *whole* bunch of honored people, not highlighted or anything. Just there. But I seriously—this year, I just don't really care that much.

I just want to get out of here. And I'm trying my hardest, I'm just doing what I have to. But I'm personally okay with that. Like, I don't feel like I'm—you know. When I go home and I look at my report card, I'm not in tears. I still just want to get out, and I'm happy that I'm almost there. Now maybe in *past* years, I would have been distraught about a bad grade, or trying harder. But my parents just want me to get out of here too. All of this trouble that I've been in this year. They are really just trying to get me out of this school.[7]

The anthropologist asks her why she has been in so much trouble this year.

'Cause I want to leave more than ever! I'm realizing that at this school, I'm not learning anything relevant. I don't like the staff. I don't like being told when to go to the bathroom. It's annoying. My parents know that if I am set on doing something, I'm going to do it regardless. And I'm very stubborn. And they just want me to graduate now. So glad to be getting out of here. I feel that I am much too old to be constantly told what to do and when to do it, raise your hand, da-da-da-da-da. 'Cause, you know, technically, I'm an adult. And they always tell you, you know, you can't talk to adults like this and that, but they can talk to me like that? I am of an age to be considered an adult, so you treat me like an adult, and I'll treat *you* like an adult. I can be very, very rude. I can be *extremely* rude. And very mean. That's only when I feel like somebody's being rude to me, or trying to put me down. Then I will be a very smart-ass. And I am very, very, *very* good at it. *Very*. I will *talk* my way through a lot. And I can keep an argument going for a very, very long time. Especially with an adult. They feel that they are somehow superior. Or they think that they can just tell me something to do, and expect me to just do it. I realize that there *are* younger children here but, as a senior, I feel like I deserve special privileges.[8] You have to get a pass to walk everywhere, and, you know, no headphones, you know. Cell phones. I can understand the cell phone thing in class, but in

the hallways and things, you cannot have on your headphones,
in the hallway. Or during lunch. Not at school, period. . . . Like,
sometimes, like, at the library, I would work a lot better with my
headphones on. You know? Listening to music, I'm, you know,
more focused. Um . . . it was a lot easier to, you know, to come
back. You know? If I don't want to go to a certain class, that's *my*
choice. And I know the consequences, and I shouldn't be forced
to stay here, if I don't want to.[9]

Clearly you are frustrated, angry, and experiencing a level of self-
loathing that has its origins in the intersecting constraints of race
and gender, with gender being at the forefront of what is irking you,
especially as you are experiencing who you are after the involuntary
dissolution of your relationship with Dee Dee and the widely known
accusation that you were the aggressor—you stole her man. Add to
that the fact that you are not sufficiently challenged academically,
and you get a very, very unhappy high school student. When describing the main teacher deficiencies at UGRH, you tell the anthropologist that two critical features are missing:

I think that school officials need passion and experience. I
remember my Chemistry teacher last year. He is very, very
passionate about chemistry. And you know he cares about
all his students, and really wants you to grasp that concept or
whatever . . .—and he gets frustrated when students *aren't* as
willing to learn. And I think we need to have more teachers like
that, even though *I* was personally annoyed by it.[10]

Class-Based Muscle and Frenemies

It is not surprising, then, that during your first two classes on this important day, you are unable to quell your excitement or to keep your
mind from wandering, remembering all the fun you and Dee Dee
had, the multiple ways you were able to mend many of the problems
you had when you were friends. It is extremely difficult to dislodge

that memory, to breathe, and to truly feel that you belong unconditionally somewhere here at UGRH. Beyond today, you want to be with your friends, but you *did* promise your mom that you would be more engaged in your schoolwork during this final push toward the end of the year. You insist that you earned a 1450 on the SAT, which you recently took at a school out of state, thanks to the help of one of your dad's muckety-muck friends, but you made your mom and dad swear not to tell anyone about your performance.[11] Like most parents, you think, they want to go around telling their friends how smart their daughter is as a way of affirming their superior and more effective parenting practices and/or the value and validation of their excellent gene pool. You, on the other hand, are just hoping that you won't have to take more of those damn boring AP classes with the nerdy White kids while your Black friends are consigned to the "regular curriculum." Plus, you want to avoid envy from your White peers, who will inevitably insist that your exam was probably scored by an affirmative-action officer (or his or her equivalent— just kidding), and from your Black peers, who will accuse you of "acting White."[12] You're so sick of this never-ending conflict, of having to juggle everyone's expectations in order to be acceptable—to no one, apparently.

It's only a few weeks until graduation, and being able to start a new life for yourself—and not for your parents, for once—is supremely appealing. This makes you giddy with anticipation. You are seventeen, but in your mind, your parents still treat you like a baby. As a self-identified Black, middle-class student at this predominantly White suburban high school, you are looking forward to graduation, for sure, but you're really just looking forward to having more time to date once you're done with this school stuff. It's true, your primary goal, much to your mom and dad's dismay, is to snatch up a husband as soon as possible. Getting married, being someone's wife, has always been your greatest (and, frankly, your only) ambition. You can't think of anything more exciting and rewarding for your life.

Nadine (Dee Dee) would have something to say about how boy

crazy you are. Even though—or maybe because—she *is* your BFF, you got into a physical fight last year after you started hooking up with her boyfriend without her knowledge. Yes, you have to admit that they were still dating, but he was "hot" and you really liked him, and he didn't seem to be really into Dee Dee that much anymore. (That is your assessment, not hers.)

Dee Dee virtually lived at your house rather than her own prior to discovering that you were secretly dating her then-boyfriend, Kyle. She was beyond furious when she discovered that you had betrayed her in such a personal and vile way, and she refused to speak to you again after she confronted you and you told her that what she had been told was in fact accurate. You thought she knew or at least suspected that you were dating her boyfriend, but, much to your surprise, she appeared to be totally blindsided by your betrayal. (Did her "blindness" have its genesis in her unconditional trust in you? Was she a victim of believing that because you were more middle-class than she, you would never be guilty of violating *the* hegemonic gender rule, Thou shalt not date your sister or friend's boyfriend/husband/lover, aka the first rule of the girl code?) You still cannot force yourself to revisit the pain and tears that formed in her big, luminous brown eyes the afternoon when she confronted you and you had to admit that you were dating her boyfriend. Even though you are still dating Kyle, a year later, you continue to feel as if a part of you died that afternoon, when the brightness in her oversized brown eyes suddenly disappeared as if switched off, making her look even shorter than her diminutive five feet. Dee Dee was more than your BFF; in many ways she was the real sister you never had. She adored you, and you thought highly of her as well, or at least you thought you did. Your parents treated her as if she were their daughter, and she was always at your house. In hindsight, you recognize your hypocrisy, and almost a year later you are able to acknowledge that your behavior had its origins in your sense of entitlement and/or class privilege. As you reconstruct your relationship, there was a class-based bias in your interactions with her. Dee Dee was—and remains—lower in class status than you, and that entitles you, in your mind, to have what she thinks belongs to her. She did not know (and still does not know—and initially neither did you), but the price of your friendship was her boyfriend. She feels betrayed; initially, you felt entitled. It was her confounding response, her unmitigated rage that compelled you to even begin to consider why she was so angry. After all, she was your BFF and "roommate," not so much because she wanted to be but largely because she had such an unstable family life: her mother and father were never married, and their sexual and parental relationship ended for all practical purposes when she was in elementary school. When the betrayal occurred, her mother was dating a man whom Dee Dee did not like, her father was living with a woman who did not like her, and she and her younger sister and two younger brothers were competing intensely with each other for the little love and attention their parents had left over for them.

Dee Dee has always lived in upstate New York; you have not. She is growing up in a two-bedroom apartment in a single-parent household, with a younger sister and two younger brothers. Her life is filled with lots of happiness, but it is also chaotic and largely improvised. In an effort to be like your family and her perceptions of the normality of American society at large, Dee Dee focuses on the ways her family does not conform to what is seen as normal. She wants what you have, because she sees her family life as deficient and what you and your family have as normal.

Blacked Out in the Middle Class

You, Keyshia, live with both your parents and a younger brother in what your parents idealize as the American dream: a four-bedroom, three-bathroom house in a suburban development, known as Idlewood, with meticulously maintained gardens in the front and back yards, including a wooden gazebo in the backyard, overflowing with hundreds of flowers and winding vines—hosta, wisteria, morning glory, clematis, and more—that your mom and dad, especially your mom, take such pride in. The family home—under your mom's unrelenting supervision—is their pride and joy, and they work hard, very hard, to make it comfortable and safe for you and your younger brother. They, especially your mom, are committed to a house-proud ethos and devote much of their nonwork and weekend time to making the family home the envy of the family's kith and kin.

You do not mean to suggest that your dad is not involved in creating and maintaining the family nest; he is. It's just that he seems to think that his work outside the home is both more demanding and more important. You think the longer hours have something to do with it as well. As one of only two Black scientists in his company (there was one Black female in his department, but she became ill and left the company just as your dad began working there), your dad was in many ways a pioneer at this level in the company. You remember the intense conversations your mom and dad engaged in around the dinner table on a nightly basis, conversations that focused on race and, to a much lesser extent, gender (or at least as far as gender is connected to femaleness was concerned).

Your past history includes both private and public school prior to coming to upstate New York. Your parents have always been professionally employed; Dee Dee's have not. Her mother works at a job that pays just above minimum wage (she works as a nurse's aide in a local hospital, you think); her father lives in the Rodman area, but he is not now nor has he ever been consistently in her life, and he is not and never has been married to her mother. Despite these boundaries and other obstacles, between her overnight stays at your house and her maternal grandmother's apartment outside the UGRH school district, she was at least doing well enough in her academic work to be on track for graduation with you this summer.

Everything about your friendship changed once she knew you were dating her boyfriend. She was so displeased about your relationship with Kyle that she even opted not to reclaim the clothes she left at your house. Indeed, until a little more than a month ago (almost an entire year), she would not have anything to do with you, and I do mean nothing: no phone calls, e-mails, text messaging, visits, or any other contact. She refused to speak to you or even be in the same room with you. You remember the day she walked into your English classroom at the beginning of the fall semester and saw you there. She abruptly left the classroom, never to return. You concluded that she requested and received a new assignment.

Ironically, Dee Dee assumed that she needed you because she is class inappropriate: a lower-class Black girl in a predominantly White suburban high school. What a joke. What she did not even begin to appreciate is that as a middle-class Black girl, you feel keenly the inadequacy of "not being Black enough" in this same environment.[13] Among the Black students at UGRH (and perhaps in many other predominantly White contexts), being what is perceived as authentically Black trumps one's class position—at least that is the case among the Black students. It was a hellishly painful journey, forcing you to conclude that being authentic meant being real or unadulterated Black.[14]

This realization compelled you to revisit your memories of a brief tenure as a middle-schooler at a private school in suburban Maryland and then a longer time spent in the public schools in Columbia, Maryland. You will never forget the alienation and isolation you endured in those schools. Most of the Black kids avoided you, primarily because you had strong relationships with the White kids, especially the White girls. The conflict got so bad that your mom bought you a book by a successful Black journalist in Colorado (you don't remember her name—something that begins with an R) called *My First White Friend*.[15] Reading about the racial (not to be confused with academic) struggles of this journalist in an elite, predominantly White suburban school and community was like looking in a broken mirror. The person you inevitably saw was you, not the journalist.

What Dee Dee did not (and still does not) know is that you needed her (and still need her) as a friend more than she needed or needs you. Her friendship and support shored up your connection to the larger Black student population (especially among the Black females) at UGRH and eased your feelings of inadequacy, in your class-based Black identity.

> The Black girl clique is *nothing* but *drama*.[16] I'll chill with them a little, but I cannot abide the drama. They're talking behind each other's backs. . . . And that's kind of stupid 'cause that's like elementary stuff. For example, they'll have someone call, and you'll talk about the other person, see what the other person says, then you—the other person who is listening will confront them, and then *they'll* lie, and then—it's just a lot of backstabbing and stupid stuff. I don't do house parties. I just like to chill out. Like, *I* don't want to go anywhere specifically to fight someone. You know? It kind of—you go out to have fun, not to engage [in physical] fighting. Macing. You know? Everything. They are fighting about boys! He's *my* boyfriend, why are you talking to him? Why are you looking at me like that? Her outfit is ugly, and—you know? Stupid stuff like that. It's especially the case if you're cute. If you're pretty, somebody wants to fight you for no reason, especially if you're nice, too. Like, you can't be nice. 'Cause people will take that as weakness.[17]

No one ever accused Dee Dee of not being Black enough. But they sure accused you of that inadequacy. This was the case even when she began dating that White guy this year; she was still seen as "authentically Black" in a way you could never claim. She has what you and apparently most of America thinks of as the authentic Black experience: she comes from a broken home (her mother is her father's baby's mama, not his wife); her two younger brothers do not have the same father as she and her sister do; neither of her parents went to college. (Both of your parents are college educated, and they have been married since before you were born.) Indeed, Dee Dee is so Black that, to use Lonnae Parker's line, "when [she] get[s] into a car, the oil light comes on."[18] You desperately want to be Black enough, and so you fight the perception that you are not. At the same time, you also want to be embraced by your White peers as well, especially the ones in the AP classes you take (AP English, math, and government), which leads to more contradictory behaviors and practices.

> I prefer to go to the White parties rather than the Black house parties because it's a place to chill. There's music and stuff, but no dancing. There's no—not a lot of dancing. If there's dancing, it's just a few people—most people are sitting around, you know? . . . Not like dancing.[19]

Unknowingly, Nadine is a key participant in your efforts to be more engaged in the Black students' activities at UGRH and in your reclamation project. Her class status (or is it her lower-class status?) is implicated in your decision to choose her as your BFF and in your willingness to model for her a (Black) middle-class life. This brings you to the confrontation and attempted resolution of the cataclysmic fight between you and her a year earlier.[20]

"The Fight"—Keyshia's Version

You have just completed your first two classes and a study block, and you head for the cafeteria where you and Dee Dee have agreed to meet during the second lunch hour—not just as it begins at 11:15 but at about 11:25. You are so excited and so scared that you are aware of your heart beating and you believe that you can actually see its movement beneath your green V-neck cashmere sweater (your mom gave it to you for your birthday the year before). Your palms are slippery with sweat and you sense sweat on your brow. Yet despite your fear and trepidation, at the designated time, you leave your study hall on the third floor in the Z wing of the building, retrieve your book bag from your locker, and head downstairs to the first floor and the student cafeteria. You see her before she sees you. She is near the middle of the cafeteria talking to the woman anthropologist. (You did not know that she too had agreed to participate in the study—OMG!!—this is not good news.) You slowly approach them and say hello. Dee Dee's huge familiar smile is so reassuring; you feel your heartrate go from a hundred to almost zero. But the anthropologist confirms your worst fears: she says that she would love to talk with both of you later today (apparently, Dee Dee has told her that she is meeting you for lunch). You both respond to her request almost simultaneously: why not together—now, you ask? She gently says no and agrees to meet you after your lunch meeting in order to make individual appointments to talk with each of you separately. She smiles at both of you and wishes you both a good lunch. (You reason that Dee Dee has told her more than you have about your friendship, and that does not make you comfortable or happy.) The anthropologist tells both of you that she is going to wait for you in the main office and then turns and leaves the cafeteria.

As she leaves and you turn and face each other you realize how much you have missed Dee Dee and how the serendipitous presence of the research woman may have been helpful in lessening the tension you both were experiencing. You both start to smile and then laugh as if you had never had the fight.

You both remove your book bags, one shoulder at a time, and put them on the table near where you are standing. Dee Dee says she does not want the awful, greasy pizza they serve in the cafeteria or any of the other regular, predictable entrees on the menu. You agree, and you both decide to get in the line for the cookies, chips, sodas, ice cream, and other snacks. After about five minutes in the snack line, you both get what you want to eat and head back to the table where you left your book bags.

Perhaps it was because you were so engaged in trying to salvage your erstwhile friendship that you failed to notice the hostile stares of the White girls who are standing near the table. Not Dee Dee. She appears to see them right away—long before the two of you get back to the table. As you get near the table, you recognize them too: they are some of the cheerleaders—the school's iconic females—though they are not in uniform. You know that Dee Dee does not like the tall blonde one, Kirstin. That is not your issue. You are ambivalent about her for other reasons. You have seen her—repeatedly—with one of the star Black players on the school's boys' basketball team, and you know that the two of them are dating because you have seen them together at several of the chill parties you and Kyle attended at the end of last school year. You also have a gym class with her this year, and although you are not friends by any means, you are polite to each other. Your gym teacher sometimes puts you together on the same team, which you have to admit annoys you a little, not because of who she is but because she is just a cheerleader, and you actually play on a sports team and, at least here at UGRH, are known as a real athlete.[21]

Regrettably, it is Kirstin who tells the two of you that you cannot sit at the table you have chosen; she says that the table belongs to her group because they sit there every day. Her tall, lean frame dwarfs all the girls at the table, especially Dee Dee. You are torn, compelled to silence by your friendship with Dee Dee and your acquaintance with Kirstin. You say nothing, but Dee Dee does not seem to have an off-button. She responds immediately and talks nonstop, telling all the White girls, but specifically Kirstin, that they cannot keep the two of you from sitting at the table. She even dips her hand into her just-purchased bag of potato chips and throws them across the table at Kirstin. None of them appears to reach her, falling harmlessly on the table and floor.

That is when you hear Kirstin call Dee Dee a "stupid nigger." Suddenly, the room becomes totally silent; even the people sitting at the surrounding tables appear to have heard that part of the conversation. As you are trying to determine how to respond, you see Dee Dee run around to the side of table where Kirstin is standing and reach up and slap her on the face with such force that Kirstin staggers backward, though she manages—somehow—to retain her balance. Her body slumps toward the table, her face showing the imprint of Dee Dee's small hand, her face turning from red to a splotchy purple. She then begins to cry, and all the teacher monitors in the cafeteria appear to freeze in place. The room is suddenly, strangely silent, except for Kirstin's sobs. Like magic, Mr. Kanker, one of the assistant principals, suddenly appears, rushing Dee Dee out of the cafeteria; you don't remember which adults help Kirstin leave the room—if any. Your memory failure does not extend to your vivid recollection of the panic you begin to feel as all the other White cheerleaders follow Kirstin, turning right as they exit the cafeteria, toward the main office. That's when a kind of fear that you have never experienced before cloaks your body, evoking a paralyzing panic as you realize the predicament you (and Dee Dee) might be in.

You are finally able to unfreeze your muscles (and your mind) and move your disoriented body. Without really thinking about it, you make a surreptitious run to the main office to let Kirstin and her White girl posse know that you are not to be blamed for or associated with what Dee Dee did in the cafeteria. You seek to assure them that you are just an innocent bystander.[22]

Later, when the anthropologist asked you to tell her what you witnessed that day, your account was quite different from Dee Dee's and from the accounts of many of the students (and some of the adults) in the cafeteria. Dee Dee insisted that the cheerleader called her a "nigger–bitch." That is not what you heard. You are sure that Kirstin called her a "stupid bitch."

A few days after the cafeteria fight—after Nadine had been suspended for five days and nothing was done to the cheerleader, the White girl—when the anthropologist asked you to recall what happened between the two females, first you told her that you consider Dee Dee a very good friend, but . . .

> I did think that the cafeteria fight was funny—as it was
> happening. It was something we could laugh about later,
> but— . . . I do feel that Dee Dee was just *looking* for a fight, like,
> she wanted to fight . . . I don't know why . . . And I usually don't
> have, like, a good friend that stays over [at my house] or— . . . But
> she's my only friend that I have *ever*, like, had sleepovers with and
> talk to, like, multiple times a day.[23]

You assured the anthropologist that you did not see any injustice in what happened to Dee Dee in the wake of the fight. Indeed, you shared the perception of many of the school officials that she got off easy by getting suspended for only five days: she should have known better.

> I could see if it was—if they were fighting back and forth— ...
> Like if the *girl* was trying to fight her. But— ... Dee Dee basi-
> cally instigated the whole thing. So, you know, ... Five days is for
> a *mutual* fight—I think. But if ... if the girl had done something,
> like, offended her in a serious way, but she didn't. So I think five
> days is fine.[24]

Although you were very much aware that among segments of the students in the cafeteria that day (and even some of the teachers), it was widely believed that the White girl had indeed called Dee Dee a "nigger bitch," not a "stupid bitch," you were not persuaded that you were wrong.[25] And when the anthropologist told you that she remained unclear about what caused the fight, you told her, "Kirsten called Dee Dee a stupid bitch."[26]

As was the case when you dated Dee Dee's erstwhile boyfriend last year, she had no idea that you took this position. Since you were both involved in the altercation in the cafeteria, should she question your friendship? You don't think so. You experience a twinge of guilt, but you suppress it and move on.

The fight in the cafeteria compelled you to recall how often the anthropologist used the word "bystander." Was she describing you? Prior to the altercation between Dee Dee and Kirstin in the cafeteria, you were not sure you knew what she meant. After the cafeteria fight, your mind kept rewinding, going back to the fact that she saw you as you came into the office shortly after the fight to tell the White girls that you were not to be seen as promoting what Dee Dee did to Kirstin. You wish she had not been there; she witnessed firsthand your betrayal of, duplicity toward, and deception of your BFF—again. Did she say that the people who watch the fights at the school are not innocents but enablers, fueling the conflict? You wish you could remember what she said because you had a conversation with your parents that same evening regarding what you thought was the anthropologist's incredibly naive understanding of what it means to be either the victim or the perpetrator of violence. Are people who stand by and do nothing but watch a fight guilty of promoting violence, you wanted to know? Since most of the physical fights between two or more Black girls or a Black and a White girl at UGRH are observed by a largely White audience, you desperately wanted your parents' opinion because you just could not believe that this was a legitimate way to view violence.

A version of this conversation occurred at the dinner table. (At your house everyone eats dinner together, unless there is a preplanned social or academic activity.) Your mom and dad were so happy that you were actively engaged in the daily family ritual that night and that you had jettisoned your recent sullen, pregnant silence that they jumped into the debate with unusual exuberance. Your dad took a more skeptical position, insisting upon using what your mom repeatedly refers to as his "math approach" to life: identify the problem and factor in only the relevant issues, and, voilà, the problem is solved. He argued that conflict is physical in nature. Period. If a war is occurring, he insisted, knives, bullets, bombs, and other markers of war are evident.

Your mom also (mis)understood the gender-specific nature of girl fighting—albeit differently than your dad did. She at least recognized that female aggression and conflict are often unacknowledged and are widely underreported. Nonetheless, she, too, failed to fully appreciate your view of the problem—or the anthropologist's. She reminded you that you are not going to school in order to make friends or to become popular; you can do that later, she insisted. Your goal is to get an education. Your mom (a high school science teacher) denied your social reality and thus, in so many ways, mimicked your dad's approach. She insisted that you just ignore the haters. She explained that you are young, Black, and smart and that that should be celebrated. You are fully aware of the female haters and the fact that most of the hating has to do with boys, dating, and looks, or, put differently, hair, skin, and bones. You love your parents, and you are absolutely certain that they have a rock-solid marriage. Nonetheless, like most of the adults with whom you have interacted over the years, your mom supports your dad's position, telling you to just ignore the gossip, competition, and meanness, and do your schoolwork.

When the anthropologist registered surprise that you did not empathize with Nadine's outrage at being called two of the vilest terms used to describe a Black female, you restated your assertion that Kirstin, the cheerleader, did not call her the n-word; the only terms she used were "stupid' and "bitch." Furthermore, you insisted,

> that was only after Dee Dee, you know, was throwing things at her. . . . And calling her names. A lot of kids—like, I, if I was the [White] girl, I personally would have been upset—a while ago.[27]

When the anthropologist asked you to clarify your assertions that the fight was "funny" and that there was an "audience," you backtracked, acknowledging, "Well, there wasn't really an audience until Dee Dee punched her."[28]

Getting the Hell out of Dodge—*Right Now*

Your parents insist that you enroll in college immediately after high school, especially given the fact that you have been accepted at one of the Ivies. They are so proud of you. However, they fear that you are more concerned about your peers' approval than you are about academic success. You insist that they seriously misunderstand your motives. Indeed, they are in denial. Matrimony is the most important goal in your life; for you, Keyshia, this is the ultimate female achievement. Your mom and dad chalk it up to being boy crazy—but it's so much more than that. You are constantly on the phone talking about or talking to boys. Your parents set the house rules, though, not you, so it's not like you haven't tried to keep the boy-talking to a minimum in their presence. You'd prefer to use your cell so they can't overhear your conversations. But if it's before nine in the evening, you have to use the house phone; you are free to use your cell only after nine because it's free then. Technically you should be focusing on your homework all evening, but you are very, very good at your schoolwork. You always get good grades, except when you don't submit homework assignments—which has been quite often this year. You just don't care about it, and you don't see what all the fuss is about.

The point is, all you've ever wanted is to get married and have a family. You want a guy who loves you and wants to take care of you, a guy who will protect you and treat you like a princess. This goal is a constant source of conflict between you and your parents. Neither your mom nor your dad appears to realize the fierceness of the competition among the girls at school, especially for the attention of Black guys. The Black guys are the "it" guys, the school's most prominent sports stars and the ultimate signifiers of what it means to be masculine.[29]

At school, though, Black guys' unique status as the school's strongest, most visible public service workers (i.e., the students whose job it is to bring widespread attention to the school through their performance in the most popular extracurricular activities, such as football and basketball), combined with an imagined hyper-masculinity, makes them exceptionally alluring for the female students. The vast majority of the girls at UGRH, regardless of race or ethnicity, want to date a Black guy, despite—and sometimes because of—their parents' disapproval.

Meanwhile, the racialized nature of America's social life means that these are the *only* guys that you—a Black girl—are unconditionally allowed to target for dating, for potential sex partners, and for long-term mates. Your brother's non-Black male peers would experience varying degrees of disapproval from all segments of the school population if they dared have an open relationship with you or any of your Black girlfriends. You have chosen to date White guys before (and somewhat even now, maybe?), but the dating cauldron in which you are forced to survive when you date a White guy just gets too hot. Your own sense that you shouldn't be doing so works on your psyche, buttressed by the almost unanimous condemnation from your Black girlfriends and the "brothas"—even those dating White girls. Add to this your own sense of not being Black enough, and you exist in a social purgatory. But occasionally this is the cauldron in which you have sought to find a mate or, at the very least, to learn the skills needed to attract one later if you are forced to delay marriage—as your parents so desperately want you to do.

You and Nadine have recently made an effort to repair your broken relationship, which was ruptured by your decision to go out with Kyle, her boyfriend at the time, and to keep it a secret from her. You couldn't really help yourself though. There was something that you are still unable to put in words that was so appealing about him. Not only was he a big man on campus, but his body image—not to mention his big baritone voice—validated his social status. In addition to being a star basketball player, he was also rumored to be a "street pharmacist," and guys who have access to drugs are hugely popular among the girls at school. They tend to have a lot of money, and often that money gets spent on their girlfriends. You really loved Kyle; just seeing him, even at a distance, your body became unsettled, your palms got wet with your sweat. But he was a senior—a year older than you and a year ahead of you in school—and graduated last year, so you don't see each other often now. Those late-evening phone calls are typically between you and him, but more as friends now than anything else. You are still carrying a huge torch for him though. Your parents, especially your mom, cannot stand him; she hates the grounds he walks on. You think your dad and some of the other family members have urged her to rein in her contempt for him because they fear that her reactions just might make you feel even more attracted to him. So you have to admit that she has moderated her reactions when his name is mentioned or he calls on the house phone. With her Ivy League credentials and her status as a science teacher in a high school in the area, she thinks he is "well beneath you." You, on the other hand, think it doesn't really matter. He is currently living in California, trying to become a hip-hop artist. Nadine, like you, is also a senior this year, and she just found out that you are bringing him as your guest to the senior prom. What a downer for her! Maybe she won't go to the prom this year. All this is just too much to bear. You hate to even contemplate the fight you are going to have with your parents when you tell them that you are going to your senior prom with Kyle, Dee Dee's ex-boyfriend.

Like your peers, female and male, you seek to highlight your attractiveness to the opposite sex, especially given the centrality of matrimony and family in your life's goals. Having a boyfriend is a constant, often unavoidable, issue in your life. Male companionship, for you, suggests normality and belonging. You are constantly working your angles to keep guys interested in you, which would validate your friends' and family's claim that you are a beautiful girl.

Equally important, however, you seek to remain connected to the Black community. *Your* personal Black community frowns upon your dating so much; you are convinced that White girls don't have to work as hard to get ahead, so they have the freedom to spend more time engaging in social activities. Struggling to maintain this dual citizenship in Black and White is wrecking your personal and academic life. As a Black female in a predominantly White high school, you are essentially required to embrace norms and values that, perhaps unintentionally, signal your disconnection from the Black community.

You have read about, and your parents have told you stories about, the Black (and White) color hierarchy—the "brown-paper-bag principle"—that exists, historically and contemporarily, consciously and unconsciously, in the Black community.[30] So you are totally, totally intimate not only with socially approved discrimination but also with Black-on-Black discrimination, especially as it affects Black females. You are convinced that your saving grace is the unusual color of your eyes.[31] Your weird Uncle Marvin often tells you the story of how when he was a young man, he went to call at the house of a woman he was trying to date. The mother of the woman met him at the front door, saw his dark-brown skin, and yelled back into the house, "Did someone order coal today?" He was mortified.[32] He probably tells you this story to ground you with the awareness that color prejudice is not confined to men or to women; both are involved in its perpetuation.

You don't care. In your family and at church, you are described as a very pretty girl. Indeed, your mocha skin is not the lightest among your female friends, but it is also not the darkest. With the combination of your long black "arrogant hair" and your unusual eye color, you're not bad looking—by the reigning Euro-American standards.[33] You are keenly aware that these standards valorize long, straight, preferably blond hair; eye color that is much lighter than the dark brown common among people of African ancestry; full lips, but not too full; bodies so thin that breasts protrude dramatically (a feature so desired that you know several White females at UGRH who have already had breast implants;[34] you conclude that breasts are the only part of a female's anatomy allowed to be big); and tiny hips devoid of "junk in the trunk."[35]

Being pretty is one thing; nevertheless, you have noticed that when you go out with your lighter-skinned cousin, whose White mother is married to your Black uncle, you tend to disappear. You feel invisible to others around you, attracting no male attention whatsoever. Your cousin does nothing to provoke this. You don't think she is any prettier than you, it's just that she exists as a lighter variant across the brown color spectrum, and in her presence, you aren't noticed. Combined with her much straighter hair and tiny body, she is a boy magnet—and in her presence you become a wallflower. This pattern is too pervasive, so much so that you have started to play the avoidance card. You have given up going out with her if you really want to attract male attention.

You feel sorry for your darker-skinned female classmates, although they probably don't want your sympathy; they get virtually no attention from the males at the school, except when one of the guys needs help with homework or, more often, wants his hair braided. You are amazed at how often you see these "sistahs" braiding both the star athletes' hair and the regular brothas' hair. Even more alarming, you have begun to notice a response in some circles to the competition for male attention. These darker-skinned sistahs have resorted to forming an unnamed sorority, bonding with other girls like themselves to put greater effort into attracting guys.

On the flip side, you have also observed more weight gain among some of these girls than among the girls who are able to get male attention more readily.[36] What a shame, you conclude.

As stated, the brothas' overwhelming popularity with girls of all racial or ethnic identities makes it difficult to attract their attention. You have learned, surreptitiously, that in order to maximize your chances of being the "chosen one," you have to surround yourself only with a posse of darker-skinned girls—those who do not have long or White-looking hair. Being the lightest in the group doesn't always work, but it helps more often than not. You have started to take advantage of this dynamic at lunchtime. In order to demonstrate your desire to be identified as "girlfriend potential," you and your best Black female friends always sit at the Black Table in the cafeteria; admittedly, the table is gender segregated too, but it does get you closer to the brothas. A tiny minority of Black students sit with their White friends or with other Black girls or boys who do not want to sit at the Black Table.

The brothas' almost wholesale adoption of hip-hop styles of dressing helps them present a kind of male swagger that is appealing to the vast majority of the girls at school. Braided hair, dreadlocks, do-rags, long baggy jeans, massively oversized (pink) T-shirts, and meticulous attention to every detail of their attire (including how their shoe strings are tied, for goodness' sake!) are all attractive attributes of street fashion that the girls pine after.[37]

Your mom, grandma, and other adult Black females in your family keep telling you that when they were young, braided hair, huge T-shirts, and do-rags were feminine ways of self-presentation; men would not have been caught dead with their hair braided, not to mention stuffing their bodies into the kind of attire now popular. Such nostalgic old folks' talk annoys you. The church ladies— women who have traditionally chronicled and enforced norms and standards within the Black community—are exasperating to listen to. Don't they know that there has been a sea change in gender and race relations in America, you wonder? You can't imagine living in a blatantly, outwardly segregated society.

The point is, your parents and grandparents talk about being forced to live under the reign of Jim Crow and mass incarceration.[38] As young adults, your parents and grandparents were severely limited in whom they could and could not date and marry. You often remind them that these kinds of legal and extralegal constraints no longer exist. Today's dating practices, you argue, are both much less constrained and much more complicated and nuanced, with most adults (and, much to your surprise, your non-Black peers as well) unable to decipher its complicated structure and rules. You admit that today's Black males *are* freer to date outside the race than are Black girls (at least, that is the case at UGRH), but Black girls could opt to date outside the race, too—if they were more willing to withstand social disapproval and help break down those barriers.

Despite this greater social openness toward dating, the general practice of you and most of the other Black girls at your school (except for people like Dee Dee) is still to go into "the ghetto" to party on weekends. This would horrify your parents, so you just don't tell them. In this social world, in the ghetto, there are fewer non-Black people and the cultural rules are widely known and understood, even if you, as a suburban Black girl, don't know them all. You are free to hang out with whomever you please, and you don't feel any remorse in doing so. Plus, a lot of the guys are really hot, and you get plenty of attention there, so that dual-citizenship problem that you confront at school is not as crucial an issue as you party with Black peers.

At school, you and most of the other Black girls consciously choose to limit your dating to Black males. A few Black girls, like your erstwhile BFF Nadine, opt to date outside the race, but they are rare. You've done it, but it was difficult and, in the end, too hot to handle. Many White girls, in stark contrast, don't let a little thing like social disapproval get in the way of their desire to date the brothas. Almost daily, a different White girl, or sometimes two, will sit at the Black table, behind a brotha she is dating (or wants to date). You find it odd because if you were she, you'd feel uncomfortable. She's always in a seat that is either pulled up behind her boyfriend (presumed or desired) or in a seat at the edge of the group—always adjacent to him, of course. She's obviously marked as an outsider by her skin tone right away; everything else just furthers her exclusion. The chosen brotha poses coolly, in a way that suggests he is not interested, but he is.[39] Everyone at the table acts as if she is not there—including him. You basically feel sorry for her.

The sexual attraction between White girls and Black guys is evident elsewhere, too. You remember how frustrated the anthropologist was by the failure of her efforts to get the female students to talk with her during lunch hour. She was resoundingly unsuccessful. Why? The Black Table afforded the Black students a space to have a daily reunion, but so did the hallways (and to a lesser extent the classrooms), where they congregated more covertly. They were unanimously unwilling to give up this valued space and time to talk with a boring researcher.

The dark classroom in the Red-Light District supervised by Mr. Wallace (see chapter 2, "Romance in the Red-Light District") is a case in point. You, Keyshia, find this the most desirable space in the whole school building and bolt for it as soon as the second-hour lunch bell rings (and after you have had a chance to check out the Black Table) as often as you can. This is also the safest place to go if one desires to avoid the intrusion of the principal, assistant principals, counselors, teachers, and Mr. Sienna (aka "Officer Friendly"), who never come to this section of the school unless specifically paged, in order to maintain the fake claim that freedom reigns.

Lunch is the ostensible reason for the daily gathering in Mr. Wallace's classroom, but voyeuristic and unfulfilled sexual desire is the *pièce de résistance*. The male desire for seeing, smelling, and touching human flesh is apparent and unavoidable here. Because this is unabashedly a hypermasculine space, their sexual hunger makes you and the other girls who invade it prey to the third power. No matter. Like you, many Black girls and a few White girls who desire a pseudo-exotic experience often find themselves the center of attention here, but everyone treads fairly lightly. Had these desires been even partially acted upon by the male students, the school would have been at the center of a major sexual and moral disaster. The motives of these male and female students are diametrically opposed. Because most of the females are coming of age without the guidance, validation, or support of their fathers (that is not your excuse, Keyshia), they are seeking validation of their desirability as women and as human beings, while the males are, simply, most often, seeking sexual gratification.

You, Keyshia, remember the day when one of the alpha male football players posted a sign on the classroom door that said, "Hos get in free."[40] He wrote the letters with a large black felt-tip pen on a regular sheet of notebook paper. Since Mr. Wallace rarely ventures outside the room during the two lunch hours, he didn't see the note until it was too late. The door was pushed open with a kind of authority that indicated something was askew. Swooosh!! A hulking White male walked quickly toward Mr. Wallace's desk carrying the sign as if it were a grenade, closely followed by two coworkers. Their looming presence filled the room, and a sudden hush fell. Students engaged in animated conversations around their desks or lingered on and around the radiators along the windowed wall, male and female bodies in such close proximity that it was difficult to tell where one body began and the other ended; they all felt the chill of fear and anxiety.

Mr. Terence, the aide who entered first, asked Mr. Wallace if he knew the sign he had in his hand was posted outside his classroom door. Mr. Wallace's face turned beet red and he had difficulty finding his voice. Mr. Terence told him that it had been brought to his attention by the librarian, Ms. Gilderhead. Everyone laughed nervously, and Mr. Wallace regained a little of his composure. While all the male teachers and students think Ms. Gilderhead is hot, they admit that she is one of the most annoyingly diligent rule enforcers at the school. Her persnickety behavior irritates other women (so much so that they generally can't stand her), but the males give her a free pass because of her looks, highlighted by the short pencil-thin skirts she wears showing off her well-proportioned legs and ankles, her blond hair, and her large, turquoise-blue eyes.

Ms. Gilderhead absolutely abhors what she imagines is going on in Mr. Wallace's classroom during the official lunch periods. She has repeatedly tried to persuade the administration, especially the principal, Ms. Ferragotta, to either monitor the behavior of the students who congregate in this classroom during the official lunch hours or to forbid them to gather there at all. She is convinced that this classroom is ground zero for everything that's wrong with your school, Keyshia—and with all American schools and all young people. She is outraged that nothing is being done to uphold standards that she thinks are essential to academic excellence. She doesn't know whether to direct her anger against the students, against Mr. Wallace, or against the administration. She keeps her role at the school in focus, though—probably on the advice of her friends and colleagues—and avoids confronting the issue as she wants to because it could get her into trouble and could possibly damage her career.

On this Friday, the dated green signs posted on St. Patrick's Day were still hanging grotesquely on the door, making it more difficult to see the offensive sign that Mr. Terence now had in his hands. However, Ms. Gilderhead was able to pick it out from all the other signs because of her constant surveillance of this classroom door. She was returning with her lunch from the cafeteria when she noticed it. Horrified, she rushed to the library, where she put down her paltry lunch (celery, yogurt, and an apple), put on her stylish reading glasses, and immediately called the principal's office. After three rings, one of the White school secretaries, Ms. Long, answered the phone. Ms. Gilderhead was disappointed; she had hoped that the Black receptionist, Ms. Redding, would answer.[41] She said that she had to speak with the principal immediately. Like most of the other females at the school, Ms. Long did not like Ms. Gilderhead's obsessive commitment to "law and order." She responded tersely that Ms. Ferragotta was not at her desk at the moment. Ms. Gilderhead told Ms. Long that someone should come and remove what she described as "a pornographic sign on Mr. Wallace's classroom door." Pornography? Pornographic sign?? The image conjured up in Ms. Long's mind was appallingly horrifying. She felt her hands begin to shake as she dialed the walkie-talkie of the community aide workers. Given the number of calls she had had to make this week in connection with all the fire drills and bomb threats connected to the fears of another 9/11 attack, she was operating on her one last good nerve. Ms. Long kept wondering why Ms. Gilderhead did not go into the classroom and tell Mr. Wallace about the violation. This puzzled Ms. Long—but not you, Keyshia, nor the anthropologist. Why? Because both you and the anthropologist are keenly aware of the indirect, hegemonic, female-specific linguistic practice widely embraced here, and in other predominantly White social spaces as well. This narrative rewards female social agents for avoiding rather than embracing confrontation.[42] This is the case at UGRH as well.

The Anthropological Postscript

Unlike Nadine and the majority of the other Black females at the school, Keyshia, by virtue of being Black, is erased from the widely shared perception of what it means to be the child of a solidly middle-class family. Although her family life is a perfect reflection of what it means to be middle class in America, at UGRH, this is widely (mis)recognized when embodied in Black bodies. She began to flounder academically during her senior year, but the collective response of school officials closely approximated watching a train wreck. They were very much aware of her changed academic performance, but instead of intervening by first calling her parents and advising them of the seriousness of the problem and then following up by utilizing appropriate social services, the general response was to frame her problem as entertainment, to watch her fall and try to get up and fall again and slip deeper into the abyss. Moreover, the almost complete absence of adult Black professionals exacerbated her problems because too many of the adult (White) professionals saw her problem as normal for a Black child and felt no compulsion to act on her behalf. Keyshia's teenage logic and the adult professionals' inadequate engagement merged to create the toxic brew that fueled her inadequate academic performance and reinforced what has been identified as the "adultification" of Black children's bodies.[43] While Keyshia was economically different from many of her Black peers, she reached out—more than they did—to her White peers, playing a sport that no other Black girl at UGRH played, attending parties with an array of similarly placed White peers, performing in class in ways that she imagined her White friends performed, and, recently, embracing the partying and leisure practices affiliated primarily with her White friends (such as going to parties with no music).

Ultimately, Keyshia is beyond class consciousness and dreams of a life that is embedded in traditional, hegemonic norms and gender-specific values. As her narrative reveals, she is deeply ensconced in a life where normality is an unending and uncritical preoccupation. Unlike her same-sex parent, she wants no part of an adult world of paid employment or a life sans husband and children. She rejects her mother's life in part because she defines it as abnormal and a tad too difficult, even though it is freighted with conspicuous consumption. Like most of her school peers, she has embraced the gender-specific hegemonic images, values, and norms that have flooded her life since birth and, perhaps unintentionally but at the same time profoundly, she has rejected the nonnormal and nontraditional components of her mother's life: professionally paid employment. How Chloe responds to a perception of normality as the ultimate form of social and economic protection is the subject of the next chapter.

CHAPTER 6

Chloe

GOLDILOCKS, AND GIRLS WHO ARE NOT

Today I went to the mall with my brother and we saw two girls
from school. The two girls were black and they were arguing with
each other about who was going to do the rest of the driving. It's
funny because both of these girls are out of school so I wouldn't
trust either of them to drive me. When we walked by my brother
and I just laughed at how stupid they sounded. The one girl who
looked younger wanted to drive and was yelling at the other girl
to let her drive. When my brother and I had passed them we
turned back to look and they were grabbing at each other for the
keys. It may have been playful but it didn't seem like it. I don't
have therapy today so when I got home I relaxed.

—Chloe's journal, 7 May 2005

The anthropologist remembers how much she wanted you, dear
Chloe, to be involved in her study of female aggression, bullying,
and competition. She recalls how she wanted to learn why—and
how—the childhood narrative you were taught and what you have
learned have compelled you to be blindly committed to the rewards
of the society's dominant narrative of individual responsibility and
inadequacies but was unable to acknowledge or recognize the structural—or power—issues[1] that made you so angry that you turned it
inward, inadvertently fueling your frequent bouts with depression.[2]

Family in Zebra Stripe

You are seen as a Black girl by everyone—but you.[3] Your primarily
White friends see you as Black; the Black peers you seek to avoid at
school see you as Black and wonder why you are always trying to

"act White"; your family members, including your mother, see you as Black; and the people in your suburban church community think of you as a Black girl as well. Nevertheless, as your diary entries indicate, of all the identities you could choose, Black is your least favorite—but the one that you cannot dislodge. You are as close to White as any American of African descent can get: your mother is socially defined as White. The only Black people you love unconditionally are your father and your little brother. That love does not extend to other people defined as Black. You care about your Black relatives, but you see that as a social obligation and is not the same as the feeling you have for your father and brother.

You love your father unconditionally, despite, or maybe because of, his Black skin. He has always made it clear to you that you are his little princess. You can twist him around your little finger without much effort. Anything you tell him you want or need, he makes heroic efforts to get for you. Last year, he bought you a used car because you told him you wanted a vehicle in order to be like the other kids at school. Your mother was adamantly against the idea, arguing that the family was in such shaky financial condition that there was no way to pay for something that was not absolutely essential. Her wishes were ignored—again.

You love everything about your father: his thick, arrogant black hair, super dark brown eyes, and wide, crooked smile. His oversized hands and chocolate-brown skin merged with his six-foot-three frame constantly remind you that he was a football star in high school whose dreams of playing professionally ended abruptly with a knee injury. He works so hard to protect the family he created. He retired from the military last year after serving on a submarine for more than twenty years. When you were growing up (you just turned seventeen), your father was only home for short periods of time, and then it was back to sea. Now he works as a police officer in one of the nearby suburban towns. You don't remember him ever working an eight-hour day; he is always working. His absence from home has fueled the current estrangement from your mother. He actively seeks ways to avoid having to interact with you and your little brother in her presence.

You sense that he no longer loves your mother. You also sense that she knows this and has become ill as a way of dealing with this loss and in an effort to regain his attention. Fortunately, Nana, your maternal grandmother, lives down the street and is very much involved in your life. Consequently, when your mother goes into one of her frequent and extended periods of drinking and depression, your grandmother can help you take care of your little brother. That, however, does not include getting him up in the morning and making sure that he gets breakfast, takes a shower, brushes his teeth, and is ready when the school bus arrives. That's your job every weekday morning.

During these periods when your mother is concurrently present and absent, Nana comes by at night to make sure that your brother's clothes are in order. Apparently, everyone thinks *you* can make it on your own; you are only four years older than your brother. She prepares him a sandwich for lunch the next day and makes sure that there is something for breakfast. He looks more like your mom's side of the family. Both sets of grandparents adore him. Despite Nana's intimate involvement in your lives, you have always viewed your relationship with your brother as closer to being his mother than his sister. The responsibility of taking care of him has been almost exclusively yours for so long that you don't remember a time when you were not in that role. The adultification that suffocated your childhood was forced, not a role you chose or one into which you grew. No one takes care of or shows any concern for or about you except your father, and he is rarely home. Your pain and confusion are virtually invisible to everyone but you yourself. Not only do you suffer, but your suffering goes unnoticed. This is the primary reason for your massive depression.

Suturing Love, Loss, and Border Crossing in a Landlocked Social Space

Your mother and father met while in public school in the urban area that fueled the growth of the suburban community in which you were born and now live. Ironically, during their childhood and early adolescence, the schools in the city where they both lived were less segregated than they are today. A greater number of the Black and White kids took classes together. Tracking was not the huge problem it is today. Your father was the star of their school's football team; your mother was the captain of the cheerleaders, all of whom were White. Your parents took some classes together, too. Their friendship evolved into courtship, love, and marriage despite their racial differences. And, some twenty years ago, that was really risky. Neither of them went on to college. They got married; he joined the military, and she became a housewife. After you were born, they were able to purchase a house using the benefits provided by the GI Bill. Your father did not want your mother to work, and at that time in her life, she thought she shared his views: the man works to earn the money; his wife stays home and rears the children. Jokingly (or was it?), on more than one occasion she has told you that your father is a traditional kind of guy; he did not (and still does not) want a wife who does not view motherhood as the most important, even the only, role she should occupy. But, unfortunately, this is what appears to have unglued her emotionally.

Your mother is the kind of woman, you assert, who needs more than two children and an absent husband to feel fulfilled. Add to this the loss of so many of her friends when she married your father because they did not approve of interracial marriage, and you have a perfect recipe for isolation. Her depression and alcoholism were predictable responses. When your mother was in school, she was the center of attention: the beautiful, slim cheerleader with long blond hair who captured the attention of virtually every guy at school but chose the star athlete—your father. Everyone, including him, was convinced that he was headed for an NFL career. Since all the teachers and other school officials were White, including his coaches (Black people were thought unqualified for such jobs when your parents were in high school), your father's parents, especially his father, believed he was headed for the big league. You never met your paternal grandfather—he died the year you were born—but you have seen pictures of him. Your father is a perfect replica of your paternal grandfather, whom everybody talks about endlessly. Like your father, he was a military man, one of the Tuskegee Airmen, you've been told. (What's a Tuskegee Airman? You've been planning to look that up, but have yet to get around to it.)

Your father's mother, Grandma Harriett, is alive and doing well, but to your way of thinking, she's a bit strange. The most visible marker of her strangeness, as you perceive it, is her practice of continually humming, off-key, Negro spirituals that are unfamiliar to you. As a young girl you would attempt to engage her in conversation in order to stop the buzzing sounds, which is how you defined her humming. You were only partially successful. As soon as she answered your questions, which she always did with great patience and sincerity, she would resume humming. You were only trying to distract her because you found the songs annoying, even frightening, compelling you to confront and embrace her profound loss as it was articulated in the songs she sang and as it was inscribed on her body and embodied in her posture and speech. When you mentioned this to the anthropologist in one of your many interviews, she said that such humming is a gender-specific practice (which does not mean that males do not do it, she said; some do, but it is much more prevalent among Black women) that is not as widely practiced today as it was during the official enslavement of African Americans and during the Reconstruction, Jim Crow, and civil rights periods of American history. According to her, humming to disguise and/ or minimize the stress in their lives was a common Black female way of being, especially among women beyond their teenage years. She suggested that it might have emerged as a way to cope with the inordinate stress in their lives as well as to mask what they were really feeling about the violence and loss sutured to their female bodies.

This exchange between you and the anthropologist forced you to think about Grandma Harriett not only as an old lady but as a young woman, a mother, a wife, and a worker. Reluctantly, you remembered that in addition to having married a man who was more than twenty years her senior (her family tried to get her not to marry him, as your mother's family tried to keep her from marrying your father, though for different reasons), she gave birth to five children, the oldest of whom is your father. Her other three sons are all in prison. Her only daughter, Aunt Wilameena, married your mother's wealthy brother, Uncle Bradley, after your parents were married.

Unlike your mother, who agreed with your father that she would stay home and rear their children, Grandma Harriett returned to her teaching job shortly after the birth of each of her five children. She had struggled so hard to attend college, and she shared a sense of collective identity with the African American community. In addition, her husband, your grandfather, was a military man whose long absences and relatively low salary, like that of your father, left her with the primary responsibility of rearing their children. Moreover, because she was born before the civil rights movement (which the anthropologist tells you was the second emancipation for African Americans), Grandma Harriett's anger (an inappropriate female emotion, by the way) and disappointment are so pervasive that in her presence your nose tingles.

You don't know why or how to explain that when you are in her presence, she seems to be a partitioned or divided person: one part above the ground, the other below. On the one occasion when you talked with your Aunt Wilameena about this, she dismissed your concerns and responded by saying that her mother has two stomachs: one an organ for ingesting food, and the other a receptacle to contain and restrain the violence and loss that has permeated her life. You are never quite sure whether to take what Aunt Wilameena tells you seriously. After all, she married your uncle for his money, and that is a real source of hidden conflict between the two of you. She does not realize how much you resent her for being what you see as a gold digger.

> Happy Mother's Day! What a day it was. We went out to lunch with about 16 of my family members. Nothing really interesting happened but my aunt did get an attitude. My aunt (Black) pulled me aside and told me not to worry about her life any more and that it was none of my business, this after the previous day she

came to me, as an adult, and told me that she was going to divorce my millionaire uncle. The family knew from the beginning that she was a liar and only wanted the money. She told me that she had never loved him. This just about sent me through the roof. How could you have two great kids (my cousins) with a man you don't love!? Well of course I made the mistake of telling my non-trustworthy mother and look where it got me, in the corner of the restaurant being lectured by a witch who I am embarrassed to say is my aunt.[4]

Nevertheless, your aunt's claim that her mother is camouflaging the manifold losses she has endured rings true.

Bifocal Violence in a Racialized, Gendered World

According to your aunt, who sees herself as being the direct opposite of her mother, prior to the transformations fueled by the civil rights movement, Grandma Harriett was a social studies teacher in one of the predominantly Black high schools in her community. After integration, the most desirable jobs were given to White teachers; she was demoted to teaching at the junior high level. Finally, frustrated and weary beyond her years, she retired the very first day she became eligible.

During the early part of her career, Grandma Harriet's enthusiasm and passion for social justice had fueled her teaching practices. As a social studies teacher, she taught students the meaning of race, juxtaposing its putative biological nature with its social construction, creating a smorgasbord of mixed race and caste identifications, misunderstandings, displacements, and longings. According to Aunt Wilameena, one of her mother's favorite topics of discussion in the history classes was a theory she had learned in college: the nation's insatiable quest for cheap labor, both past and present, fueled racial exploitation. This analysis supported her claim that the rapid growth of the prison system today is not caused by a rise in crime but, rather, by a need to warehouse huge segments of the

Black male population in order to make it impossible for them to compete with White males for the society's most valued, stable, unionized jobs, jobs that enable men to marry and provide for their families. She sympathized with the Black Panther Party during the heyday of the civil rights movement, admiring from afar women like Elaine Brown, Eldridge Cleaver's wife Kathleen Neal Cleaver, and the progressive philosopher Angela Davis, who were active in militant organizations.

Aunt Wilameena insists that like so many descendants of enslaved women before her, Grandma Harriett believes she is destined to live a life flooded with violence and loss, and the only way to demonstrate her power is to endure. The humming she does that annoys you so much permits her to live in the ruins of what she calls "bone memory," existing as both a corpse and a living, breathing person, masking the excruciating pain of being both here and not here at the same time. A massive chill runs down your spine as you hear your father endorse this explanation.

Aunt Wilameena goes on to recount how Grandma Harriett taught her children, including her and your father, the history of Black people in America, consistently highlighting two features: the nation's demand for unpaid or low-paid labor and the continuation of the unique, mixed caste–race status of people of African ancestry. Aunt Wilameena tells you how she hated those lectures, which she endured while sitting on the floor between her mother's knees having her hair braided. What her mother said was not what she was taught in school and not what she wanted to believe. Nonetheless, Grandma Harriett would press on, telling her daughter how important it was for Black children to have an accurate knowledge of their history and the social conditions of their ancestors, who were the only people on American soil to be officially enslaved—or put another way, prisoners before there were prisons.

She would tell her brothers to disregard the claims of rising criminality in the Black community, insisting, instead, that the prison system was the most recent stage of the "peculiar institution." Slavery, she argued, was "peculiar" because it extracted labor from a population that was deemed ineligible for citizenship. When slavery was officially abolished in 1865, its absence opened up a big hole in the race–caste system. To quell the potential hemorrhaging this void produced, the northern practice of segregating free Negroes was transplanted to the South, where it was embodied in the Black Codes, and transformed into the Jim Crow laws.[5] This system was effective for almost a century, she continued. Massive numbers of Black people migrated from the rural South to the urban North, where they were confined to ghettos, under- and unemployed, and disempowered, until the situation exploded in the streets of America's largest cities during the 1960s.

By this time, Aunt Wilameena says, she was dying to escape because she did not think her mother knew what she was talking about. She knows that her mother was valedictorian of both her high school and her college classes. She also knows that her mother was repeatedly accused of "acting White," of being "uppity," and of "not knowing her place" when she was in school. The last straw was her mother's assertion that the prison system is the contemporary form of involuntary servitude. Like all the previous "peculiar institutions"—slavery, Jim Crow, and ghettoization—the prison system is the latest way in which Black male, and to a lesser extent Black female, labor and competition are contained in postmodern America. The chain gang, in which Black men convicted of no more than vagrancy, that is, unemployment, were forced to build the various states' infrastructures and to labor in the iron furnaces and steel mills, has gone the way of the rest of industrial labor, Grandma Harriett suggests.[6] Aunt Wilameena regards this as her mother's most outrageous assertion: that the idleness of contemporary prisoners is the quintessential postmodern example of the self-perpetuating cycle connecting cheap labor with social marginality. You and Aunt Wilameena groan—at the same time—at this outrageous claim.

Although you and your Aunt Wilameena were born a generation apart, neither of you has ever had a Black teacher. At predominantly White schools with all White teachers, Black students, like you and Aunt Wilameena and her brothers, are taught the same lessons as their non-Black peers: crime is a problem of the inner city, and Black males are accurately characterized as "deviant, devious, and dangerous."

Grandma Harriett's homeschooling opposes this narrative. She has always made two powerful claims that Aunt Wilameena rejects out of hand and that your father's younger brothers disregard, though your father is not so certain. First, Grandma Harriett says that in addition to ending racial slavery in 1865, the Thirteenth Amendment allows the continuation of slavery for those convicted of a crime. What? How crazy is that? You have taken history classes in elementary, junior, and senior high school, and none of your teachers, a couple of whom graduated from Ivy League colleges, have ever made such a preposterous statement. It never occurred to you to examine the discrepancy between what your "crazy" Black grandmother asserts and what your White teachers say, until the anthropology person suggested that reading the Thirteenth Amendment[7] might verify the accuracy of your grandmother's position.

The second claim your grandmother made, much to the chagrin of Aunt Wilameena and her younger brothers—though not your father (at least not now)—is that the rising imprisonment of Black males is intended to shore up the leaking race–caste firewall that was fractured by the social upheaval of the civil rights movement. Breaking down the walls of the ghettos, she repeatedly told her children, was not sustainable; imprisoning large numbers of their inhabitants was the government's solution. Among today's Black males, especially those in the lower class, going to prison is so common that it hardly carries a stigma. Indeed, some appear to view it as a rite of passage—until they get there and find that, according to a chapter you read in the book *Fish: A Memoir of a Boy in a Man's Prison*, which was assigned in the anthropologist's seminar on race and gender, gender roles are involuntarily assigned based on each individual's physical strength and ability to dominate others.[8] You discover, to your horror, that even within all-male prisons, replication of the gender roles that operate in the larger society is rampant.

You have heard snippets of these debates between Grandma

Harriett, your dad, and Aunt Wilameena many times. But you have scrupulously sought to avoid their discussions regarding whether or not her sons (their brothers) were unjustly convicted and subsequently imprisoned for smoking—not even selling—crack cocaine. One is serving a prison term for burglary, probably related to his desire to buy drugs, you surmise. Although you try not to identify with the problems of people regarded as Black, even when they are your relatives, you are unable to avoid hearing their conversations. Grandma Harriett has repeatedly bemoaned the injustices that culminated in the imprisonment of her beloved sons. You don't know the specifics of your uncles' situations because, to be honest, you have tried not to notice how much it hurts your grandmother and your father.[9] But you don't get what they are arguing about. As you see it, the issues are crystal clear: individuals have a responsibility not to put themselves in situations that might cause the police and other law enforcement people to think of them as suspects. It never occurs to you to think that your uncles may have been the victims of a racialized system that has too many laborers and not enough jobs. You conclude that your Black uncles are solely responsible for the predicament in which they currently find themselves. You blame them for putting themselves in situations where they were thought of as participating in illegal activities. What other possible explanation could there be?

When you were younger, you were more adamant about this opinion. Now that you are dating and going out with friends, most of them White, you find that you are often in situations where drugs and alcohol are not only smoked and imbibed but sold, bartered, and otherwise exchanged. You don't condone these illegal enterprises, but you are there, and on rare occasions you have reluctantly taken a puff or two, just to fit in. This part of your social life sucks. You are by no means a saint, but drugs—beyond alcohol—are just not your thing. Since most of the guys who want to date you are those you meet online, you have no way of knowing anything about them except what they choose to tell you. You have no opportunity to observe them from afar. This is a powerful drag on your social life because most of the peers you socialize with view indulging in pot, crack, cocaine, and other drugs as ordinary—like breathing.

When you told the anthropologist about your uncles' incarcerations and your grandmother's theory (what little you know about it), she suggested that your grandmother's viewpoint, like her practice of humming whenever she is not interacting with others, might be interpreted as a "Black female way of being." That got your attention in a major way. Since you do not desire to be socially identified as Black and you work so hard not to perform Blackness, you made a mental note to yourself never to hum to yourself or espouse crazy/radical theories because you want to avoid anything that might remotely link you to the revolting idea that you are Black— even only partially.

Eschewing All Things Black

Grandma Harriett lives in the city, and you don't like going there because you are afraid of all the Black people who live in the city, though not in her immediate neighborhood. Even though your grandmother's neighborhood is clearly identified as middle-class (the relatives call it a "Cadillac" neighborhood, meaning it is expensive and very, very nice), your fear of an imagined Black horde means you don't get to see her as often as you did when you were younger and your father took you with him to see her. Your father tells you that his father's (your grandfather's) frugality and life-insurance policy, combined with the GI Bill, enabled him to purchase this house in this upscale neighborhood. To this day, only one other Black family lives on the block. While nothing bad has ever happened to you personally or to anyone you know when you have been at her house or playing with your cousins in the neighborhood, you are fearful, and despite the fact that you now have a car and could easily drive there to see her, you don't. The exception to this rule is if your Black cousins, Aunt Wilameena's daughters, Keria and Temeka, go with you. You certainly would not go there with only your little brother, who might be mistaken for a White boy. When you talk on the phone with your dad about your fears, he says you're crazy to worry; no one, he insists, will do anything to hurt you—especially in your grandmother's neighborhood. You sense his annoyance every time you talk with him about this issue, but you constantly defend your unwillingness to visit your grandmother by telling him how scared you are to go into the city.

Grandma Harriett claims that her mother named her after a character named Harriett whose life is chronicled in Pauli Murray's book *Proud Shoes* because she saw a striking resemblance. You find that hard to believe because the anthropologist assigned the third chapter of that book in one of her seminars at the college, and you read it. The Harriett depicted is described as a beautiful woman with long, curly, jet-black hair. She has high cheekbones and very light skin because, the author claims, Harriett's father was a slave owner (a White man) who had raped her mother. Indeed, she is so beautiful that the slave owner's two sons are unable to restrain their sexual desires for her, their unknown half-sister. According to the author, their unadulterated lust toward the character named Harriett is despicable. The brothers fight each other nearly to the death to get the chance to rape and impregnate this woman, first one and then the other, each compelling her to bear his child. The enslaved community in which Harriett lives is horrified by her nightly screams and cries for help, but they are unable to protect her from the White male brothers whose father owns her and them.[10]

When you look at Grandma Harriett, you do not see even a smidgen of the Harriett described in the book. Your grandmother could not be described as beautiful; she is middle-aged, matronly, and dark skinned, and she is predisposed to a Black discourse speaking style. You do not mean that she does not speak standard English; she does. What you mean to convey is that she has a Black way of talking.[11] She does not have long hair with big curls, either; her hair, sans a hot iron, is tightly curled. She has dark chocolate-brown skin like your father, and while that looks good on him, it is not a beauty marker on her. Using the scientific knowledge you acquired in your junior high and high school science classes, you conclude

...

(erroneously) that race is a predictable genetic marker and that if your grandmother had any White ancestry, it would be evident in her phenotypic features.[12] Based on this distorted knowledge, you conclude that if some of Grandma Harriett's forebears were White, she would not be as dark in skin color; she would look more like you, or a tad browner. None of your White male science teachers (and they were all White and male) was comfortable talking about the "one drop" rule: the idea that just as one drop of black ink colors an entire glass of water, so one drop of Black blood pollutes an otherwise White individual, making him or her Black.[13] You dismiss Grandma Harriett's claim that she is, like you, concurrently Black and White. And, more critical to your life story, you conclude that race is accurately a genetically based social category.

The idea that race is a genetically defined category was called into question when you read a lengthy narrative that appeared in the *Washington Post*. This was at the behest of the anthropologist. (She assigned this material to her students, and you were in her class again that day—you sense that she is getting a little bit uneasy with your frequent visits, though you hope you are wrong; she assures you that she is not.) The journalist (whose name is Lonnae something, Parker O'Neal or O'Neal Parker; you don't remember), a self-identified African American woman, tells the story of her White cousin, Kim, and titles it "White Girl?"[14] The writer relates that she and her biological cousin Kim, whose father is the journalist's Black uncle, are kin but only under the skin, because they are living totally differently: in Black and White. Aided by her light skin and straight hair, Kim opts to live her life as a White girl. Lonnae is surprised and a little outraged. When her cousin, who (like you) has one White parent and one Black parent, comes to live with her, she discovers that Kim has refused to do what is commonly expected: embrace the one-drop rule and perform Blackness. Lonnae has to admit to herself that she chooses Black in part because some White girls called her the n-word when she was younger. In the anthropologist's seminar, she put the following segment from the journalist's essay on a machine that allowed her to merely open a book (or anything) and put it on display for her students. (You loved the novelty of this technology; none of your teachers at UGRH had ever done that with class material.)

"I had always been shy," explained Lonnae.

> A good student with long hair. Teachers loved me. And always, a few black girls hated me. "White dog," they called me—no, wait, that's what they called my sister. I was a "half-white bitch." . . . Back then, I had "A Foot in Each World" but couldn't get my head into either.

Slowly, ultimately, she chose to be Black and be proud:

> Sometimes I still hear that white girl ask me if I am black. And now I have an answer.
>   Pitch.
>   Cold.
>   Blacker than three midnights.
>   As black as the ace of spades.
>   I'm so black that when I get into my car, the oil light comes on. . . .
>   Cousin Kim still chooses white not only because she looks white, she says, but "because I was raised white" and because most white folks don't know the difference.

That essay made Parker and her Cousin Kim nationally known figures in the ensuing racial debate.[15]

The two things that struck you most about the assignment were that the college students, most of whom looked White to you, failed to show any sense of humor (you thought the writer was poking fun at such pretenses), and that they were reluctant to talk about the issues discussed in the article, especially a central issue in your own life: hair. Hair has locked you out of a White identity, to which you see yourself as entitled and which you desperately desire.

You hate, absolutely hate, the stigma directed at your Black hair.

You can't pull off passing as a White girl when you have hair that is affiliated in the public imagination with Black girls. When you were in elementary school, you would cry when the kids teased you about your hair. If your father was home, he would console you and tell you that "sticks and stones might hurt my bones but words don't bother me." He would reassure you that you were his little princess and the prettiest girl he knows. If he was not home, after making sure your little brother got off the school bus and feeding him dinner, you would go to your room and cry, using your pillow to stifle your enraged screams. Sometimes you would use your rosary to pray for God's mercy, asking Him to change your hair so you could claim, unambiguously, the White identity you think is your birthright.

This ambivalence regarding your hair was reinforced by the *Washington Post* journalist's claim that "a [White] neighbor who is married to a black man casually tells me that she hopes against hope that their child doesn't come out with nappy hair."[16] You are adamant that your hair is *the* problem, and you don't give a tinker's damn that the anthropologist keeps giving you copies of that stupid hair poem she has written called "My Love Affair with My Arrogant Hair."[17] She may be in love with her Black hair, but you—and most of the rest of the world—do not share this amorous feeling.

The *Washington Post* journalist's narrative resonated because it reminded you of your cousins Keria and Temeka, Aunt Wilameena's daughters. Like the journalist and her cousin Kim, you and one of your cousins, Keria, are darker in skin color than your other cousin, Temeka, even though each of you has one biological parent who is socially defined as White—your mother and their dad. Temeka is more like your little brother in skin color, but not in hair texture; she also has hazel eyes. Like yours and Keria's, her hair is tightly curled. Fortunately for your cousins, their father, Uncle Bradley, makes lots of money, and they live in an upscale community in the city. They have their hair done weekly and permed as often as needed to keep it straight.

The day the journalist's article is discussed in the anthropologist's seminar, you go home more confused than ever about race and how you should see yourself. For the first time in a very long time, you think about the phenotypic differences between you and your little brother. Even though you have the same mother and father, you are a lot darker than he is, and your hair is not like his at all. Once you complete your chores and make sure he has done his homework (he is painfully shy and does not like school), you go to your room and lie down on your bed and visualize all your immediate family members, but especially your Black relatives.

Raced Out of Gender or Gendered Out of Race?

You console yourself by acknowledging that even though Grandma Harriett does not look like you wish she looked, she is a great cook, and you love all the delicious foods she prepares and identifies as your father's favorite dishes. You force yourself to disavow your denial and acknowledge that your ambivalence about visiting Grandma Harriett is not only about the fear of what might happen to you if a Black person attacks you. You are also ambivalent because your mother rarely comes with you when your father takes you and your little brother to Grandma Harriet's house. This makes you feel as if you are being disloyal to your mother. When you were younger, your mother was more likely to be a part of this family outing. Now she often declines the invitation to come with you and is left at home all alone. You worry because you fear, with good reason, that in your absence she will drink nonstop to cope with the stigmatized, racialized life she is now compelled to live.

When your mother was a young woman and so in love with your father, she tells you, she had no idea that her life would turn out this way. Initially she thought he was going to be a star running back in the NFL; he was judged the best athlete at that position in the city and the surrounding metropolitan area his senior year. Scouts from the major universities, including Notre Dame, the University of Michigan, and Ohio State, came to see him play. He was truly a rising star. Relatives on your mom's side of the family have told you that they tried hard to get her *not* to marry a Black man, but she re-fused to listen.

You think (correction: you know) that your mother now regrets that decision. While the racialized straitjacket she encountered early on in her marriage has lessened enormously in the past decade, it has not totally disappeared. There are still people who look at her strangely when she tells them that you and your little brother are her biological children. Add to this awkwardness her decision not to work or to seek more education after high school, and you might get some idea of the level of her anger and frustration, all of which she is compelled to mask in order to be thought of as a nice lady. Only recently have you been able to utter the word that aptly describes your mother's primary problem: alcohol. ("My mother is an alcoholic; there, I said it.") Because she is an alcoholic, she cannot possibly do what your father expects her to do: nurture you and your little brother while he is away at work.

As you see it, your parents' unfulfilled, deeply flawed relationship has had the most devastating effect on your own and your brother's young lives. He is more affected by your parents' dysfunctional re-lationship because he was born just as it was beginning to unravel. Your father was not a constant presence in his life, and your mother was drunk and depressed most of the time. At the same time, your brother's skin color and hair have muted his affiliation with his African ancestry, enabling him to be accepted by his peers as if he were White, even though he identifies himself, unequivocally, as a Black male. Because of the saliency of features affiliated with people of African descent, your parents' dysfunctional relationship has pro-foundly altered your life and what you think the future holds for you.

Within the household, your father's long absences while he was in the military fueled your mother's loneliness and isolation. Her incessant drinking began at home—alone—and then morphed into barhopping and lots of time away from home. During the brief periods when your father would return home, there would be lots of conflict (is this what they call domestic violence, you wonder?), including yelling, screaming, and sometimes physical fighting. His relatives strongly objected to your mother's behavior as a married woman, and they told your father, even before he could get home on leave, that she was running around drinking and spending time with other men. She denied this, insisting instead that she was going out with girlfriends, and when men were present, they were either with her girlfriends (not her) or just friends, not lovers. Your father did not want her to go out at all; he kept insisting that he had married a woman who was committed to the primacy of marriage and child rearing. He demanded that she discontinue this behavior. His traditional approach to marriage and family, which your mother had found so reassuring when they began dating, was suddenly obsolete and unacceptable. She experienced this view of the world as a kind of pink jail cell that, despite its soft, gentle facade, was both reeking with violence and an inescapable prison.[18] Nana kept admonishing her to pray to the Virgin Mary (this side of your family is all Catholic; the Black side is all Baptist) and to go to confession so that her sins would be forgiven and her marriage saved.

Your father is unwilling to negotiate or compromise. He refuses to go to marriage counseling, which he condemns as "stupid girl stuff." He accuses her of being White trash, a slut, and a bitch. She retorts by calling him a nigger and a male chauvinist pig. All this goes on in your presence. As a very young girl, you heard these racial and sexual insults and sided with your father because you loved him more. He was always so handsome in his military uniform and so happy to call you his beautiful little princess. Even when your mother was not in a drunken stupor, she was not a good role model. Worse still, she appeared to favor your little brother, who looked more like her and did not raise as many eyebrows when she took him out with her and identified him as her son.

While your skin color is close to that of Vanessa Williams, the only dethroned Miss America, your facial features and hair texture unmistakably betray your African ancestry. But your language usage and your deliberate avoidance of Black females subvert that image. You used to make an exception for your Black family members, but, to be truthful, the older you get, the more you try to avoid them as well. You detest those self-identified Black girls because they make you feel as if you have to choose to be Black instead of the mixed-race person you know you are. After all, how many people choose to belong to a group that is the most stigmatized in any social context? Those people have got to be crazy, you conclude.

Your African ancestry is most clearly manifested in the tug-of-war between you and your mother over your hair and your sexuality. These issues drove a wedge between you and her. She kept trying to make your hair her hair, to groom it like her own, and when she failed, she criticized it—and you. When you were a little girl and wanted to go swimming like all the other little girls in the neighborhood (all of them White), she was frustrated when you came home and she had to spend a lot more time making your hair presentable to a critical public. Fortunately, your Black Aunt Wilameena and her daughters, your cousins, saved you from disaster by agreeing to take care of your hair and to teach you how a Black girl grooms her hair. Keria and Temeka meet the brown-paper-bag test, but they have hair like yours, blessed with arrogance. Because of Aunt Wilameena's cultural knowledge, she is able to help you.

These cousins were far less successful in resolving the gender-specific issues between you and your mother. She wants you to give up your own power and embrace the "frailty myth," the notion that women are supposed to be weak and should learn how to be, or at least seem, helpless.[19] The idea that you should remain infantilized for as long as possible elevates your stress every time you leave the house. This approach to femininity violates the gender norms practiced in the Black community. You abhor the idea of being perceived as weak, but you are not allowed to display strength, which leads to the depression that envelops your life. You are depressed because you cannot embrace the identity of the women she labels self-sufficient, your paternal aunt and grandmother, and you loathe your maternal female family members, who, as you see it, are so lathered in realms of need and powerlessness that they are too afraid to challenge anything or anybody.[20] Your mother's decision to remain in an undesirable marriage is a case in point. She is miserable and everyone in the family knows it, but she knows they would say "I told you so" if she opted to leave, and she would hate herself even more because she chose to marry exogamously, outside her privileged racial group. In many ways, she feels crucified, unable to evolve as most humans need to do throughout the life course.

Most of your White relatives, ironically including your uncle who later married your Aunt Wilameena, did not approve of your parents' marriage in the first place. They thought your mother should have married the White guy that she had been dating since junior high. His father was a local politician and had national aspirations. This guy wanted to be a doctor, a neurosurgeon, mind you. He was considered a nerd by all his peers, friends, and family. To your White relatives, though, he was a great catch. But no, your mother wanted a guy who was exciting and what every other girl wanted. Your mother imagined her life as an NFL player's wife: a huge house (dare we say mansion?), lovely kids, a nanny and housekeeper to help her in raising them, trips to every NFL game in which your father played, and baubles galore.

Although she was unable to acknowledge it, your mother craved adoration, wanted someone who appreciated seeing her perform at sports events as a cheerleader. Looking back, your mother doubts that your father ever saw her at these athletic events, but she consoles herself with the knowledge that on game days—almost every Friday during football season and even more often during the basketball season, all the cheerleaders wore their short purple-and-gold cheerleading outfits to school, and everybody noticed them.

Your mother also told you that her nerdy boyfriend had no interest in sports and barely knew what a cheerleader was. He was extremely uncomfortable in social situations but was clearly in love with her. Everybody noticed what a calming effect your mother had on him; she thought that was really strange because one of her major criticisms of him was that he was so predictable. As your mother told you the story, she did not want to spend the rest of her life pretending she was interested in the minutiae of neurology; nor did she want to live within the restraints imposed on the lives of families in which one family member (in this case her presumed father-in-law) is a well-known politician. The main problem was that nobody else wanted this guy. He was devoted solely to your mother—and his books.

Your Black relatives did not welcome your parents' marriage either; they thought your father should have married a Black girl, not a White girl. Now that you are older, you sense that, unlike the White side's objection—that your father was from a subordinate race—the Black side's objection was based on their fear of what might happen when your parents were seen together, not on some racial or human inadequacy on the part of your mother or the social group with whom she was identified. The Black side of the family lives with its memories of such nationally known killings as Emmett Till's and the thousands of lynchings connected to Black males who were suspected of consorting with White females. They wanted no part of that in their lives.

Among their reasons was the fear that your mother would not be loyal to your father. If she was accused of being involved in an extramarital affair with a White guy, the resulting conflict could have major implications for not just the immediate family but also the entire community in which your father's family is located. Unlike many Black men at that time, your father had a stable job with a predictable paycheck. In order to demonstrate that he was "da man," he bought a house in this suburban community and insisted that his wife become a housewife. That led to her becoming fatally invisible, like roadkill.

Depression and Skin Displacement

Have you unconsciously imbibed your mother's evolving preju-dices? Her uncertainties and anxieties? Like her, you are often de-pressed, so depressed that you frequently sleep for days on end. (Is depression an emotion or a disease? That is the question.) You blame your anxieties on those damn Black girls who are always try-ing to make you feel as if you should be a Black girl rather than the

White girl you seek to be. You sense this with your Black cousins, Keria and Temeka, as well. They are adamant in their assertions that they are Black. Why don't they have a problem with the idea of being Black? Is it because their mother, Aunt Wilameena, is Black?

You keep forgetting to ask the anthropologist if she knows of any studies that look at the identity issues of mixed-race kids,[21] especially females, whose mothers are White, compared to those whose mothers are Black.[22] You know several other mixed-race girls at school—two others are in the same study—and most of them don't seem to have a problem with being identified as Black. Your cousins, too, have skin as light as yours, yet they keep saying they are Black. You don't get it. Temeka even belongs to UGRH's stupid step team.

Then there is your little brother, a ninth-grader this year. He is comfortable with the designation Black and keeps trying to find ways to be identified as a Black male, including getting his hair braided and trying to make it into dreadlocks. He hates his hair, but his problem is the opposite of yours. He keeps complaining that his hair is not like other Black people's hair, and he spends so much time trying to make it look and feel like yours—which you despise. When you told him about Gregory Williams's book *Life on the Color Line*,[23] which was discussed in the anthropologist's seminar, he insisted that you take him to the library to get a copy that very day. He is a voracious reader and completed it in two nights, skipping some of his assigned homework. He might have finished the entire book in one night had Nana not taken it from him in order to get him to do at least some of his homework and get some sleep. As soon as he got off the bus the next day, he ran down the street to her house to retrieve it.

After he read it, he told you that he totally identified with Greg, the author, and his younger brother, Mike, who are told by their father, on a Greyhound bus en route to Indiana to visit their father's family, that they are not White but Black kids and that they are going to live with their father's mother, a Black woman whom they had met as a waitress in his now-defunct restaurant. They had been misled into believing they were White until their dad, who was Black, lost both his business and his wife, their White mother, in Virginia. They are forced to return to their father's home in Muncie, Indiana, to live with his Black mother in the heart of the ghetto and become Black, to perform an alien and undesired identity.

All this craziness is too much for you to bear. Earlier this year, after several conversations with your counselor at school, you acknowledged that you desperately needed help and decided to be admitted voluntarily to a hospital. You spent three weeks in the adolescent psychiatric ward at St. Rodman, trying to cope with the stresses you associate with your racialized existence and with the sense of not belonging anywhere. The hospital stay did reduce your stress, but you still have days when you feel as if you can't cope. You struggle to make do with the once-a-week therapy sessions that your counselor has arranged for you. Some weeks the stress is so great, you skip your Wednesday classes and can barely wait until therapy on Thursday. You told your counselor about the anxiety attacks and hoped that she would be able to get your schedule changed from one day to two days a week. No such luck. She claims that by law the school system can only offer you one therapy session a week.

While gender, race, and class are the three most powerful factors in your life, at this particular stage, gender—as merged to race—is the most troubling issue. The anthropologist explained that these three powerful social categories are interlocked, meaning that they do not operate as individual isolates but tend to be entangled in a virtual morass of class, race, and gender issues. White Americans tend to use their internal group filter—that is, class—as a master status to explain the behaviors and practices of individuals who are seen as other, or at least as outsiders, within the White population.[24] Imposing this kind of analysis on the behaviors and practices of populations that are stigmatized or marginalized is inappropriate because their master status is not privilege but stigma. Consequently, seeking to offer simple or one-dimensional social phenomena to explain the actions and practices of individuals who are locked in a stigmatized identity and for whom class is not the central issue not only inappropriately devalues the impact of the stigma but, in addition, diminishes such individuals' ability to adapt to their social reality. This is true for women—regardless of race—and for African Americans, Native Americans, Hispanics, and members of other stigmatized or stigmatizing categories.

As you see it, you are trying to separate from a family system to which you, admittedly largely by your own choice, have not been superglued. The racial tensions are at the core of your discomfort. You have come to realize that in addition to not wanting to be identified as a Black female, you want desperately to share your mother's and maternal grandmother's identity: you want to be known as a White girl. You shop, visit, and interact constantly with your White BFF, and you observe how seamlessly she travels through the world. You want to live like that: to be the beneficiary of doubt. When you are with your White friends, this doubt rebounds against you. At school, you have noticed that your teachers and other school officials appear to reward you for your distance from other Black students.

You remember a segment from one of the books the anthropologist assigned in the class you visited (you don't remember the title, except that it included the words "White" and "trash"). One of the book's White authors writes that moving from her mother's lower-class home after her parents' divorce into the wealthier and socially more elite home of her father totally altered her life. After she moved in with her father, put on her "good girl smile," and changed the way she dressed, she was able to pass as an elite White girl and to move almost unimpeded through most social spaces.[25] The writer notes her own disbelief at how deferential everyone was to her, an erstwhile lower-class White girl, in her new environment: for example, if a salesclerk asked her whether she had taken something and she said she had not, not only was she not further interrogated, but her questioner sincerely apologized, indicating that she was believed unequivocally.

You realize that these same kinds of things happen when you are with your White BFF. Just last Saturday night, for, instance, you were a passenger in her car on the way to the mall. The cops stopped her because she was speeding, but they did not end up giving her a ticket. Now, you know your BFF is not a pretty White girl: she has mousy brown hair, is short, and is painfully shy in public. But no one stops her in stores or other public places to search her purse, although *you* may be subjected to this kind of dehumanization and asked for your ID. While she is able to talk her way out of a ticket, you never can. When the cops stopped you for speeding last month, there was no dithering about whether a warning or a ticket was appropriate—you got the ticket.

You remember being asked to join the step team when you were a sophomore, your first year at UGRH. ReRe, the Black girl who is now the team's captain, asked you more than once. Each time you were horrified! Was she blind? What made her think that you would be caught dead engaging in such a spectacle and, more critically, that just because your skin color is not associated with Whiteness, you self-identify as a Black girl? More than any other activity that Black females engage in at UGRH, participation in the step team compels a girl to perform what is seen as Blackness, which you want no part of. Unlike you, the step captain is from one of the newcomer families, and apparently she did not know that you hate the idea of being associated with anything considered Black. In her efforts to convince you to join the group, she told you that one White girl, Brittany, had already agreed to become a member. You wanted to scream at her, *Look at me, I am a White girl, too, and, if I join, there will be two White girls on the team.* But you did not. You smiled politely and made up some flimsy excuse about having to take care of your little brother on Tuesday and Thursday afternoons for the remainder of the semester. What a dingbat. This silly Black girl looked at you and assumed, based on your skin color, that you were Black.

I went to school today which was a ton of fun because we had a Substitute. Everyone was being loud and crazy and the Substitute loved it. Two of the girls that sit next to me (both White) had fun talking to me. They kind of tease me because a boy in the class has a crush on me but I don't mind that they tease me, we are friends. There is a very annoying (Black) girl that sits on the other side of

me. She never shuts up and always thinks she is right. We were
reading a poem and the Substitute asked a question and the girl
got it wrong. For once. Well everyone started laughing at her and
eventually she told them to shut up.[26]

This is what annoys you most: nobody will allow you to be who
you want to be. You love science, and even though you don't have
the best grades in the world in biology, you are convinced that you
know enough about genetics to know that your genetic makeup
disqualifies you for the category Black. Everybody keeps telling you
that you are Black and female. You don't have a problem with the
female part; it is the practice of defining you as Black that you don't
like. You know you are not Black. After all, one of your parents is
White. You are not completely crazy. You realize that your father
is Black, and that inevitably means that you are at least partially
Black. Since you are only partially Black, you are frustrated because
you are not able to choose between the two identities but are
compelled to be Black. While your skin color is not light enough
for you to be identified as White, at least not to the average person
(Aunt Wilameena keeps telling you that you look like a young Lena
Horne—who the hell is that?), you think it is your Black hair that
undermines your efforts to be seen as White. You have thought
about buying a wig or a weave, but that is not socially approved by
either your parents or your school peers.

You don't want anyone else to define who you are and then
compel you to accept their definition. Because no one will allow you
to choose your identity, you take out your revenge on other Blacks,
especially Black females. (Remember the play at Feeder High School
called *Sweeney Todd* where the protagonist, the barber, displays his
anger and misplaced aggression by killing indiscriminately, making
everyone suffer for the pain he experienced when his wife was
unfaithful with that crazy, lecherous judge?)

At school, you engage only in activities that do not mark you as a
Black girl. You tried to become a member of the cheerleading squad
but were unsuccessful because, as one of the coaches told you, you

do not have bouncy hair. Bouncy hair? What the hell does that mean? You certainly do not wear your hair in any form other than straight or, as they say in the biz, relaxed. You would not be caught dead with your hair in any other style. Being denied a spot on the cheerleading squad because of your hair was a horrible disappointment. You cried all the way home. When you tried to tell your mother about it, she was drunk and depressed—again. No response. So you went down the street to Nana's house and told her. Unfortunately, she seemed to agree with the coach. You are convinced that you are right to see double when it comes to your family.

While you have dated and will date Black males in the future, you work hard not to become friends with African American females, primarily because you don't want their image to rub off on you. You never, ever sit at the Black Table; you refuse invitations to join the step team, and thankfully the Black girls no longer ask you to do so; you don't play basketball or sing in the glee club or the gospel choir. Instead, you are a member of the swim team (and you make all the practices, even though it means that you are constantly struggling with your hair even when you wear a swim cap), sit with your White-only gal pals on the other side of the cafeteria, and become anxious when Blacks are in your classes.

Only one of the teachers at the school is Black, so you do not have to be concerned about how they perceive you. Since most of the teachers know your mother is White and you have no friendships with Black girls, they often will give you the benefit of the doubt, which they do not often do for Black girls in their classes. You have noticed this pattern repeatedly. Your impressions were validated when the anthropologist told you that she was amazed at how often your teachers' evaluations of you included the statement that you are a very nice girl. Working to create and maintain this image is stressful, but you have chosen this way of demonstrating that you are not Black.

You remember the day the anthropology professor invited you to be a member of her study; you were overjoyed, honored even. But you remember even more keenly the fact that once, after a long, revealing interview in which you shared with her so many of your frustrations, especially those regarding your complex racial identity and family life, she invited you to visit her undergraduate seminar about race and gender at the university. You sat in several times. Looking back, you realize that she wanted you to get a perspective that you did not have at the time and would never get in any of your high school classes.

Being in a college classroom was a daunting yet exhilarating experience. During your first visit, the students appeared to be so sophisticated and knowledgeable as they talked about their home-work and social activities; you wondered if you would ever be in this setting as a matriculating student. The class of about twenty was made up mostly of females, with only about five males. Various racial and ethnic groups were represented. As you remember it, one of the activities included posting students' journal entries—anonymously—on some kind of machine that permitted everyone to read along.

You recall the jolt you experienced as several students shared their extremely personal stories about race and gender. The two that stand out in your mind were Latino/a students' entries detailing their response to taking Spanish as a language class in high school. Both students shared their versions of how, as native Spanish speak-ers, having to suppress their native pronunciations and opt instead to mispronounce the words as their teacher and their peers did caused them great pain. When they looked back on the experience, both concluded that they were participating in the degradation of their native language. They attributed this problem to the fact that their Spanish teachers were nonnative speakers and did not or could not replicate the sounds. They both indicated that they had felt compelled to violate their native knowledge in order to fit in with their peers and to obtain the approval of their teachers.

These stories had an impact on your thinking about racial identity. Finally, however, you concluded that your situation is substantively different from the issues discussed in the anthropologist's seminar. This is your story and you are sticking to it, despite the evidence she offered in class regarding the centrality of language in people's folk understanding of culture.[27] Ultimately, you tell the anthropologist, your greatest desire is to have your life be uncomplicated by race and all these crazy issues. You absolutely hate the idea of having to see the world in Black and White, especially within your own family. You realize that your parents did not marry across the color line in order to make your life a living hell; they just fell in love and got married. The reality is that you were not included in their decision making. If they thought about children at all, it may have been as part of their desire to create a world that was less marked by race for the next generation. In choosing to marry each other, they intended to blur racial boundaries, to participate in the construction of a color-blind society. But if your experience is generalizable to the children of other interracial couples, this strategy is not working. In Black and White America, your parents' children are Black. Is this the case for other children whose parents married or had children across racial lines, you wonder? While there may be cases where the children of marriages like that of your parents are free to be who they want to be, you suspect that your and your brother's situation is the norm. You wince with the discomfort you feel when you have to think about the implications of your conclusion.

All this stuff about race and your inability to cope with it is what led you to spend three weeks in a wing of the local hospital known as "the partial," which offers day treatment for people who are having mental health problems, including depression. You strategically decided to spend the required three weeks just before spring break, committed to the cause of trying to heal yourself. You didn't return to school until after spring break, which means that you didn't see your friends for four weeks.

An Anthropological Postscript

The critical problem for Chloe is that both in her "abnormal"—zebra-striped—family and at UGRH, she feels displaced in her own skin, unable to be identified as she desires (White) and, instead, compelled to be what she desperately does not want to be: Black. As her narrative documents, Chloe embodies what it means to have a displaced identity, with its concomitant loss of connectedness and mental well-being. Interestingly, she is inadvertently complicit in this massive self-displacement, primarily because she wants to be normal (which for her means White)—which she cannot be—and indistinguishable from the socially identified hegemonic part of her family and, by extension, of UGRH and the nation.[28] Her gendered self desires to be socially identified with the females in her maternal family; her overwhelming love for her father complicates her disdain for all things Black. Indeed, it is her desire for normality—which she misrecognizes as the embodiment of banality—that repeatedly fuels the injurious impact of her depressed condition, compelling her to acknowledge her bifurcated reality. Struggling not only to navigate but to transform this unsustainable social reality, she descends into an even deeper abyss when she approaches school officials seeking support in handling the cultural and social problems in her personal life. Those problems, instead, are fueled by the hidden reproductive tendencies of America's system of public schooling and its endemic structural violence.

Ironically, Chloe embraces—unconditionally—the rigid racial categories that dominate and structure American social life with one exception: she wants to be identified as White, and if that is not possible, she will accept biracial. She learned these racial categories prior to coming to school, and they were then buttressed— uncritically—in this academic environment; her view of these racial categories is self-reinforcing, with profoundly negative consequences for her mental well-being. Her consignment to the margins of social life in her family and at school forces her to seek therapy as a way out of the emotional cul-de-sac in which she finds herself.

One of the other biracial girls, Sophia, is typically defined as White—not because of her skin color—by her Black peers, but, unlike Chloe, she wants to be embraced rather than marginalized by her Black peers. After trying to gain their acceptance, she ultimately concludes that the Black students reject her, and she sees herself as being very, very different from what one anthropologist identifies as "regular Blacks."[29] Like Chloe, Sophia is also primarily defined by the texture of her hair:

I have always been on the Dean's List . . . even after the Black kids gave up on me. . . . Well, I remember I used to watch these TV shows, like they have on now, like, all mixed people, and they talk about how people will ask you, "So what are you? Are you Black or are you White?" And I remember I sat there, I was like, nobody asked *me* what I was. They decided for themselves. Like, "Oh, look at her." Like, I kind of do that myself, like, 'cause there *are* lots of mixed kids like me in this suburban area, so— . . . Like— but most of the mixed kids that *I* still talk to are very white, in their identity. . . . It's almost ridiculous. And I'm afraid that I'm kind of like that, and I don't want to be that stereotypical Black person that wants to be White. And I want to be just happy with myself, and not conform to anyone's idea of what I should be. . . . But I just find it ridiculous when you start—like, my mom told me that there was a psychological study they used to do, with young Black girls and boys. And a lot of—like, when they'd put a Barbie doll in front of them, and they'd always choose the White Barbie doll, because for a very long time Black people wanted to be White. And I just didn't—I don't want to be like that. But when I grew up, it was very difficult—you couldn't—it was hard . . . to choose a group. . . . Because the Black kids pushed me out. I just went to the one group that chose me—well, not really chose me. . . . Unlike the Black kids they didn't deny me admittance. . . . The Black girls didn't accept me. . . . Well, for—well, like, in the sixth grade— . . . It was my hair—well, it's straightened right now. . . . But before, it was very curly and soft. . . . And this girl, she would pick on it. She picked on me ruthlessly, all of sixth grade. . . . I remember the first time she talked to me, we were sitting in an assembly, and she pulled my hair really hard. So they started—her and her girlfriend started screaming in my ear, so I was like, "What's your problem?" They called my hair nappy, said it was, you know, really bad. I was like, "It's not *my* problem." And so for the rest of the year, they just picked on me ruthlessly. . . . And I tend to be very patient with race stuff and those kinds of things, you know, back off, don't wake up sleeping giants. . . . When you anger them, they can be really—mean. And finally she just . . . I heard her start picking on my friend. And that just pushed me over the edge. . . . So finally I confronted her and I asked, "*What* is your problem?" And she . . . said—you know, I can't even remember what she said, but she you know those tables that have those octagons and very sharp edges? . . . She pushed me. I fell into these chairs, and my head barely just— Was very close to the edge. . . . I would have split my skull on the edge of the table. So I basically calculated my odds as I lay there among the chairs. . . . So I high-tailed it out of there. Which I'm really ashamed of now, because I would—it made me look like a coward. . . . So I just ran and told, and, really, nothing happened. The principal—she didn't do anything. Even though I'd been repeatedly reporting, hey, this girl is picking on me, could you do—something?, they didn't do anything. I mean, not a thing. Not a thing. And I was thinking, 'cause they have a no-tolerance policy on violence, you'd think, "Ooh, you almost hit a girl's head on the edge of the table." "Maybe we should do something." No, she—nothing happened. [Similarly,] . . . when I—but, like, in eighth grade, when I had—seventh grade, I had a—bad I was having very bad hearing problems. . . . I was practically deaf, half of the seventh grade. . . . Before I got my surgery . . . I had liquid going up in my ears and my lungs. And it's still there. . . . That's why, when you hear— . . . sounds like I'm breathing really hard, even though I don't even notice it. . . . But, yeah, I was practically deaf. And this boy Sean . . . we were five, we were young, you know. But he took my chair, so I took it and he took it back, and he was sitting on it. . . . He took juice and shot it on me, and then I ran after him, we ran. . . . We were running down the hallway, and Ms. Junior was screaming at me, "Stop! Stop! Stop!" And I'm practically deaf, I couldn't hear her, so I kept going. Because Gene [another five-year-old classmate] just suddenly stopped, I'm like, "What?" And then she was screaming her head off, I'm like, "I didn't even hear you." So when we got in the room and I told her "I'm practically deaf, I did not hear you" . . . She went crazy on me, and put me away for—in the detention center for two weeks. And it's like— . . . It was just ridiculous.[30]

You, Chloe, share with Sophia a lack of acceptance by your desired racial group, and their rejection has profoundly affected your self-perceptions and your important school and familial relationships.

Chloe is not defined by UGRH officials and most of her peers as just a "regular Black." She (and to a lesser extent Sophia) is nonetheless marginalized and consigned to a kind of social purgatory at the school, which denies her what she seeks most: gender-specific normality.[31] This lack of a sense of belonging and her insatiable quest for elite status is a primary factor fueling her depression. It is this burning desire for acceptance by those she thinks are her most important peers that has propelled her to an unhappy place where she blames herself for being "admit[ed] but left out"[32] How and why Ally, a White girl at the school, sees herself in similar ways and, like Chloe, is struggling with a social dis-ease is the focus of the analysis in the next chapter.

CHAPTER 7

Ally

SIZE MATTERS

I'm four feet 11 and I'm going to heaven [and] it makes me feel ten feet tall.

—Evie Tornquist Karlsson, "Evie and RSJ Help
Women Celebrate Being God's Gals"

You, Misrecognized in Your Own (Despised) Body

It is another typical school day in Rodman: cold, overcast, and snowy, with more of the same expected tonight, tomorrow, and the next day. Not having experienced anything different, you think that this is normal, the quintessential definition of this season of the year. You cannot image experiencing Halloween, Thanksgiving, or Christmas in Arizona, Florida, California, Hawaii, or any context where there is no snow as a marker of this season of the year.

Your mom's familiar, soothing voice has gently called you several times to remind you that you have to be dressed and ready to get on the bus by 6:50 a.m. You finally force your imagined oversized body to move, to leave the cocoon of your warm bed and get into the shower, in order to get dressed in fifteen minutes. You do all this without looking in a mirror. Mirrors, as you perceive them, are your first enemy of the day, so you hate them, not just because they remind you that not only are you not "four feet 11 ... and [not] going to heaven," but also because they compel you to acknowledge that you are both too fat and too tall to be thought of as "pretty," the most valued marker of idealized femininity. And in the tape that keeps going around and around and around in your head, it is imperative to be thought of as pretty because only pretty girls get to heaven, that is, get chosen to be someone's date or mate, and often even an appropriate employee.[1] In addition to being thought of as being very nice, pretty girls are petite in both size and height, at least as you see them. You embody only one of these characteristics: you are very, very nice. Indeed, you are so nice that most people, especially your friends, take you for granted. You go on to tell the anthropologist why you think being nice has made you a target of female angst, not just among the girls who often bully you at school but even among your friends.

> All throughout my schooling I have always had friends. You
> know two groups of friends. But I've found that usually, in the
> two groups of friends, I've become the person that's easily picked
> on. . . . I would become sort of like a target. And then I would
> stop hanging out with that group of people, because it just got too
> [problematic]. Every time we were together, they would pick on
> me. That type of thing. So I always had friends, and I would have,
> like, some *close* friends. But usually friends just kind of, you know,
> just keep passing and going.[2]

A seventeen-year-old White American female with what you self-describe as "pasty white skin," you loathe your self-image. Add nondescript mousy brown hair, gray-green eyes, and a body that stands about five foot ten and weighs about 175 pounds, as you see yourself, you might as well be seven feet tall and weigh six tons;[3] hence your aversion to mirrors. Brushing your teeth and combing your hair are the last items on your morning hygiene list, and you hurriedly look at your image and learn, much to your chagrin, that nothing has changed overnight: You are still the overweight, too tall girl that you were before you went to sleep. Regrettably, you have not become the beautiful princess you were in the dreams you had last night. As you rush downstairs to gulp down the milk and hot cereal that your mom invariably has waiting for you (you adore her because she never fails to make life so easy for you—loving you unconditionally and getting far less than your best in return), you make a silent commitment to be a better person at school today in order to make your dreams of becoming a beautiful girl come true. Your mom tries to engage you in conversation but you are too self-absorbed, too reeking in both self-pity and self-loathing to be responsive to her small talk. You ignore her efforts to engage you in a conversation about the neighbor's dog and hope she will understand—again—that you are having a PP (pity party) and feeling really sorry for yourself. A few days ago, one of your female friends described you as being narcissistic and self-absorbed, concerned only about your own needs and desires. That hurt *so* much, and you cannot tell your mom about your friend's hurtful words.

Despite your friend's assessment of you, that is not how you see yourself in relationship to your peers, including your close friends:

> I think I am too nice to people. I (laugh)—I can rationalize not getting upset with people, in my mind. So people see that, as one of my friends told me the other day. But I just like to avoid conflict. So I'm not—I don't bring things up. And people will start to understand that they can walk all over me.[4]

You grab your coat, scarf, hat, and book bag and run to board the oncoming yellow school bus, which you will barely make. You hear your mom saying something that is bound to be helpful, but you cannot make it out; you are closing the door on her words because you have to get to the bus stop prior to the arrival of the bus. Most of all, you disregard the lessons constantly reinforced by your mom: practice good posture, stand up tall. You consciously ignore her suggestions and bend slightly forward—just a little bit—in order to make yourself look shorter; standing tall is not your goal. You loathe the idea of being the tallest girl (you dare not think about your size ten shoes) in your science classroom, in your gym class, on the school bus, everywhere. As you board the bus this morning, you also avert your eyes to avoid the surveillance you routinely observe in the eyes of your peers, to avoid seeing who is on the bus and the disgust you imagine in your schoolmates' eyes as they look at your oversized body. You button your winter coat from top to bottom in order to mask its perceived girth. You move as rapidly as possible to a seat in the rear, next to one of the few Black girls (there are only two Black students who routinely ride the school bus, both of them female; you wonder why the seat next to this girl is almost always vacant, as if it has a reserved sign on it, which you choose to ignore), who seems to be closer to your size and whose body is more like your image of yourself, hoping to make abundantly clear the color and racial contrast: you are White; she's Black.[5] OK, you admit that you are not nearly as large as you were before you lost all the weight in tenth and (especially) eleventh grades, when you had to be hospitalized and received extensive treatment in a clinic.

> I spent three months in that clinic, so that I could get over this sickness, like, get it under control. 'Cause it started off with me losing too much weight, and then putting it on and binging, purging, and then it just got to where it—I don't know, it would have thrown things off in my body and it became dangerous. So they had to like, get it flattened out. . . . I'm perfectly fine now, there's nothing wrong with me now physically. . . . I am not exactly normal, like some people. 'Cause it's hard to go back to a complete normalcy. I kind of just eat, like—really every day it's different. I'll eat totally different every single day, so that's how it is now. . . . It's about, like, how I'm feeling. It's, I feel, based a lot on, like, what emotionally I'm feeling.[6]

You are still very uncomfortable with food, and you try to explain that to the anthropologist. You recall the first time she asked you if you were able to see a relationship between how your friends treat you and the fact that you developed an eating disorder. She said she wanted you to help her understand why you had such a torturous relationship with food, why you not only did not want to consume food but defined food as a vital enemy.

I think a lot of, like, my friends sort of—I don't know, it's so hard to 'splain. Like—I don't know. I feel like I'm never on an equal level with the friends that I have, because they've all, like, always pushed me sort of down. . . . I really don't know if it's all in my head, or if it really happens, but I feel like that's how it is. Like, my friends just—like, maybe it's the way I look or the way I act or the way I am. I don't really know what it is, but . . .[7]

Initially, you did not understand, did not appreciate why the anthropologist tended to ask you questions with such obvious answers. Is this really what anthropologists do?, you want to know. (You've never met an anthropologist before so you are unable to make a comparison; hell, you had never even heard of Margaret Mead, the iconic anthropologist whom this woman keeps referring to.)[8] She surely knows that you are not just overweight, you are *fat!!!!*, a condition you have endured all your life, and fat girls are not the objects of lust in America. Although your parents assure you (and they have pictures to prove it) that you were not born fat and did not begin to become fat until just before you started kindergarten, you have no memory of your nonfat body. Your first school memory is being not only the fattest but the tallest girl in your class and therefore being consigned to the end of the girl's line—always. (Your dad seeks to humor you when you whine about this situation by noting that at least you are not taller than the tallest boy in your class.) Your parents, especially your mom, would constantly assure you that you would stop growing and that what she initially talked about as "baby fat" would evaporate.

Everyone in your family, especially your parents and maternal and paternal grandparents, became hypersensitive to your food sensibilities, seeking to assure you that you were loved not for what you looked like but for who you are. However, despite their Herculean efforts, you still suffered under the omnipresent spectacle of the violence affiliated with conforming to the normality of female-specific height and weight. This is what you would have to make the anthropologist understand. It's what your dad was referring to when the anthropologist called your home number for the first time and talked with him about your involvement in her study of gender-specific aggression, bullying, and competition. One of his first questions was whether she was aware that you had a eating disorder, trying to subtly make her aware of what he and your immediate and extended family sees as your major problem.

Family Life on the Beige Side of Town

Your life is boringly middle class. Your mom and dad were married before your birth. The older of their two children, you have incomplete memories of the privileges affiliated with being the first-born child—and grandchild. For the first six and a half years of your life and prior to your brother's birth, you have vague but vivid memories of the way everyone doted on you, especially your maternal grandmother and grandfather. They made you feel that they loved you unconditionally and that the way you looked or any other conditions were unimportant. You and your BFF, Sam, were the little girls these adults adored. You are not quite sure when things changed; but they did. Maybe it was when your younger brother arrived—just after your sixth birthday—or perhaps it was when Sam's mother died.

You live with your parents and younger brother in a nondescript three-bedroom Colonial, with a living room, a small dining room, a bath and a half, and a partial basement. The exterior of the house is wrapped in white aluminum siding that, if truth be told, desperately needs to be replaced and stands on a street that is indistinguishable from most of the streets in the suburban Rodman community. The steps up to the front door are in need of repair (which is only clearly visible when you are close to them, and not so visible from the sidewalk). One of the things your mom constantly includes on your dad's honey-do list is the repair of the front steps. This has been ongoing since you started high school—almost three years ago. He just never seems to get around to doing it. Recently, she has begun to threaten to hire a mason to make the repair. He repeatedly re-assures her that he not only can do the work and save the family money but is going to do it—real soon. This inevitably ends the discussion.

Your mom is the family's primary breadwinner at this time in your life. (As you think about it, she always has been.) She has worked for the same company for about ten years, you think. (You admit to the anthropologist that you are not sure.) You do know that she has always been in the food services business, but you don't know if she has worked continuously for the same or different com-panies. You also know that she has worked in food services for the same university in the area for several years. She is the manager of the food services program at her current worksite, and she is a good cook, if one likes what is widely known as comfort foods—and you do.[9] She makes a mean spaghetti and meatballs, fettuccine Alfredo, meatloaf, macaroni and cheese, shepherd's pie, creamy soups, sauces, biscotti, and more.

Your dad works episodically and at a variety of odd jobs. You find their relationship a little bit strange, but it seems to work for them. You know your mom loves him and that he feels needed, despite his lack of full-time employment and his failure to complete the honey-do list—a failure that is a perennial source of (muted) conflict in the home. There is very little open hostility in your family, and except for a handful of verbal and physical fights between you and your younger brother, noise is nonexistent; everything is so quiet, very quiet.

You live on a quiet street among quiet people who are virtually indistinguishable from each other. They are all White, they all go to work every day, and they all go to church on Sunday. Everyone in your home community appears to like the same things and to do the same things. No one seems to be different, and that, ironically, is what seems to be critical to the building of community in your neighborhood: the absence of diversity—nothing and no one is different.

Food and Rage: In and Out of That Order

You share the information about your family with the anthropologist in your effort to disabuse her of the wrongheaded notion that there must be something going on in your family or immediate community that led you to the unhappy relationship you have with food and the attendant predicament in which you find yourself. *No!!* You want to scream the word at her, but of course you don't. You are much too nice to do that. The fact is, there is nothing different in either your immediate family or your community, despite the fact that sameness is both unscripted and predictable. Everybody knows and obeys the rules. Everyone also knows everyone else. And until you became ill with your food aversion more than a year and a half ago, no one had ever done anything that was that unfamiliar or strange in your community. (Did you mean on your block, the anthropologist wonders?) You shocked everyone in your immediate community with your unusual relationship with food and the attendant change in your behavior. It was not until you began to tell your story to the anthropologist and to see diversity up close and personal for the first time (after all, she is African American, and you had never engaged with anyone of African descent over such a long period of time) that you began to have an appreciation for how your struggle with an illness uncommon in your community may have marked you as different. And you realize that the way your community saw you as different parallels the way you had perceived Black people and other people who were not members of your immediate community. In the wake of your struggle with anorexia, for the first time in your life, you've begun to fully appreciate—in reverse—how embodying a dominant gender-specific norm not only facilitates social acceptance but fuels status mobility to boot. There were no Black or Brown people (except the one Latina and her biracial family at your Catholic church, whom you did not know) in your severely monochromatic, racially circumscribed world.

You realize that when someone meets you for the first time and has no knowledge of your history, it is hard for him or her to fully understand how sick you were last year, the year before, and, to a lesser extent, this year. Indeed, you quickly realize that that is the anthropologist's issue: she just does not have enough of the historical picture to fully understand. Sealed in a synchronic image of who you are today, initially she fails to comprehend why you are always smiling—you smile as a way to signal your desire to be accepted, to minimize hostility. Indeed, smiling signals your unhappiness rather than any joy. Therefore, you are not at all surprised when the anthropologist mentions that she has never seen you sans a smile—and has never, never seen you in the school cafeteria, has never seen you with a single item of food during all the times she has seen you in class, in homeroom, in the hallways, with friends, or any other time. During this particular interview session, you make her fully aware—for the first time—of how much you eschew food, not only in private but in public spaces as well. You tell her:

> No, I haven't gone to lunch since, like, the tenth grade. (Laugh.)
> I don't—I don't like to sit and watch people eat, it's just—I don't
> know. I still feel uncomfortable in a big room of students eating
> food. But I can always handle myself. It's not to the point where
> I can, like, forget and really have to avoid situations. But I will
> choose not to be around people who are—you know, all sitting
> together eating and stuff.[10]

Although you are not "fat" or anorexic when the anthropologist meets you and you agree to participate in her study, she tells you that she has talked with your friends and peers, your counselor, and other adults at UGRH, and they have validated what you tell her: you are still struggling to recover from a crippling case of anorexia.

She tells you that these individuals also tell her that you are repeatedly victimized by female aggression, bullying, and competition. You have to admit that you are a tad annoyed to learn that so many people at school see you as a victim and, more importantly, would tell a strange Black woman something that causes you so much pain and humiliation. That is not the image you would choose for yourself. The first identity you would choose for yourself is a simple four letter word: "nice." Admittedly, you desperately want to be seen as "nice," hence the perennial smile, but you do not want to be thought of as a patsy or a pushover, and yet that is how others seem to be identifying you.

Every day during your designated lunch hour, you struggle to figure what to swap out for it. Since you do not eat lunch in the cafeteria (or anyplace for that matter), you are almost always available to talk to the anthropologist. Indeed, you are happy she wants to talk with you in order not to have to find something to do to keep you from feeling so alone when all your friends are in the cafeteria—or some place—eating. At this stage of her research study, you meet the anthropologist at the designated room on the second floor (in the spring when the weather was nice, the two of you went right outside and sat on one of the more remote benches). She turns on her tape recorder and just listens to you as you vent (including crying tears so freighted with your anger that as they run down your face they burn your chubby checks) your suppressed rage about your weight, your height, and especially your friends, all of whom seem to take your friendship for granted, abusing you psychologically.

Initially, she did not share with you all that anthropological stuff about how important food is in a culture, any culture. That was probably a good thing because you were so wrapped up in your pain that it never occurred to you to ask her anything about why she was not eating during lunchtime. You wanted and needed someone to really hear your concerns; she appeared to be willing, and she certainly was available. Plus, she was so strange to you that you found it easy to assume that because she looked different from 99.9 percent of the people at school, she was a safe stranger, someone you could tell your secrets to without fear that she would violate the promised secrecy. This was your first sustained interaction with a Black American, and although you were unsure about how you felt about "those people," you concluded that it was her strange status coupled

with her perceived lack of knowledge of anyone (or anything) you
knew today or might know in the future that fueled your willingness to be so open with her about your feelings, beliefs, ideas, and
problems.

You could sense her genuine empathy, see the pain she felt for
you reflected in her muddy brown eyes (why do they all have such
dark eyes, you wonder?), and feel her regret that she was powerless
to alter your undesired social condition. Yet this did not deter you.
You talked and talked and talked—and talked—despite the fact that
she could not alter or change the constant themes in your meetings
with her. Each time you met with her, you reminded her of how
awful you felt about your weight and your desire to change your
reality. On one (and only one) of those occasions, she did something unusual in her interactions with you: she mentioned a book
called *Fat Talk* and promised to bring you her copy to read.[11] She
summarized it, briefly, noting that she was confused by the realness
of your situation. The author of that book argues that despite the
widely repeated claim that dieting is such a major problem among
contemporary teenage girls, "fat talk" is largely a ritualistic practice,
with most teen girls' diets lasting from breakfast to lunch. She said
that the author concluded that these girls use "fat talk" ("Am I too
fat?") to bond with each other in order to cope with the hegemonic
gender-specific expectation that women and girls must be thin to be
seen as beautiful, desirable, gender appropriate, and unquestionably
eligible for the most prestigious female-specific prizes: marriage and
motherhood—in that order. (Or is it motherhood and marriage?)
She asked if you would read it and let her know if you agreed with
the author. You told her you would, but you indicated right then and
there that you don't agree with the claim that teenage girls are essentially just talking as a way of bonding with each other. Maybe
that is true for teenage girls who are not really fat, you assured her,
but with girls like you who are already fat or have been fat, there
is real, overwhelming pain affiliated with being overweight. You
have to admit that when you recall your many discussions with the

anthropologist—both formal and informal—you had no real answer or answers for her questions about why you both loathe and
love food; you just know that you are fat, have always been fat, and
hate being fat.

Living with (and Lacking) the Most Important
Female Status: Beauty

Despite your remarkable progress in overcoming some of the most
devastating aspects of your relationship with food this school year
and many years before, you are still unable to free yourself of your
conviction that you are not only too tall but, more important to
your way of thinking, too heavy for any boy to think of you as someone he would want to date.[12] You remind yourself that that is not the
central issue in your life; you just want to look normal, like Kristin
Chenoweth, a petite, Tony Award–winning blonde Broadway
actress, as she proudly sings the lyrics of the song "I'm four feet
11 and I'm going to heaven [and] it makes me feel ten feet tall."
Embodying the lyrics of the song, Chenoweth is supposedly only
four foot eleven. Or, alternatively, like the well-known morning-
television host Kelly Ripa, who at five foot three is much taller than
Chenoweth but still, like your BFF, Sam, a reasonable height—for
a girl.[13] At five foot ten you are the average height of the American
male. Add to that a size-ten shoe and you are inconsolable. Are you
really a girl, you wonder? You realize that lots of males are taller
(and lots are shorter) than the average, but that is of little comfort to
you. You cannot think of any advantages affiliated with your weight,
height, or shoe size. If you were thin (willowy) rather than obese
and the height you are, you might be considered appropriate for a
modeling career—if, in your case, you could also camouflage both
your face and your hair. (This is your self-assessment, not that of the
anthropologist; like your mom, she keeps telling you that you are
beautiful inside and out. You desperately want to believe her, but
you don't.)

I have always felt like I was a fat girl. Fat and ugly girl . . . basically, like, since when I was four and up, I've been having really negative feeling about the way I looked, which I really don't know where they came from, because I had a really supportive mom. Who didn't wear makeup, and never forced the ideal girl things on me. They just kind of happened to me. I—it might have been the fact that I've been friends with and have known Samantha (Sam), my BFF. (Laugh.) She's always been so little, and she's always tended to have been—I guess, skinner than me. When I was little, I thought she was prettier than me. And I guess it sort of just—everyone I was surrounded by, I just always got this feeling that I was just—just not as good as everybody else. And when people say nice things about me, you'd think that that would boost my self esteem, but I just automatically saw that as just lies, . . . people trying to make the fat one feel better.[14]

Your image of you compels you to be totally repulsed by your appearance. No amount of encouragement and or praise from your friends and families overrides your belief that there is anything socially redeemable about you. For example, your mom is an unconditional cheerleader in your life. Her cheerleader uniform is permanently attached to her body, as is your dad's—to a lesser and different degree. On a daily basis your mom chronicles what she thinks of as your beauty, skills, intelligence, and so on. She repeatedly tells you that you are beautiful, intelligent, thoughtful, nice, and kind. She praises you profusely for being such a good girl; a wonderful friend and a good student. She tells you this against a nonfeminist backdrop. Your mom, at about five foot three, is just so ordinary—not into makeup, stiletto heels, or anything like that. Pleasantly plump, she exudes marriage, motherhood, and traditional values.[15] Your father, at six foot one, also tells you that you are beautiful. You experience their praise as self-serving, on the part of both of your parents. After all, how does it serve them to argue that they created an ugly duckling? They created you and are invested in your success, so they are compelled to see only the good in your looks and your accomplishments or lack thereof. At least that is how you translate their behaviors and practices.

The following excerpt from the anthropologist's field notes captures this conundrum for you—and for her.

Of all the girls with whom I've spoken, Ally is the one who has not mentioned "boy" or "boys" as the first priority in her life (although her misery and self-loathing is premised on the absence of male attention). And—and maybe that's because she's *not* an attractive girl—as she defines herself. She's very homely looking, and she's very insecure and smiles *all* the time, especially when she is in pain, which is most of the time. *I* see this as a sign of her trying to make herself acceptable to other people. She talked with me again today. It is so interesting to see how this young woman, who is *not* in the top part of her class but who is doing pretty well in school, navigates and negotiates what she sees as a gender-hostile social context. It seems that one has to work very hard to be able to do that successfully at UGRH. This is especially burdensome because her BFF, Sam, according to her, is absolutely driven to be an honor student. Although Ally described Sam as her best friend, I'm amazed at how she allows her friend to walk all over her. She has such negative feelings about Sam—this girl that she identifies as her best friend. It's amazing! The amount of anguish, fear and hostility she harbors regarding this girl—her alleged BFF—is concurrently common and amazing.[16]

You tell the anthropologist:

I've known [Sam] since I was three. And we just, like grew up together. And I'm not sure if we're friends because we really like each other— . . . or it's just because we've just been friends for so long. (Laugh.) But she is one of the people that is really into herself. And she'll kind of do the tear-down thing to other people too.[17]

Learning to Lose—In Order to Win

The anthropologist recorded the following in her field notes in response to the interview just quoted:

> Ally talked and talked about how she disliked her friends, especially her BFF, Samantha, and how they and she treats her.[18]
> Listening to this particular student and several of the other girls, this BFF or best-friend relationship that girls get involved in very early on in their lives appears to prepare them for many of their adult relationships, including marriage. Typically, a woman's best friend is the person in whom she confides everything. Invariably, the girl, like Ally, feels that their best friend is not living up to her end of the agreement. Ally does not like most of the things Samantha does. But Ally does not say anything to her about what she does that annoys her. Her anger is underground, misrecognized and hidden from her friend. Ally is the quintessential example of this practice, i.e., how females at *this* particular school seem to value suffering. She said to me in one of our last Thursday interviews, where she cried for most of the interview because she was so angry at Samantha, that it was better for her rather than Samantha to be unhappy. And, of course, when a girl *does* this, i.e., cries, one thinks that it's sadness, and everyone wants to comfort her.[19] Given our gender-specific enculturation, we certainly should do that—as I did with Ally yesterday. But the more important thing is that [among females] crying is often a sign of anger, not sadness. She is really, really angry at Samantha. And I can't *tell* her she's angry at her BFF. That's the key issue here. Ally kept saying, for example, "Why should I hurt *her* feelings? You know, make *her* feel bad? I—you know, *I'd* rather be the one who feels bad."[20]

You think you are being a good friend by not telling your BFF, Samantha, what she does that makes you unhappy. For example, you hate the fact that she is so preoccupied with getting good grades and being identified as an achiever. She appears to want to be the best in everything; you don't. You think of her as being too pushy, as being aggressive. Indeed, you tell the anthropologist that a big part of your reluctance to tell your friend that she is annoying in so many ways is rooted in your empathy with her loss. Samantha's mother died when she was very young (you think she was either three or four; you've forgotten her exact age), compelling her father to take on the mother role for her and her two younger brothers. You empathize with this loss because you are so connected to your mom. When you think about your mom not being in your life, you realize what a big hole exists permanently in the life of your BFF, and you are motivated to forgive her for anything she does that annoys you. You feel more than sorry for her: you pity her. This pity forces you to find excuses for what you consider to be inappropriate actions and behaviors on her part.[21]

Not just Sam, but all of your friends' perception of you has both shaped and transformed your self-perception, not only of your personal characteristics but of your academic goals and ambitions. You shared with the anthropologist how much you had wanted to go to college in elementary and middle school, but not now during your senior year in high school. The following is a snippet from her field notes:

Ally's not planning to go to college, at least not immediately after high school. She's decided she's going to wait at least six months—one semester. And then she'll probably go to one of the local universities, including the one where her mother works. Tuition costs are very high. But because her mother's an employee, Ally will get to go there tuition free. This is amazing and something that I think she'll take advantage of—eventually.[22]

Because you and Sam have been friends virtually all your lives. Her parents live on the same street in a house that is virtually indistinguishable from your parents' house from the outside, leading you and her, as young girls, to think, when you played with each other at either house, that you were in your own home. Moreover, while she is so much shorter than you (at four foot eleven) and weighs so much less, she seems unsuited to have either a physical or mental fight with you. Even in grade school, you have always been much taller than all your female friends and enemies. Now you are five foot ten, and though you now weigh about 175 pounds, prior to your two-year bout with anorexia, you weighed a lot more, and a lot more than Sam.[23]

An Anthropological Postscript

Ally misrecognizes the violence that is implicated in her unsuccessful quest for weight and height normality. She blames herself totally for her abnormalities, especially her obesity. Like most of the other students at the school, she would never go home from school and say to her parents that she was a victim of violence on any given school day, unless she was involved in a physical fight. Like Nadine (see chapter 3), she only recognizes violence that is physical. Her desire to embody the normalized, hegemonic images of gender-appropriate size is not equated with violence. She does not even recognize what she is forced to endure as gender-specific, structurally sanctioned aggression, bullying, and competition.[24] Instead, she attributes the fact that she doesn't match what is socially and culturally mandated as evidence of her own shortcomings, for example, as evidence of a lack of will power. Her rendering of what is fueling her anorexia, for example, is her inability to control the amount of food she consumes on a daily basis. If she could control her food intake, she reasons, she could and would be happy. Here, I have to admit that she did tell me that she received so much more male attention when she was thinner. Apparently, the frailty embodied in her thinness made her less threatening and a more desirable female commodity.

Ally is the quintessential example of that I've seen at *this* particular school: first, these teenage females are often conflicted about the meaning of female friendships, forced to embrace the idea that their friends are also likely to be their enemies or frenemies; and second, they appear to be abundantly rewarded for suffering.[25] One of the ways this is manifested is in the widespread practice of crying. When Ally cried during our several interviews when talking about her BFF, Sam, and other gender-specific conflicts in her life, I understood her behavior as indicating anger, not sadness.[26] Ironically, I was supposed to misrecognize it as sadness, not anger. I never acknowledged to her that I understood her tears as anger; it would have been inappropriate to do that. And that is the key issue here. Ally repeatedly asked the rhetorical question, "Why should I hurt *her* feelings? You know, make *her* feel bad? I—you know, *I'd* rather be the one who feels bad."

As Ally's narrative suggests, she is actively implicated in the gendered mandate that idealizes or normalizes smallness in the definition of what it means to be female. She embraces the hegemonic narrative even though it means that she must starve her body of the essential food and nutrition needed for good health and even life. Ally's narrative is more reflective of the White girls at UGRH than of the Black girls at the school, who are more likely to resist this dominant narrative and who, by resisting, end up with bodies that make them ineligible as the embodiment of the dominant idealization of femininity.[27] Interestingly, these oversized bodies do not make them ineligible for motherhood, but it does diminish their potential to be selected as some male's wife. As Ally understands, albeit at an unconscious level, her weight is far more important than her height (although her posture suggests that she seeks to minimize that as well). Consequently, she has learned—and is reluctant to unlearn—that she exists in a world where four foot eleven to five foot seven is the female-specific norm, and that means she is never going to get to heaven.

Ally also realizes at an unconscious level how important it is to be identified as beautiful and gender appropriate. However, like the vast majority of the Black girls in my study, she sees herself and is seen by others as not embodying the normative image of femaleness. Consequently, like the Black girls at UGRH, she is unprotected, compelled to fly solo (sans the support of males) because she is normal in neither height nor weight, and she is not going to heaven, or anywhere else desirable, primarily because she does not embody the female normative standard: short and thin. As the data presented here suggest, the female quest for thin bodies and shortness is only partially fueled by the desire to be beautiful. A more important driver than the desire to be beautiful is an unconscious quest to be protected and selected in a heterosexual, male-dominated social system.

Excavating, Resuscitating, and Rehabilitating Violence— by Another Name

Misrecognition of the violence embedded in what is widely believed to be "normal" social practices pervades our culture and all aspects of our nation's institutions, including our schools. It is this misunderstanding that both masks and fuels the gender-specific violence so rampant in our society. It is also the focus of the study reported here. As the narratives in this book reveal, most people seek to be "normal," assuming this designation will render them "invulnerable," protecting them from what is deemed "abnormal."[1] Thus, this book offers the reader the opportunity not only to interrogate the idea that normality is neutral but to think of it as a socially approved form of violence—a violence that is habitually misrecognized. More specifically, this book questions what is taken for granted: the banality of normality.

But what is normal, and is it banal? Moreover, if it is banal, can it be linked to the kind of violence—aggression, bullying, and competition (ABC)—manifested at UGRH and other social contexts? Is "normal," by default, what is socially expected or accepted and, therefore, uncontested? Is it, as anthropologist Jules Henry noted so many years ago, the feel-good social status?[2] More broadly, is what is deemed normal the central organizational framework for all relationships and institutions in American society? For example, during official Black enslavement, slavery was seen as normal, especially in the South. Most people—enslaved and free—did not challenge it, even though it made many of them uncomfortable, especially the enslaved. And, as incredible as it seems, a few enslaved people "evolved" and began to think of slavery and their enslavement as normal, that is, as appropriate for who they were: captured and enslaved Africans in a foreign land where everything affiliated with power and goodness was controlled by people who did not look like, think like, or work like them and who in no way shared their history. Similarly, prior to the passage of the Nineteenth Amendment, when American women—of all races—were not allowed to vote or own property, many of them thought of their exclusion from important rituals and social practices as normal, and when some of their female peers opted to challenge these constraints—women like Harriet Tubman and Susan B. Anthony—they were skewered not only by men but by other women, labeled with unflattering names and isolated from the community of women. The fact that the social constraints on Black persons and on women were lawful (that is, state sanctioned) and viewed as "normal" during a particular historical era in no way absolves either the state or the individuals who enforced them of the deliberate harm—the violence—they inflicted.

This leads to a second important question evoked by this book: Is "normal" what is affiliated with what is dominant—at any given time—and therefore constructed as "natural"? In a context of dominance and subordination, is it normal or natural to seek affiliation with the powerful and to avoid—as much as possible—being identified with the subordinate? More concretely, are the young women in the narratives in this book who are defined as subordinate or different (and by extension not normal) more likely to seek identification with men, the dominant and normal, than with other subordinates, especially other women? Likewise, are people of African ancestry more inclined to disidentify with other Black people and to seek, instead, to be linked to the norms and values of the dominant: White people? In our unending quest for status and recognition, what I call in this book "statusitis," are we—all of us Americans—inadvertently complicit in reproducing rather than eliminating inequality?

These questions were provoked by the headwinds metaphor in this book's prelude. By merging Bourdieu's notion of habitus and its structuring impact—largely misrecognized—to illuminate the conundrum in the lives of the (Black) women who give birth to, nurture, and support the (Black) girls at UGRH, I reveal what is often overlooked in schools and other cultural environments: the pervasive, masked violence, especially among and between persons gendered female.[3] The ethnographic narratives presented here document the deadly impact of this structural violence and how adolescent females cope with this reality. The powerful omnipresence of the headwinds fuels the perception that Black girls are bullies, not the bullied. The White girls are seduced by the trade winds and taught to believe that they are nonracial and are simultaneously seduced to see the major obstacle in their lives as gender inequality. Paradoxically, what is officially defined as normal academic and social practices, particularly what is narrowly defined as achievement, mindlessly presumes that all these young women share (or ought to share) the hegemonic trade wind habitus; they don't. These practices not only for the most part ignore (or privilege) the effects of their different habitus but also strategically use this information as evidence to disregard or overvalue it for inclusion in the existing school curriculum.

The narratives of the Black girls—that is, the practice of routinely consigning them to the less rigorous academic components of a gated, walled-off social space—reinforce and perhaps, unintentionally, reproduce their families' (especially their mothers') typical but undesired social and economic reality. By contrast, the narratives of the White girls—whose habitus is generally seen as more aligned with the goals and objectives of the larger society and of the school's curriculum, extracurricular programs, and other academically oriented activities—are closely allied with what is officially defined as "normal."[4] The misrecognition and ubiquity of the violence embedded in these differential practices and expectations are at the center of this book.

By juxtaposing the ways one navigates the structural violence embedded in a headwinds versus the ways one does in a trade winds environment, I am able to contextualize the effects and consequences of performing in an academic habitus that has as its official mission the fulfillment of the needs of the current diverse student populations—both those negatively affected by the headwinds and those whose lives are supported by the trade winds, despite the power and incursion of the state-sanctioned hierarchical social structure.[5] At UGRH, this goal, the fulfillment of students' needs, is achieved by compelling all students to embrace the official, trade wind habitus. The paradox is that at this public school one is more likely to achieve this goal by *not* acknowledging the existence of a habitus characterized by racial bias and or gender discrimination within and among the diverse student communities. Students who are victimized by gender and/or racial discrimination are rewarded for pretending that these issues do not exist at the school.

The social conditions I unmasked at UGRH suggest that academic progress is much less likely for those who face into the wind than it is for students whose academic progress is fueled, shaped, and structured by the support of the trade winds. Unlike headwinds, trade winds are imbued with a kind of wind DNA that promotes human survival; headwinds are not. Consequently, individuals caught in the most severe trade winds are unlikely to even notice its existence, able to virtually float along as the wind pushes them forward, so much so that they "do not feel the wind; it feels [them]," propelling them, so they arrive at their goals virtually effortlessly.[6]

In this conclusion, I revisit the primary goals of this book: to excavate, resuscitate, and rehabilitate the meaning of violence by centering the normality endemic in symbolic or structural violence and summarizing the way unconscious, albeit deliberate and often misrecognized, human intervention alters the efficacy of a hegemonic trade winds–rich social context. I do this in three ways: first, by *excavating* the way the Black and White female study participants are influenced by a gender-specific violence informed by their divergent habitus; second, by *resuscitating* the way both groups of girls shared—albeit differentially experienced—gender subordination connected to their unending quest for normality but were differentially rewarded and punished for embracing or violating this hegemonic gender-specific script; and third, by *rehabilitating* the meaning of violence by focusing not on the harm inflicted on the victims of physical violence but on a parallel, misrecognized kind of harm, which is inflicted primarily, though not exclusively, by gender-specific language—regardless of the user's race, class, or other such categories—on females.[7] Thus, by acknowledging a nonphysical meaning of harm, I am able to illuminate and document the effects of the violence embodied in the nomadic, everyday practices sewn into the idea of friendly fire, the central focus of this book.[8]

First, while I have repeatedly referenced the widely used cultural categories of race, class, and gender, I am keenly aware of both their intersectionality and their chameleon-like existence, reflected in their "nomadic subjectivities," which shift and intersect with different contexts and social locations.[9] The importance of this characterization cannot be overstated. Further, while it is fairly routine to excavate and resuscitate the role of violence in postcolonial and even in what is known as postracial contexts, resuscitating and, by extension, rehabilitating its meaning to include female specific "warfare" is not.[10] In this text, I expand the meaning of violence by deploying Bourdieu's (and others') theoretical argument, which privileges not just words but language, judgment, images, and so on.[11] I begin here with a discussion of why it is so important to *excavate race*—a major cultural category that is, at the same time, socially constructed, deeply flawed, and socially taboo.

Excavating Race—Another Kind of Violence

In anthropology, especially archaeology, excavation is typically associated with the scientific effort to find or uncover or recover something that has cultural value or significance. The language unique to archaeology is embraced here not because I am an archaeologist but because, as the opening vignette of this book reveals, when one lives in a world structured by and sutured to an omnipresent headwind (which everyone who is not directly affected by it has little reason to believe exists), excavating headwinds (a metaphor for stigmatized race) is a far more challenging task, a task made even more difficult by an official commitment to "color-blindness and sameness," that is, a refusal to see race as a color. However, unlike the typical goal in an archaeological excavation, to retrieve and analyze material artifacts, my goal is to unearth race as both a biological and socially constructed fiction, normalized, perceived as harmless or at the very least banal, and therefore an underground (or suppressed) but extremely powerful symbolic category. Thus, in all its "nomadic subjectivities," the goal here is to garner a deeper understanding of the trade winds and the headwinds by those directly affected by them.

This exhumation inevitably entails nonphysical cultural products, such as emotional labor, and is a critical initial step. This is a much more laborious, contested, and subjective project than most academicians and other professionals are willing to acknowledge. Indeed, there is a widely repeated axiom that goes something like this: "You cannot change what you do not acknowledge."[12] Moreover, like other researchers—including, for example, Keith Sullivan in *The Anti-Bullying Handbook,* Mica Pollock in *Colormute,* L'Heureux Lewis-McCoy in *Inequality in the Promised Land,* and Frantz Fanon in two seminal books, *Black Skin, White Masks* and *The Wretched of the Earth*—I have chronicled here the ubiquity of the violence affiliated with race (sometimes known as ethnicity) as a powerfully stigmatized/privileged, misrecognized, underground and/or (often) hidden social issue in the lives of Black (and Brown) peoples, specifically the female students at Underground Railroad High.[13]

The irony is that at this research site, even when the issue of race (and race merged to gender) surfaces in either physical confrontations or in the perceived banality of words and images, its unwelcomed outing is often not only denied or unacknowledged but suppressed because the bystanders and, in some instances, even the combatants themselves, resort to the practice of identifying the "victim(s)" as assailant(s) and the "assailant(s)" as victim(s).[14] In other words, the typical response of the adult and peer-group bystanders is to frame the issue in the language of static binaries, as a conflict between a good person and a bad person, and to punish the latter, not the former.

The most prominent example offered in this book—the physical fight between a Black girl and a White girl in the school cafeteria—is premised on the fact that the girl identified as the aggressor, the Black girl, Nadine, was the victim of vile, racially degrading language that dehumanized her both from a racial and from a gender perspective. In striking contrast, her White protagonist, Kirstin, who uttered the disputed but nonetheless violent words, was identified as the victim rather than the assailant primarily because she responded to the altercation not with physical violence but with tears.[15] While the Black girl, Nadine, agrees with the hegemonic definition of violence as physical, what she also knows, subconsciously, is that at UGRH, race is such a taboo issue that to even allude to its historical (not even its contemporary) manifestation or existence makes one eligible for unmarked isolation and alienation—the subtlety of the dissimulations missed by virtually everyone directly affected.

Moreover, just as Lyn Mikel Brown points out in *Girlfighting* regarding the conundrum facing White girls at her research site, at UGRH the Black girls who are at least marginally acceptable are those who, like their White female peers, deny or mask the existence of race as either a biological or social construct or some combination of a fluid, contested, constantly changing lived reality.[16] Paradoxically, both the Black (and White) girls are punished for acknowledging the pain and stigmatization of a stratified racial context and are rewarded, instead, for embracing a fictional color-blind social order.[17]

Interestingly, as the narratives in this book reveal, the most academically rewarded female participants—adults and students—are the ones who are the most committed to distancing themselves from the idea that race and/or the intersections of race and gender are issues in their lives, either at school or elsewhere.[18] They are the students who are most likely to believe that their achievement is the direct result of individual effort, that we live in a color-blind social world. Self-identified White females were rewarded for misrecognizing that Whiteness was a privilege or benefit that, like the trade winds, promoted their greater academic success. For example, in her book *White Kids,* Mary Bucholtz acknowledges that for the nerds or the most academically successful White students at Bay City High, eschewing the linguistic and all other "cool"-related Black practices fueled their achievement.[19] However, this was not without some undesired consequences. Bucholtz insists that being branded with a (totally) White identity was a more complex "racial matrix" because of its more complicated, episodic connection to an "ideological . . . [Whiteness] associated with cultural blandness and lack of coolness, while at other times . . . [being] viewed as the embodiment of racist hegemony."[20] All other ethnoracial student groups at the school, she asserts, were less constrained in this way and were therefore far more willing to embrace their less privileged identities. Outside the school context, similar social practices are at play.

Perhaps this was also a contributing factor to what I observed among the White female students at UGRH and to the apparent defensiveness I detected on issues connected to race and gender, including the way their perception of the subordination affiliated with being identified as female stymied their goals and aspirations. As a group, these females were extremely uncomfortable talking about race as a site of either privilege or stigma (especially privilege) and about the associated benefits and harm. Both of the White girls' narratives included here, for example, reflect enormous conflict regarding Whiteness: Brittany embraces a Black rather than a White identity and seeks to pass for Black—nomadically in this context; Ally, on the other hand, because of her failure to measure up to the idealized, petite White female body image, exists in a sea of self-flagellation and anxiety that is so disfiguring that it manifests as anorexia.[21]

The White girls responded very differently than did the Black and biracial girls when it came to race talk, both privately and intraracially. Despite their reluctance to talk about race, the embodied power affiliated with the White girls' various "shades of whiteness" was an invisible shield that protected them from the attempts of the Black girls and other students of color to eliminate—or at least lessen—the inequality gap in achievement.

Given the contextual conundrum chronicled here, how do we

negotiate the movement from excavating to resuscitating a racial discourse that makes everyone, in particular those community members historically imbued with power, uncomfortable to the point that they are unable to engage in a conversation about race, highlighting the way(s) that it privileges and stigmatizes? The next section offers some preliminary thoughts on the importance of resuscitating the violence affiliated with this silence.

Resuscitating Race—Another Kind of Violence

The civil rights movement of the 1960s resuscitated race as a central dehumanizing issue in the lives of African Americans, breaking the violence embedded in the silence that was misrecognized as peace, primarily because of the absence of ongoing planned, public resistance on the part of Black citizens. Originally published in 1961, John Howard Griffin's book *Black Like Me,* chronicling his life as a White man passing as a Black man in the South, had very little impact on policy making or on the attendant structural violence he identified in glaring and chilling detail.[22]

During the heyday of the Jim Crow era that immediately preceded the civil rights movement, the Black and White communities held very different views regarding race-related social and economic conditions and regarding the meaning of violence, with the vast majority of White citizens insisting that race and its attendant inequities were not major issues in the lives of either community.[23] Not surprisingly, their domination of the major apparatuses of power meant that their claims carried the day. In contrast to these official claims, a very different picture slowly emerged in both the literary and historical narratives of Black (and some White) scholars and writers of that era, with the overwhelming majority of these narratives recounting the horrific violence of a seemingly pastoral and peaceful section of the American dreamland.[24] In order to get the opportunity to have their grievances acknowledged and/or listened to, Black southerners complied by embracing the hegemonic claim of intimacy and friendship and the dominating trope that they were not only the perpetrators of the most horrific violence extant in the country at that time but the embodiment of such violence.

Amazingly, despite Black people's intimate knowledge of the headwinds that structured their lives, most did not embrace Fanon's recommendation of using "violence as . . . therapy for a cultural disease brought about by colonial subjugation."[25] Americans of African ancestry who embraced the civil rights movement opted, instead, to practice a major dictum of their Christian religion: "turning the other cheek," accepting, unconditionally, "nonviolence," or peace, as the watchword of the movement. Framing their social movement in the idealization of Christianity and the philosophy of Gandhi, they were able to resuscitate the meaning of violence in the court of public opinion, thereby altering the perception of the region and the violence therein.

The gated nature of the academic lives of the Black and White girls at UGRH reveals a similar need to resuscitate a parallel kind of "intimate apartheid," that is, lives lived in close proximity but with enormous differences in social and cultural practices and interactions.[26] Although the two groups of girls attend the same school, the capital affiliated with their preexisting social lives is differentially acknowledged, accepted, evaluated, and officially (mis)recognized, compelling them—at least in the school context—to act as if their habitus are undifferentiated. Consequently, when their academic performance (the third rail of education: the Black–White achievement gap) is addressed but this differential persists and social interactions are still vastly different, school officials and potential future employers attribute the differences to individual inadequacies and failures rather than to the structural or symbolic (or even a hybrid of the two) violence connected to the hegemony of an ever-changing normality and the girls' unending quest to embody it, whatever it is at any given moment.[27]

As I have chronicled in the narratives in this book, one of the critical features of most cultural systems is their persistence in the face of major social and economic upheavals and the attendant demographic shifts.[28] Following William Faulkner, who insists that not only is "the past never dead, it is not even past," the teenage girls—sixteen, seventeen, and eighteen years of age—who made up my research population were committed both to the dominating gender-specific cultural messages and to an accompanying, albeit misrecognized, belief that rituals, routines, or traditions that are widely practiced, especially by the most elite segment(s) of their peer and family culture, are by definition at the very least harmless.[29] As the culture's most recent members seek to embrace generationally specific practices and behaviors, caught in what Janet Moone identifies as the tug-of-war between two identifiable social processes, "maintenance and change," these female rookie adults seek both to be acceptable to the normal cultural practices of their parents' generation and, at the same time, to embrace the dominating practices of their age cohort.[30]

Examples of this are endless. In the American context, it is evident in many segments of the southern United States, where loyalty and reverence to the Confederacy and especially the Confederate flag are often part of the region's social identity; it is also visible in the foot-binding practices in ancient China. Female genital mutilation in some parts of Africa and some parts of Asia and the Middle East and, prior to Western colonization, the potlatch ceremony among the Northwest Coast Indian populations are also examples of the collision between and asymmetrical merging of past and present. All these practices, rituals, and/or traditions are learned and widely practiced by older generations and are passed on—generation after generation, largely unaltered or only partially altered—to their children, who at least partially embrace them. Among the adults, these mores, rituals, behaviors, and so on are not only not typically seen as harmful or evil and rejected out of hand, but are often framed as sacred and carefully taught to their children, who are rewarded for embracing them. Unfamiliar influences and the desire to be seen as generationally appropriate sometimes prompt the children and younger generations to alter these traditional practices, but rarely are they completely transformed.[31]

As the ethnographic narratives reported here reveal, the ubiquity of racialized, gender-specific violence is not an aberration; rather, it is emblematic of what is "normal" at Underground Railroad High, and perhaps in the nation. The unacknowledged existence of female-specific aggression, bullying, and competition is exacerbated and repeatedly fueled by the fact that it is simultaneously largely invisible, misrecognized, and, paradoxically, highly rewarded. Female-specific ABC is rewarded through our misrecognition of its existence, our commitment to not seeing it or to rendering it benign rather than harmful when we are compelled to acknowledge its existence—a critical component of the kind of violence that is the focus of this book. It is so often misrecognized because, as I repeatedly note in the narratives included here, our cultural institutions only recognize aggression, bullying, and competition that is embedded in physical violence. (This is clearly revealed in chapters 3 and 5, where both Nadine and Keyshia acknowledge that no adult in the cafeteria was willing to be an advocate not just for fairness but for social and moral justice.) Admittedly, female-specific practices are in some ways racially differentiated, with those most often affiliated with Black females more closely aligned with maleness and masculinity. At UGRH, for example, bodies gendered female that violate this social norm, that is, that engage in physical violence, are severely punished, with the ongoing double-layered "fight"—one physical and one nonphysical—between Nadine and Keyshia and Nadine and Kirstin an outstanding example. All the other narratives reveal how ABC shapes and alters the lives of the female subjects, even those who are at least partially conscious of the distance between the literal meaning of the hegemonic gender-specific race and gender narratives and their lived reality.[32] These binaries are inevitably breached, and the identified "gender-role infringement" leads to sanctions more severe and problematic because female students are unquestionably expected to eschew behaviors and practices typically aligned with males and masculinity.[33] This is a central trope in the lives of the female students at UGRH who cannot unconditionally claim an elite White identity.

As noted above, the cases of Nadine and Keyshia are emblematic of how teenage girls deploy their limited or more literal (mis)understandings of the hegemonic gender narrative and often, unwittingly, reproduce the professed undesired gender subordination, albeit somewhat altered from earlier configurations of these same social issues.[34] Moreover, this gender misrecognition is tethered not only to class but to intraracial and interracial issues. The narrative of the lower-class Black girl Nadine chronicles how she is subjected to ABC by her BFF Keyshia, not because Keyshia is perceived as mean or powerful, a trope typically assigned to women who are identified with these practices, but because she is perceived by both girls to be the person in this friendship duo who is socially and culturally designated to be emotionally powerful.[35] Keyshia feels entitled to Nadine's lower-class friendship and friends, including her boyfriend, primarily because of Nadine's lower-class status and the attendant distance from what Keyshia deems normal: Nadine's "abnormal" family life, massive poverty, lower academic dreams and achievement, and so on. Mimicking the historical racialized practices between lower-class White women and elite White women, in this intraracial conflict, class trumps what these Black girls have learned about gender.

However, their class and intraracial issues are catapulted to a more toxic level when Kirstin, the White girl, and her posse are added to the mix, and their misrecognition makes race appear to be the only issue fueling the reported "fight" in the cafeteria; it is not. Gender and class are also salient issues in this instance of ABC. Kirstin and the other White girls do not offer a class response to the two Black girls. Their primary perception of them is that they are Black; they assume that that is all they need to know. The White girls feel entitled to all the social space in the cafeteria other than the Black Table because they have sat there in the past (sans the presence of Black bodies), and they feel that the Black girls are out of place because they are not at the Black Table. At the table that both groups of girls have chosen, there is more than adequate space for both groups to sit without being in close proximity to each other, but apparently this is not acceptable to the White girls, who insist that the table is theirs and that the Black girls cannot share it—even though they would not have to interact with each other. This leads to the following questions: Is this situation emblematic of what anthropologists have noted repeatedly regarding food and intimacy, that one does not eat with people who are not one's equal, except in instrumental contexts (such as at work)? Have these teenage girls unconsciously learned this cultural message, and are they reproducing it here? Does a similar response pattern exist in other American social contexts?

The first "fight" during the civil rights movement centered on food: the native populations and the Freedom Riders quest for the right to eat in and occupy White public spaces in the presence of White people.[36] Are Black people and other historically marginalized groups similarly resented or marginalized when they are finally permitted to attend formerly all-White segregated schools, universities, parks, department stores, restaurants, movies, theaters, and other public spaces? Is the issue about space or about entitlement and the exclusion it entails? Is our response as researchers and as American citizens adequate when we focus our analyses primarily or exclusively on the behaviors and practices of individual actors in asymmetrical social and cultural settings, leaving the impact of legal, economic, and other policies uninvestigated or, at the very least, underinterrogated?

Brittany's narrative also illuminates the violence at the core of the narratives presented in this book, but for very different reasons. Although her case is exemplary, it also violates the hegemonic, White-elite gender norm that says that Whiteness is not only an unambiguous example of privilege and power; it is also the embodiment of nice. This is so pervasive that, as I have identified it here, White elite females (and some males) make demands by asking questions.[37] Despite her recent arrival and her lack of involvement in any physical altercation, Brittany is not perceived as being nice because she is identified with the "rhetorically nappy" speech practices of African American females.[38] The adult females at the school who view her as White like themselves are aghast at her "inappropriate" racial speech performances and attempt to restrain her by telling me—a stranger whom they see first as Black, second as female, and third as an anthropologist who is studying their school—that Brittany is guilty of deliberately appropriating a Black female discourse style, maybe even a Black identity. Are they trying to say she is guilty of identity theft? The answer to this question is unclear. In Brittany's social world, the White boy is as strange to her as he would be to most of the Black girls at the school. At UGRH, school officials and her White peers identify her as White, based on the normal critical markers of a White identity (skin and/or eye color, hair texture, academic performance at her erstwhile school and the attendant GPA), an "identity confer[ring] tangible and economically valuable benefits [that are] jealously guarded as a valued possession, allowed only to those who [meet] a strict standard of proof."[39] However, because Brittany has not been involved in any physical altercation during her short period at this school, her White interlocutors equate her appropriation of the Black discourse style as prima facie evidence that she is trying to "pass" for Black and feel that therefore, by her very voice, she is guilty of female-specific ABC.[40]

However, as a newcomer to this strange, overwhelmingly White social context, she fails to fully appreciate how her linguistic practices make her appear too adultlike to be embraced as a White girl, or at least as an appropriate elite White female.[41] Having grown up in a predominantly Black environment and having learned and embraced Black cultural sensibilities prior to arriving at UGRH, she is routinely and resoundingly bullied by the predominantly White student body and, ironically, by the adults as well, primarily because of her perceived zealotry toward, overidentification with, and inappropriate class performance of Blackness. Repeatedly accused of "talking like a Black girl" when she is simultaneously recognized as a White girl, she is skewered in the school's public square by teachers and other school administrators, whose responses signal to her school peers how they are to react and interact with her. Struggling to deal with her mother's decision to grant her father custody in order to break her attachment to the inappropriate Black kids in her inner-city school and, at the same time, experiencing peer rejection for the first time—not just from the White students but from the suburban Black students as well—she is ill equipped to handle the unfamiliar gender-specific ABC. As Bucholtz's analysis on the intertwined relationship between language and identity demonstrates, the shift in the linguistic or discursive practices at UGRH is inextricably intertwined with the racial, gender, and class practices of the White kids at this high school.[42] She is identified primarily by her "inappropriate" linguistic practices; her skin color, hair texture, and dress styles are subordinated or secondary identity markers in this context. Brittany's experience supports Bucholtz's assertion that language is critical to identity construction. It is, she insists, used to create, mobilize, and transform one's self-perception and one's perception by others.[43] Brittany's language practices are identified with African Americans, especially African American girls. At this school (and one could argue in America more broadly) this discourse style is viewed as too direct, "aggressive," and by extension it is defined as embracing physical violence, a gender-inappropriate cultural practice.

This may explain why it was extremely difficult to get beyond the idea of physical violence as the central criterion of Blackness. School officials interpreted my requests for appropriate study participants as inevitably Black. In their view, Black females were the only females at the school predisposed to embrace—unconditionally—physical violence, the only violence the vast majority of the adults (mis)recognized. Being (mis)recognized as a Black girl made Brittany guilty of what most adults and students at the school recognized as "aggression," or the desire to harm another, since her way of talking (for example, saying "I am not going to do that" rather than "should I do that?") did not embody what Lisa Delpit identifies as the "veiled use of power," or what I describe here and elsewhere as the "language of uncertainty."[44]

A similar conundrum is revealed in the narrative that chronicles Chloe's life story and, by extension, the life story of many of the other biracial girls. Chloe's presumed connection to a Black "skin-ship" compels virtually everyone to misrecognize her as biologi-cally "Black" even though she disavows any cultural connection to Blackness.[45] Like Brittany, Chloe is engaged in an insatiable quest for an identity unbounded by race, an identity that is "normal." The child of a Black father and a White mother (as were all the biracial girls in the study results reported here), she longs to be seen as nor-mal but feels misrecognized not only by everyone at UGRH, espe-cially by the Black female students, but also by the social categories put in place by the larger society and by which she is forced to live. This has caused her enormous emotional pain, so much so that she has spent a huge amount of time trying to recover from massive bouts of depression, which she connects to the misrecognized vio-lence of gender-specific ABC. She desperately wants to be unteth-ered from the never-ending racialized constraints in her life—the constant forced options: are you Black or are you White? But sur-prisingly, she constantly asks herself and others, "Why can't I just be me?" I had no answer. My inability to give her the answer she sought diminished my standing in her eyes.

Being socially defined as Black is what annoys her most; nobody will allow her to be who she wants to be. Why does Chloe insist on being White, or at the very least, not Black? Indeed, Chloe's con-signment to a Black identity has made her so depressed that she thinks of herself as physically sick, making Blackness a dis-ease she has to overcome.

Ally is also victimized by a similar dis-ease, reflected in her tor-turous relationship with food. She loves food but realizes that if she wants to be seen as gender normal and capable of attracting her male peers' sexual interest and desire, she has to learn not to act on her love of food. She is well aware that she cannot alter her biologi-cally challenged too-tall body, but she thinks she can (through sheer will power), modify the size of her body. The last time she success-fully achieved her goal, she became ill and had to be taken to a clinic in order to recalibrate her life. She loathes the idea of being identi-fied as a fat girl and a too-tall girl. As chronicled in her narrative, she compensates for these "abnormal" features by suppressing her anger and despair, smiling all the time and being very, very nice.

Rehabilitating Violence by Redefining It as—Another Kind of Violence

So how might we rehabilitate the meaning of violence, especially as it affects persons gendered female at UGRH and elsewhere?

As I chronicle it here, the ubiquity of gender-specific violence—the invisible yet deliberate intent to harm—is a deeply hidden component of female identity formation. This kind of violence is fueled and sustained among females not because the practitioners are inherently mean or amoral or immoral but because they are rewarded for embracing this kind of masked conflict by a seemingly innocuous but powerful organizational framework endemic to gated communities (including educational settings): exclusion. Because exclusion is not gender specific (individuals gendered male and female both embrace it) and is rarely physical, in educational settings it is generally seen as a benign (albeit very important) social practice legitimized by its perennial connection to quantifiable measures such as demonstrated physical skills and prowess, SAT scores, GPAs, attendance data. Typically, what makes exclusion a particularly insidious practice among females, especially teenage girls, is the way it is broadly expanded to include many nonquantifiable features that are defined from the perspective of the powerful: class identification, level of beauty, sexual behaviors and practices, and, the ultimate, niceness.

By breaching established boundaries between two distinct disciplinary genres—ethnography and narration—I am able to suggest here that we rehabilitate the meaning of violence to include the symbolic, demonstrating, in the process, how the students' divergent habitus are subordinated to the greater power of the school's and, by extension, the state's and nation's structurally sanctioned rules and regulations. In rehabilitating violence to include more than the physical form (for example, to include fear, hunger, exclusion and

marginalization, pain and suffering, and the like as instances of violence), perhaps we can all rethink the mistaken assumption that individuals gendered female are neither violent nor conflict averse.[46]

As the narratives included here reveal, the students gendered
female at UGRH tend to eschew physical violence and to opt instead for its symbolic form. They do not avoid physical violence
just because they have been carefully taught that it is gender inappropriate; they also respond in this way because they are rewarded
for allowing others to protect them and are severely punished when
they attempt to protect themselves.[47] State-sanctioned, official protectors include male relatives (fathers, brothers, husbands, uncles,
male cousins) and official protectors (police, firefighters, teachers,
and other school officials) and, typically, any "responsible" adult
male. But as the narratives included here also document, the absence of such protection can and often does have disastrous results.
For example, both Enique and Nadine sought to protect themselves
by resorting to physical violence in response to a symbolic form of
violence and paid an inordinate price. Their attempts to self-protect
had unpredicted, unexpected, and unacceptable—even humiliating
and degrading—consequences.

Contemporary and historical assumptions and expectations about
gender-specific normality can be found in every aspect of American
public and private life. Inarguably, America's obligatory system
of schooling is the one remaining institution that the nation re-
lies on most to convey these ideals, to officially certify that what
is practiced therein is state-approved and gender appropriate. In
this book, through the five ethnographic narratives offered here, I
have explored how this normality is engaged and practiced among
a group of Black and White females. Though these girls see themselves as having an undifferentiated gender identity, they do not
see themselves—and are not seen by others—as sharing a common racial (or class) identity. The girls who claimed African ancestry also saw themselves as being permanently assigned the role of
the other and as being the recipients of undeserved and undesired

marginalization. By contrast, the girls who self-identified as having only European ancestry not only do not identify with the Black girls but, as other researchers have noted, seek repeatedly to distance themselves—both spatially and socially—from all girls whom they identify as totally Black or as inappropriate shades of White.[48] Yet despite the ubiquity of this social dynamic, virtually none of the students (and none of the teachers, to my knowledge) sought to alter or even alleviate the situation.

As the narratives included here demonstratively reveal, in some instances, perhaps fortuitously, the legally constituted rules and practices of the school and community impel both desired and undesired gender-specific behaviors and outcomes that, most often, reinforce rather than transform the school and the larger social environment. By carefully crafting these narratives, I have managed to chronicle why it is important to rehabilitate our understanding of violence to explicate the central tenets of symbolic violence, fueled by what Bourdieu identifies as *méconnaissance,* or misrecognition.[49]

Ultimately, by revealing how these girls' individual lust for what is defined as normal or normality merges with what Julie Bettie identities as the fluidity of class formation, they are unwittingly complicit in the reproduction of the intersectionality of race, class, gender, and other forms of unmarked social violence.[50] In this conclusion, I argue that violence—not the physical kind—is in dire need of rehabilitation at UGRH, despite the "niceness" of the behavior of both students and adults, the spotlessness of the physical plant, and the mantra of being totally committed to eradicating all forms of injustice. By engaging in the effort to rehabilitate what we mean by violence, we will all engage in questioning what is seldom interrogated: the banality of normality, here known as violence by another name.

Acknowledgments

Writing a book can be, and often is, a life-altering experience. In writing academic books, where the researcher is dependent on the labor of others, physical and/or emotional, the "I" in the idea of researcher is forced to become an un- or underacknowledged collective "we." Not surprisingly, when my initial, inchoate thoughts fueled the research on which this book is based, the fact that the labor of others is routinely undercompensated became a permanent fixture in my professional life. Thus, from the moment of gestation to the emergence of this book, I have incurred enormous indebtedness, compelling me to struggle with the following questions. How do I repay the people who voluntarily and involuntarily supported my work? How do I appropriately display my gratitude for their support beyond this page in the book that documents the reported findings?

A mentor once told me that in academia (I would add, in all of social life) a debt is not paid until it is acknowledged. But is it paid even then? As I see it, debt and indebtedness are not that easily resolved. Indebtedness between individuals (and groups) with different pedigrees is far more nuanced, enduring, and problematic. This is exacerbated by the seemingly universal claim that achievement is an individual accomplishment, and if the "achiever" is unable or unwilling to acknowledge her indebtedness, there is no debt.

I only know that I am indebted to an army of people, some who deliberately intended to help me and others who did so unintentionally or involuntarily. In both situations, I benefited: I learned and grew professionally, and for that I am grateful.

My first and most serious gratitude and indebtedness is to the suburban school district that was the site of the study reported here.

More specifically, I am grateful to the students who participated in this study, their parents and peers, their teachers and administrators, an array of counselors and other professionals—for example, social workers and psychologists—and the workers who cleaned the floors, cooked the meals, drove the buses, and dispensed bandages and pills at the school. A special thank-you is extended to the person whose unconditional support paved the way for me to do the study at the school (you know who you are) and to the woman I identify in this book as Ms. Redding, the Harriet Tubman in my success at the school. Simply saying thank you to all these unidentified but supportive people, who cannot be named because of the confidentiality agreement between me and school officials, seems profoundly inadequate. But, unfortunately, it will have to do—for now.

My second most serious indebtedness goes to Peter Demerath and the anonymous readers whom the University of Minnesota Press chose to review my manuscript at various stages of the process. To these colleagues, I am eternally grateful. Their comments, suggestions, and belief in the work chronicled here both reassured and alarmed me.

My third most serious indebtedness during the time I worked on this book is to the people who freely supported me at my worksite and elsewhere, even when it was difficult and/or problematic. They include Rogaia Abusharaf; Linda Allen; Ashley Anderson; Nancy Ares; Alexinia Baldwin; Michael Barney; Lynn Bolles; Edward Brokenbrough; Lyn Mikel Brown; Oliver Cashman Brown; Berthenia Coltrane; Eileen Daly-Boas; Katherine Detherage; Michael Eric Dyson; Tyler Dzuba; Margaret Eisenhart; Doug Foley; Iris Carter Ford; Sam Fullwood III; Donna Harris; Ruth Harris; Faye Harrison; Bernice and Herman Howard; Kay Hunter; Frederick Jefferson; John L. Johnson; Renee Larrier; Joanne Larson; Joloire Lature; Nick Long; J. Lorand Matory; Henrietta Moore; Diane Morse; NIISYF; Joe Pasquarelli; Hoang Pham; Evelyn Phillips; Ghislaine Radegonde-Eison; Luisa-Maria Rojas-Rimachi; Arlette Miller Smith; Dena Swanson; Yvonne and Peter Tolliver;

Eve Tuck; Cheryl Wall; Frank, Nathan, and Alexis Weathers; and Deborah Gray White.

For making me stronger and more determined, I am grateful to the members of the Susan B. Anthony Institute for Gender and Women's Studies, the Margaret Warner School of Education, and the Department of Anthropology and the Dean's Office in the College of Arts and Sciences at the University of Rochester. I am also profoundly grateful to Dean Mary Ann Mavrinac, whose employment made it possible for me to regain access to the academic resources housed in Rush Reeves Library.

I also express indebtedness and gratitude to the University of Minnesota Press, Pieter Martin, and his assistant, Anne Carter. The Press's decision to publish my book altered the course of my professional life, and for that I am grateful.

Finally, I am eternally grateful for the support of my family of orientation, especially my sister-moms, their children, and their friends. And in the tradition of many African American families, friends become fictive kin with all the rights and responsibilities of kinship. On this solo flight, I am beyond lucky to have a flotilla of friends (and even a few frenemies) who profoundly support and challenge me daily.

Notes

Introduction

1. I am indebted to one of my neighbors for the "cement gray" characterization of the winter weather in upstate New York.

2. Bystanders and what is known as the "bystander effect" (Sullivan 2000; Coloroso 2003) are critical to the idea of female aggression, bullying, and competition, especially since females tend to limit their aggression, bullying, and competition to other females. Sisterhood—a dominating trope in female identity construction—is generally seen as a seamless lovefest, with females living in idyllic harmony with others of their gender. This partial truth elides the jealousy, hostility, and competition that exist even among blood-related, same-sex siblings, often in ways that mimic the "intimate apartheid" chronicled in this text (Bourgois and Schonberg 2009).

3. Enique did not use the words "critical mass." What I understood her to mean was that she did not like being alone in unsupervised spaces in the wake of the fight she had had with a White female peer almost a year earlier.

4. As I hope will become crystal clear, the kind of cruelty, aggression, and brutality discussed in this book is not the kind of gratuitous violence that suddenly erupts in mass murder, killings like those that occurred at Sandy Hook Elementary School in Connecticut, at the University of California at Santa Barbara, and in the mass slaughter of nine church worshippers in South Carolina; like the ethnic cleansings in Bosnia and elsewhere; like guerrilla warfare in Nicaragua. Instead, the kind of violence that is the subject of this book is virtually invisible, often unnamed, in that it is built into the fabric of our society; "part of the routine grounds of everyday life and transformed into expressions of moral worth . . . the most violent acts consist of conduct that is socially permitted, encouraged, or enjoined as a moral right or a duty" (Scheper-Hughes and Bourgois 2003, 4–5). In this context, "most violence," Scheper-Hughes and Bourgois argue, "is

not deviant behavior, not disapproved of, but to the contrary is defined as virtuous action in the service of generally applauded conventional social, economic and political norms" (5).

5. The word "adaptation" is used here in the anthropological sense meaning the process by which populations—human and nonhuman— are able to alter their traditional behaviors and practices in order to meet current social conditions, making it more likely that they will be able to survive extreme circumstances (Diamond 1997, 55, 236).

6. In this book, I use "African American" and "Black" interchangeably, except in those instances when I am referring to people of African ancestry from other parts of the colonial and African diaspora.

7. Formal interview, 2 April 2005.

8. As I write this book, the word "bullying"—unspecified by gender—is widely used to describe a smorgasbord of social ills, including what are known as "cyberbullying," "one-on-one combat," or attacks by a small group of girls (two to three) who once—or currently—see themselves as friends.

9. Unlike Alvin Poussaint (1972), I am much more interested in naming and describing the elided violence affiliated with the omnipresent headwinds, compelling the intragroup response to Blackness and other Black people that is indistinguishable from that of American citizens who do not identify as having African ancestry.

10. Perry 2001, 2002. Pamela Perry's astute observation affirms what most readers of this book will understand: one of the major features of high school is Exclusion, with a capital E, in an unending variety of forms. This is especially true in the case of persons gendered female. Girls appear to be much more adept at and preoccupied with cliques and appropriate groupness than their male peers. See also Hall 2000, 630–43; Leek 2013.

11. L. Brown 1998, 2003, 201.

12. Ward and Edelstein 2005, 15. See also Butler 2011.

13. I do not mean to suggest that I am so naive that I do not believe that there are no students and no adults at the school who are mentally challenged and who might, therefore, be capable of being biologically predisposed to practice meanness (the thug term for female violence) despite culturally appropriate efforts to mediate this predisposition.

14. "Spinster" is the term silently used to refer to successful women in the American context (Bolick 2015); Leta Hong Fincher (2014) uses the term "leftover women" to describe the same women in China. Fincher's varied data compel us to acknowledge that while we are taught to see

power as most visibly manifested in numbers, the contemporary gender imbalance that favors boys in China (and other Asian cultures, including India) is the result of a state-sponsored one-child rule. Combined with a preference for boys and a tendency to abort a female fetus, the fact that there are so few women in that age range does not impel females to a place of power. Instead, these professionally successful women who have not found a man to marry by their late twenties are labeled "leftover women."

15. See, for example, Ferguson 2001. See also Long 2007; Foucault 1977.

16. See, for example, Low 2001; Oakes 2005; Hacker 2003; Shumar 2004.

17. Following Moone 1983, 241, I argue that *maintenance* and *change* are two social processes that coexist. This is probably the best way to view the ongoing fight for gender equity in our country, with the intellectual and elite segments insisting that inequitable gender roles are no longer a reality (although many of them are the strongest proponents of maintaining these roles, especially for children widely labeled "other") (Ostrander 1984), and with the majority of the remaining segments of the society on a continuum that is freighted with traditional child-rearing practices and gendered expectations.

18. Gladwell 2011; Hacker 2003; Massey and Denton 1998.

19. Long and Moore 2013a, 2013b. See also Robbins 2006; Gladwell 2011; Demerath 2009; Fordham 2013a; Long 2007.

20. In a recently released report, Kimberelé Crenshaw (2015) offers a devastatingly chilling analysis of this underacknowledged differential.

21. Wilder 2013.

22. Low 2001, 45.

23. See, for example, Hwang 2005, which vividly chronicles White parents' removing their children from a predominately Asian American high school in California because they feared that the Asian students were altering the standards that the White student population had established. See also Barlow and Dunbar 2010; C. Harris 1993; Staiger 2004, 2011; Lareau (2003) 2011; DeCuir-Gunby 2006.

24. C. Harris 1993.

25. Bourgois and Schonberg 2009. See also L. Brown 2003; Low 2009.

26. Fordham and Ogbu 1986. See also Fordham 1993, 1996, 1998b, 1999.

27. The intersectionality of race and gender are major cultural categories and central issues at the heart of this book and will be defined and explicated in chapter 1.

28. See, for example, the recent police beating of Ersula Ore on the

campus of Arizona State University, a Texas state trooper's demand that Sandra Bland get out of car or he would "light her up," and the beating of a Black woman by a policeman for jaywalking near a California freeway. All this violence was state enforced and perpetrated by a (White) man.

29. See also K. Scott 1990; Das et al. 2001; Coloroso 2003; Butler 2011, 25.

30. Fordham 2007b.

31. Kimmel 2002, 42–44. See also Freire and Ramos 1993 for a parallel, albeit similar, analysis.

32. I interpret Bourdieu's notion of "habitus" to be an amalgamation of individual and structural realities or experiences that shifts and changes over time, depending upon the context. See Bourdieu 1984, 170. See also Bourdieu and Nice 2000, 42; Scheper-Hughes and Bourgois 2003, 1–31; Bourgois 2007, 7–31; Scheper-Hughes 1993, 1–10.

33. Pollock 2004. See also Touré 2012; Fordham 2010, 4–30, for a critique of the idea of a postracial America.

34. Levi 2004, 83–90.

35. Reed-Dahanay 1997; C. Ellis and Bochner 2000; C. Ellis 2004.

36. Moss 2003.

37. Ibid., 116.

38. Bourdieu 1984, 1985. I do not mean to imply that individual responsibility is not an issue in this analysis of the lives of the students I studied at UGRH. It is, but it is not the only or even the major issue. Structural violence constructs individual inadequacies. I borrow the phrase "rehabilitating violence" from Kebede 2001.

39. Clifford 1986, 6. He does not mean that they are not truthful. Instead, he rightfully suggests that like virtually all elements of social life—including race and gender—ethnographies are scripted, reiterated enactments.

40. Ibid., 6.

41. Ibid., 7. Emphasis in the original.

42. Nader 1972.

43. Bourgois and Schonberg 2009; Bourdieu 1984, 1985.

44. "Statusitis" is the term I have coined here to describe Americans' preoccupation—and according to many ethnographic studies, the preoccupation of many other human population groups—with "bling" or material things. See chapter 2 for a more detailed description of this concept. See also de Button 2004; L. Brown 1998, 2003; Milner 2006.

45. See, for example, Bourdieu and Nice 2000; Bourdieu and Wacquant 2004; Scheper-Hughes 1993. See also Crick and Grotpeter 1995; Merten 1996, 1997; Simmons 2002; Olweus 1993; Chisom and Harrington 1997; Orenstein 1993.

46. Almost everyone is able to identify a social practice in a particular context that is viewed as normal, and all members of that community are expected to embrace it as a sign that they belong to that community. Individuals who seek to eschew participating in such socially approved practices are most often ostracized, humiliated, and/or alienated from what is seen as their native group. Many disparate practices come to mind, including foot-binding among the ancient Chinese, female genital mutilation in some African countries, and snake worshiping and polygamy in some religious communities in America. Individuals who are able to embrace such painful and disfiguring normal practices can fortify their acceptance within these communities. Those individuals who are in some way identified with the community but seek to avoid participating in and/or to change these normal practices are viewed as abnormal and subjected to all kinds of overtly physical, mental, and emotional violence. Regrettably, in most instances, the only kind of violence that is recognized in the collision of these forces is what is socially defined as physical.

47. Kebede 2001; see also Fanon 2008; Schoolman and Potholm 1979.

48. See, for example, Fanon 2008; Woodson 1933; Du Bois (1903) 1994; Levi 2004; Poussaint 1972.

49. Intimate apartheid "operates at the preconscious level, expressing itself as embodied emotions, attitudes, and ways of acting that reinforce distinctions, which in turn become misrecognized as natural racial attributes" (Bourgois and Schonberg 2009, 42).

50. Fanon 2008; Fanon and Philcox 2005. See also Kebede 2001.

51. See Kebede 2001, 539.

52. Typically, "fratricide" is defined as a brother killing his brother. There is no equivalent term that identifies a sister killing her sister. However, "fratricide" is often used to encompass killing brothers and sisters. As a metaphor, that is the way in which I use it here: sisters killing sisters, embedded in the book title, *Downed by Friendly Fire*.

53. Marvin Harris (1975, 2001) argues that in hierarchically arranged social systems, the groups most disadvantaged economically and socially by their placement in it are, ironically, the ones most likely to fight for the continuation of the extant social system. See also J. Scott 1999.

54. How ironic that in order to have even a remote chance to protest the extant normality of the violence that made Black Americans eligible for de jure as well as de facto segregation, the affiliated, precipitating degradation and humiliation they endured every hour of every day, they had to agree to eschew the kind of physical violence that was what their interlopers used to compel them to obey, forcing them to be complicit in the violence imposed upon them.

55. Brettell 1996; Messerschmidt 1992.

56. For some of the most highly ranked school officials and some of the teachers and staff who were involuntary participants, I regret that my efforts to camouflage their identity beyond providing a pseudonym might not be seen as sufficient.

57. See Fordham 2010.

58. In some instances, my field notes and the students' formal interviews and diaries have been edited to conserve space, reduce redundancy, and eliminate identifying information.

59. Lewis-McCoy 2014.

60. In a recent lecture, author Lawrence Hill (2007) repeatedly notes the conflict and discomfort affiliated with naming people of African ancestry, an issue facing the protagonist in his popular book. His claim resonated in that I was often referred to in the third person by people in my presence who knew my name: "She said . . ." and not by my name (either first or last) or by my professional role. I have embraced that practice here, especially in chapter 2.

61. See Fiske (1989) 2011. See note 63 below.

62. It is important to reiterate that all names of members of the community are pseudonyms.

63. As John Fiske ([1989] 2011, 20) explains "nomadic subjectivities": "The necessity of negotiating the problems of everyday life within a complex, highly elaborated social structure has produced nomadic subjectivities who can move around [a] grid, aligning their social allegiances into different formations . . . according to the necessities of the moment. All these reformations are made within a structure of power relations, all social allegiances have not only a sense of *with whom* [emphasis in the original] but also of *against whom* [emphasis in the original]: indeed, I would argue that the sense of oppositionality, the sense of difference, is more determinant than that of similarity of class identity, for it is shared antagonisms that produce the fluidity that is characteristic of the people in elaborated societies."

1. Frenemies and Friendly Fire at Underground Railroad High

1. Typically, "friendly fire" is associated with official warfare and refers to the firing of weapon(s) that injures or kills an ally or a member of one's own armed forces. The act of harming or killing the individual(s) is not accidental but intentional because the harmed person is misrecognized. I use it here as a metaphor to describe the structurally and culturally approved, albeit often unconscious, gender-specific bullying, relational aggression, and competition that is repeatedly misidentified and or misrecognized in the varied ways the Black and White female students perceive and interact with each other, using words or language—not guns, knives, or blunt instruments—as their primary weapon in this ongoing, endless friendly fire.

2. See, for example, the work of Pierre Bourdieu, Michel Foucault, Loïc Wacquant, and Arun Gandhi, as well as of anthropologists Paul Farmer, Phillip Bourgois, Veena Das, and Nancy Scheper-Hughes and Phillip Bourgois.

3. Gandhi 2012. Symbolic or structural violence is "not the result of accident or a *force majeure*; not the consequence, direct or indirect, of human agency" (Farmer 2004, 40). See also Galtung 1969.

4. Bourdieu and Wacquant 2004, 272–74.

5. Ibid., 272.

6. Bourdieu 2004, 339.

7. Ibid., 340–41.

8. Ibid., 339.

9. Bachrach and Baratz 1962, 947–52.

10. In a recent study reported by the Pew Research Center on Social and Demographic Trends, 40 percent of women with children under the age of eighteen make more money than their spouse or spousal equivalent. Wang, Parker, and Taylor 2013.

11. Guinier and Torres 2002.

12. The word "Black" in parentheses before "female," "woman," and the like is intended both to note that this racial category is generally subordinated in most contexts and to indicate that this is not limited to this racial category, in part, at least, because of the interlocking character of the categories race, class, gender, and so on.

13. See, for example, Lareau (2003) 2011, 308.

14. Das 2004, 327–33.

15. O'Neal 2012; Murphy and Choi 1997, 97–112.

16. Choi, Callaghan, and Murphy 1995, 132. See also Foucault 1977.

17. There are two spellings of this term: "frenemy" and "frienemy." I have opted here to use the first—frenemy—rather than the second.

18. MacLeod 2009, 97.

19. Chesler 2009.

20. Fordham 2013a, 2013d; Spender and Sarah 1988.

21. Das 2004, 327–33.

22. Hochschild 1983, 7. See also 1979, 551–75.

23. Fordham 2012b.

24. Bolton 2005; Bolles 2005.

25. Rosaldo 2004. See also Lutz 1995, 249–66; Stoller 1989; Hochschild 1979, 551–75; 1983.

26. Levi 2004, 90.

27. Das 2004, 327.

28. McCall 1994, 41–52.

29. Early 1993; D. White 1985; Stoler 2000; Murray (1956) 1999, 33–44; Williams 1995; Weems 2004; Morrison 1994.

30. Two examples: AAUW 1995; Rimm-Kaufman and Rimm 1999.

31. Hossfeld 1994, 65–93.

32. See chapter 7, "Ally," in this volume.

33. Chesler 1994.

34. Kendall 2002, 91, emphasis added; Goodwin 2006.

35. Kendall 2002, 82. See also Ostrander 1984.

36. Low 2009, 79–92.

37. Unlike what is mandated in New York State today, at the time I was engaged in the fieldwork for this study, only two Regents Exams were required of all students in order to graduate.

38. Barlow and Dunbar 2010, 63–85; C. Harris 1993, 1707–95.

39. C. Harris 1993; Lewis-McCoy 2014; Barlow and Dunbar 2010.

40. Kochman and Mavrelis, 2009.

41. Ibid., 119, emphasis added.

42. Newman 1999. See also Kochman and Mavrelis 2009.

43. Maslow (1943) 2013. See also Ferguson 2001.

44. AAUW 1995.

45. Fordham 1993, 3–32; 1996.

46. Coloroso 2003.

47. Long and Moore 2013a. See also Fordham 2013a, 206–28.

48. I don't think I need to say this but just in case: Not every person gendered female interacts with other females in this manner; many do.

49. Coloroso 2003; Pipher and Ross 1994; Wiseman 2002; Lamb 2001; L. Brown 1998, 2003.

50. Simmons 2002.

51. During the proposal stage of the study reported here, like so many other researchers, I embraced the term "meanness" (Lamb 2001; Wiseman 2002; Waters 2004). As the study unfolded and I came to more fully appreciate the role of structural violence in my student participants' quest for what is identified as normal in our culture, I became more and more ambivalent about what I now think is a term too closely aligned with a biological perspective.

52. Simmons 2002, 189. See also Weitz and Gordon 1993, 19–33.

53. Lamb 2001, 227.

54. Ibid.

55. Coloroso 2003, 163.

56. Coloroso 2003.

57. Coloroso 2001, 20.

58. Levi 2004, 84.

59. Foucault 1977. See also Fiske (1989) 2011.

60. Delpit and Dowdy 2002. See also Baugh and Labov 1999.

61. Delpit 1988, 1996; L. Brown 2003.

62. Levi 2004, 83–90.

63. Kebede 2001, 539–62.

64. Fordham 1985, 1988, 1996, 2005, 2008, 2009.

65. Neal-Barnett 2001a, 2001b; Tyson, Darrity, and Castellino 2005; Tyson 2011; Ferguson 1996, 2001; Fryer and Leavitt 2004; Cosby and Poussaint 2007; Dyson 2005; Ainsworth-Darnell and Downey 1998; Cook and Ludwig 1998; Norwood 2007; Obama 1995, 2006; Young 2007; Horvat and O'Connor 2006; A. Harris 2011; Ogbu 2004, 2008.

66. Neal-Barnett 2001b, xv–xvii; Young 2007; and my collaborator, Ogbu 2004, 2008.

67. James Scott (1990) asserts that in state systems, "hidden transcripts" are laden with the deception and guise of the powerful, the elites.

68. J. Scott 1990, 1999, 2009.

69. Foucault 1977. See also Fiske (1989) 2011.

70. Conrad 2007.

71. Ibid.; Conrad and Schneider 1980; Washington 2006; Skloot 2010. See also Lovett-Scott and Prather 2014; Bowick 2013.

72. Chisom and Harrington 1997.

73. Nader 1972.

74. Pollock 2004, 2.

75. Wise 2011, 131.

76. Choi, Callaghan, and Murphy 1995; Lyotard 1984.

77. Fordham 2007a.

78. See chapter 5, "Keyshia," in this volume. There is an entire body of literature addressing the "medicalization of social problem" and as W. E. B. Du Bois argued so poignantly by asking, "What does it mean to be a problem?," for many Americans, the meaning of Blackness is evoked not by the endemic structural violence in the nation but by the imagined pervasive inadequacies of individual Black citizens and can rightfully be seen as a dis-ease that can be overcome by individual motivation, desire, persistence, and effort. See, for example, Conrad 2007; Conrad and Schneider 1980; Jones 1981; Washington 2006; Farmer 2004; Skloot 2010; Bowick 2013; Detherage 2014; Lovett-Scott and Prather 2014; Bass 2001, 219–30.

79. Crenshaw 1989, 2015.

80. C. Harris 1993.

81. Early 1993.

82. Rosenberg 1997, 80.

83. Ibid.

84. See, for example, Kimberlé Crenshaw's recent report *Black Girls Matter* (2015).

85. Ferguson 2001.

86. See, for example, Alex Tizon's memoir (2014), in which he notes how the dominant American image of Asian males compelled him (and them) to embrace "self-annihilation" in order to cope with their social placement at the bottom of the American male hierarchy.

87. See Fordham 1993; Evans 1988.

88. Ferguson 2001.

89. Grant 1984.

90. Schofield 1982.

91. Nadine's nickname and the name her BFF, Keyshia, used to refer to her almost exclusively.

92. Bucholtz 2011; Tannen 1990. See also Coates 2015a.

93. See Delpit 1988, 1996; Baugh and Labov 1999; Delpit and Dowdy 2002; Heath 1983.

94. Delpit 1988, 1996; Lareau (2003) 2011; Tannen 1990.

95. Fordham 2013a. See also Gee 2004; Delpit 1988, 1996; Foster 1989; Tannen 1994.

96. Affect embodies their fear, their memory of the endless pain they endure. Coates 2015b. See also Delpit 1988, 1996; Bucholtz 2011.

97. Coates 2015b. See also Coates 2015a.

98. Heath 1983. See also Gadsden 1994.

99. Delpit 1988, 1996. See also Tannen 1990 and Lareau (2003) 2011 for examples of indirectness or uncertainty.

100. See, for example, Baugh 1983; Kochman 1972; Smitherman (1977) 1988.

101. Delpit 1988, 280–98.

102. Ibid.

103. Choi, Callaghan, and Murphy 1995; Das 2004. See also Scheper-Hughes and Bourgois 2003, 1–31.

104. Ogbu 1981, 413–29. See also Swanson, Edwards, and Spencer 2010; Spencer, Dobbs, and Swanson 1988.

105. Ogbu 1981, 413–29. See also Stockman 2015.

106. See Page 2000 for a compelling discussion of Black bodies in "White public space[s]."

107. Lewis-McCoy 2014; Lareau (2003) 2011.

108. While Raygine DiAquoi's recent (2015) study is an analysis of "the talk" and African American males, I reference it here to assure the reader that a similar, gender-specific "talk" is the focus of the interactions between Black parents and their daughters. See, for example, K. Scott 1990.

109. Barrett 2000.

110. See Baumrind 1972; Clark 1983; Delpit 1988; Fordham 1993, 1996; Heath 1983; K. Scott 1990.

111. K. Scott 1990.

112. Ibid., 1–2.

113. Fordham 1993, 3–32.

114. Hull, Scott, and Smith 1982.

2. Last Stop on the Underground Railroad, First Stop of Refried Segregation

1. This became the anthropologist's routine on the days she went to the school—Tuesdays, Thursdays, and Fridays (and often she spent time on weekends in the community) while class was in session for her at the university. When her semester ended, she spent every day at the research site until the semester ended there in the middle of June.

2. The year before the anthropologist began the study reported here, as is the usual practice, she hired a snow-removal company to clear the snow from her driveway. In order to get to her gym class and back home in time to get to the research site, she requested and was assured that she would be among the first customers in the morning. This agreement was not honored, so she decided to simply remove the snow herself. As with most females, a central feature of her childhood enculturation was the value attached to the eschewal of hard labor, especially in a public context (though one was rewarded profusely for cleaning one's house until one's nose bled—daily). Historically, this practice is very much alive, at least in the community where she lived, to retain the image of femaleness and elite class status. Work outside one's home marks a woman as less feminine and lower class, a problematic construction, especially for Black girls.

3. At the site and in making bullet points, the anthropologist continued the archaic practice of recording field notes inconspicuously by hand in the way she had learned from one of her primary mentors, John Ogbu, during her dissertation research. She reserved the tape recorder for use in the car and in formal interviews. Today, the prevalence of mobile recording devices makes this practice seem quaint and inefficient.

4. Hair is a primary marker of femininity (see Eilberg-Schwartz and Doniger 1995). It is such an object of desire that, like female genitalia, in some parts of the world it must not be seen. In the United States it is considered normal and acceptable if it fits the hegemonic narrative of being long and straight; it is the object of inordinate desire if it is also blond. My hair does not meet any of these criteria. My African American ancestry is clearly visible in what I have described elsewhere as my "love affair with my arrogant hair" (Fordham 2007a). In discussions with trusted female friends and colleagues prior to commencing the study, I was given contradictory advice on how to style my hair. Looking back, I fear that I chose the wrong option: unstraightened.

5. D. Lee 1987; Malinowski 1932. Ideally in anthropology, once one has become a professor and acquired tenure, graduate students are deployed to do fieldwork and the professor mentors them as they seek to become members of the academy. Usually the only exceptions are faculty who opt to study abroad during the summer months or during semester-long or sabbatical leaves granted for the academic year. This is the hegemonic practice because of the laborious nature of and complexity affiliated with a research modality that entails continuous involvement with one's research population: ethnography and ethnographic research. This was not an option in my case. I elected to study female competition in a high school,

which meant that I had to be on site when the students were there: during the academic year. I was not eligible for a sabbatical, and my internal research funds were insufficient to support my absence from the classroom and my other academic duties. Consequently, not only was I revisiting what I had done as a doctoral student, but also I had no graduate students because the academic department where I was working had lost its graduate program several years before I arrived. I was, allegedly, in the "arrival" stage of my career. Most of the faculty and staff at UGRH knew this, but I sought to minimize the students' access to this information, at least initially, to make it easier to obtain the desired number of student participants. I sought to minimize the distinction between myself and them because experience had taught me that there is some unconscious and unmarked issue (*méconnaissance,* or misrecognition) at work in the interactions of "successful" Black bodies and other subordinate bodies—even teenage ones—an issue that is connected to race and gender "indebtedness" and the inability to get beyond that status.

6. Fordham 1993, 1996, 1998b, 1999; Fordham and Ogbu 1986.

7. Goffman 1990.

8. The Research Subject Review Board (RSRB) process was extremely laborious and intense. Having sought and acquired approval from similar research entities before for an earlier study (Fordham 1996; Fordham and Ogbu 1986), I did not fully appreciate the networking influence and power—that is, the underground impact—of even one well-placed, fully embraced, disgruntled individual. I had been told that the process usually took six to nine weeks. I should have taken to heart a male friend's claim that there is a "Black tax" that applies to everything, especially in areas that have a history of excluding people of African ancestry. He was right; the process took almost nine months. This was not a total anomaly. Anthropologists (and other social scientists) have reported and lamented this process that compels all members of the university community to live by the requirements of the STEM disciplines (science, technology, engineering, and mathematics) and the medical schools. This appears to be a common problem for anthropologists at many colleges; see, for example, an issue of one of the discipline's major journals—*American Ethnologist* 33, no. 4 (2006)—for several articles addressing it. Despite the commonality of this issue, the way it twisted my research agenda is noteworthy.

9. As in most American R1 universities (those classified as conducting the highest research activity), the spring semester at the institution where I work ends near the beginning of May.

10. Several people have suggested that this could have been a part of the unacknowledged hazing process that newcomers to an academic institution routinely experience.

11. "Naboh" is the term used by Yarami, the little Yanomami girl who married the American anthropologist in the National Geographic film *Yanomami Homecoming* (1994). She used it to describe her foreignness and her relationship to anthropologists and other Americans in New Jersey, where she came to live with her American anthropologist husband.

12. Low (2003, 17) defines a "gated community" geographically as "[a] residential development surrounded by walls, fences, or earth banks covered with bushes and shrubs, with a secured entrance." In practical terms, she points out, "gated communities limit access to streets and thoroughfares that would otherwise be available for public as well as for private transportation." It is the "limited access" component of her definition that informs my perception of many public school curricular offerings, including those at UGRH.

13. Loewen 2005.

14. At this school, cars are both a much-desired status symbol and a way to delay the time one has to get up in the morning.

15. Donald Messerschmidt (1992, 3) makes the case for what Margaret Mead disparagingly labeled "baby anthropologists" breaking with tradition and beginning their professional journey by studying "at home," among native peoples. As Mead points out, until fairly recently it was widely accepted that the proper areas of research for anthropologists were in cultural contexts considered foreign. Research by anthropologists in their own societies has become more widely accepted, partly because of a heightened awareness of social problems within so-called developed societies. Messerschmidt's book examines how innovative scholars applied anthropology to nontraditional research questions in urban and rural societies, in the legal, health, and education systems, and in the field of contract anthropology.

16. Collins 1991; Scheurich and Young 1997.

17. Baldwin 1985, 641–47.

18. Baldwin quoted in Ford 2010, 53–60.

19. Baldwin quoted in C. Lee, Spencer, and Harpalani 2003.

20. A visual artist friend declares that this is not unusual and is, in fact, a response to the decadence so prevalent in earlier iterations of decadent housing (Nunoo-Quarcoo, personal communication).

21. The virtual absence of the Black students as visible and eager par-

ticipants in the music and art programs at this school was unexpected, inexplicable, and troublesome.

22. These workers apparently had an official underground existence. The anthropologist did see such workers when she returned to the school after dismissal for activities such as step team and chorus practice, basketball and football games.

23. Low 2009. This concept seems to parallel Staiger 2004. See also L. Brown 2003.

24. Low 2009, 79.

25. Ibid., 87.

26. Page 2000.

27. Baugh and Labov 1999.

28. Ogbu 1978.

29. There was an overflow room across from the cafeteria where about twenty-five students met and ate lunch daily. This space was also cleaned by the custodial staff.

30. Moss 2003. I am indebted to Kirby Moss for the use of the term "paradox of privilege."

31. Staiger 2004.

32. I want to emphasize here in the strongest possible terms that there is nothing racially, culturally, or biologically wrong with Black people who are compelled or choose to live in poor areas. Poverty is not a disease—even though it causes enormous dis-ease. What I am trying to make abundantly clear is that despite my work ethic (or maybe because of it), my academic credentials, and my academic worksite, I am frequently viewed through the prism most often affiliated with an American of African ancestry.

33. Lewis 2001.

34. Mauss (1950) 1990. See also Bellafante 2013; Falcone 2013.

35. Rosenberg 1997, 79–89, esp. 80.

36. In the African American community of my youth, the term "haint" was used to describe an apparition, an omnipresent boogeyman, someone to be feared because of his (it was never a female) unlimited and unknown power.

37. While she was not assigned an office (she was only there three days a week), she was given access to the counselors' consultation office and allowed to use it on an ad hoc basis when they were not using it.

38. The anthropologist did not dare tell her that she would never be without her field notes pad and the unofficial official copies of the research

forms. She had given the human resources person the official copies prior to her first day of the project. This was nonnegotiable. The unofficial copies made her legitimate. Moreover, she was fearful of leaving her field notes pad in the possession of someone else, worried that that might compromise her ability to maintain the only contingency she promised to honor: total confidentiality.

39. All names, including the name given the community, the school, the students, their parents, the teachers, and other school officials, are pseudonyms used to protect the persons involved in the study and to honor the promise of confidentiality.

40. Included in the label "insufficiently girlie" is the idea that they are too aggressive, most often the instigators of physical fights—a marker of underdeveloped, hegemonic femininity.

41. Of the twenty-two girls in the study, not one indicated that she did not want to become a mother at some point in her life—most of them planned to do so earlier rather than later. Several of them noted that they did not want to be mothers in the near future, but they also noted that they did eventually want to become a mother—with or without a partner.

42. None of the girls who agreed to participate in the study acknowledged being gay or transsexual. At the time this study was conducted, being gay and/or transsexual was not as widely accepted as it is today. There may have been girls who were sexually attracted to other girls but who, since this had virtually no bearing on this study, did not acknowledge their "true" sexuality.

43. Interestingly, girls whose SAT scores, GPA, and other measurable, official credentials suggest that they are academically equal to their male peers and could compete with them in the widely touted, male-dominated STEM fields repeatedly opt out of those academic areas for "lessor majors" once they get to college in order to put themselves on a "sexual auction-block" (Holland and Eisenhart 1990, 128–29, 163–80).

44. For a detailed and appropriate discussion of how epistemologies influence teaching in diverse settings, see Scheurich and Young 1997, 4–16.

45. Perry 2002.

46. "Statusitis" is a term I have coined to describe the social epidemic, omnipresent in most of the world's cultures, fueled by an unrelenting, unending quest for prominence and/or recognition from peers and important others. Typically, it starts with siblings and spreads like wildfire throughout our lifetime of social networks. Murray Milner (2006) is informative here in that he attributes the existence of this phenomenon at the

high school level to teenagers' lack of control over most of what goes on in school and their desire to exclude adults from their social formations.

47. For similar material situations and parenting styles elsewhere, see Chua 2011; Demerath 2009; Lareau (2003) 2011; and Robbins 2006.

48. Academic competition with Asian Americans is a deeply fraught issue for White students and their parents. For an in-depth discussion of how the White parents at a highly competitive high school in California with a large Asian American population reacted to these students' tendency to outperform their children academically by moving their children to schools with fewer Asian American students, see Hwang 2005.

49. Fordham 2013a. The operative term here is "visibility." Like most human groups, these students want to be designated "accomplished." I am convinced that if Black students were able to achieve the academic goals of America's public schools without the unrelenting surveillance of their peers, without resource hoarding by powerful parents and prominent adults, and without the uninvited disapproval of segments of the larger society, their performance would be indistinguishable from that of their White peers.

50. Claude Steele's important work in this area (2010) has broadened our understanding of how existing stereotypes hamper and in some instances even stifle academic effort, not just for Black students, male and female, but also for all other others, including women and people with disabilities—regardless of race or ethnicity. What he acknowledges is that at this point he has not looked at conjoined stereotypes; that is, he has not asked what happens when there is more than one primary stereotype influencing one body, as in the situation of a woman who is disabled or a person who is Black and female.

51. See Milner 2006; Dickar 2008; Merten 1997.

52. Low 2003.

53. The anthropologist was baffled by the nearly total absence of Black and other teachers of color at UGRH and by the lack of any concerted effort on the part of parents to force the Rodman school district to hire such teachers. This led her to wonder if these parents unconsciously assumed that the chief criterion for a good teacher was Whiteness.

54. Field notes, 18 February 2004.

55. A much more detailed demographic picture of the school is available on the school's official Web site. However, since one of the primary goals is to maintain the privacy of the students and parents who agreed to participate in this study, the school's Web site is not identified here.

56. Field notes, 18 February 2004.

57. Field notes, Rodman Board of Education Meeting, February 2004.

58. It is ironic that in a publicly funded institution the children of the citizens paying the highest portion of their salaries in taxes are targeted for exclusion from the most elite courses and programs. In this sense, their parents pay for the children of the people who pay the smallest percentage of their earned income in taxes, making the wealthier kids the recipients of the unwitting largesse of the poor. As I argue elsewhere (Fordham 2013b) this is how the academy, broadly defined, parallels what Setha Low (2003, 2009) identifies as a "gated community."

59. Field notes, Rodman Board of Education Meeting, February 2004.

60. Ibid.

61. Staiger 2004, 161.

62. Faulkner 1951, 92.

63. Staiger 2004, 161.

64. Clifford 1986, 1–26.

65. The cafeteria was patrolled by various faculty members who had this duty on assigned days and times. This was a mandatory assignment, in ways comparable to course assignments. As many as ten professional adults were assigned to the cafeteria during each of the two lunch hours. Some others were given assignments outside the cafeteria, such as, for example, in the gym.

66. Bolles 2005, 138.

67. The location of the sentry station changed during the fall semester of the first year of the study to an area farther into the building, making it possible to go into the main office without first engaging the inside sentry and/or the sentry station.

68. Harrison 2008.

69. Bolles 2005, 138. See also Hochschild 1979, 551–75; 1983.

70. Elsewhere (Fordham 2013b) I have noted the connection between help and indebted bodies.

71. Hochschild 1979, 1983.

72. Neither this guard station nor the male sentry just outside the door was in place during the first day or the first weeks of this research. It was not until about a month after the official study began that this station was put in place. The permanent guard outside the main door came shortly thereafter.

73. E. Wolf (1982) 2010.

74. Du Bois (1903) 1994.

75. Steele 2010, 5.

76. An erstwhile White male colleague once shared with me an un-expected but compelling piece of advice: "I can say anything to my students as long as I do so without emotion." He was speaking from a male-gendered space. What he failed to acknowledge, or perhaps recognize, is that when one is gendered female, to speak with a flat affect is to speak in a lower or male register and, by extension, with power. To speak as though one has power when that is unaccepted culturally—that is, African Americans in White public spaces—is to further diminish one's value or quest for power.

77. Field notes, 23 March 2004.

78. The inflection Hawkeye employed when using the anthropologist's professional title conveyed something other than honor and respect.

79. Field notes, 14 October 2004.

80. Field notes, April 2005.

81. See Cook and Ludwig 1998. See also Ferguson 2001; Fordham 1996; Fordham and Ogbu 1986, 176–206; Shockley 1970.

82. See Schofield 1982, for a partial exception to this claim. See also Holland and Eisenhart 1990 for a similar portrayal at the postsecondary level.

83. The possible exception to this normality is the workplace or other instrumental locations. The boss or CEO, the principal, the president, and similar elites may eat with the workers on rare occasions, such as, for example, to show his or her commitment to the well-being of the workforce.

84. Tompkins 2012.

85. This is a controversial view of the working relationship between Black and White women as depicted, for example, in Murray (1956) 1999; Jewell 1993; Newman 1999; and Moody 1976 and in untold novels, including Hurston 1965; Morrison 1994; Mitchell 1936; and, more recently, Stockett 2010. The "intimate apartheid" sewn into the hegemonic narrative in all of these sources is the dominant–subordinate relationship between Black and White women. At the same time, a secondary—albeit consistent and equally important—theme is the divergent (mis)understandings of what is the epicenter of the relationship. As I argue elsewhere, among Black women, the prevailing belief is that they are employees who work extremely hard and are severely underpaid (Fordham 2012b). See also Smith (personal communication); R. Harris (personal communication).

In striking contrast, the prevailing perspective among the White women who most often employ Black women is that they are gift givers, not only helping these women survive by offering them employment but also teaching them, indirectly, how to be appropriate females; hence the transformation of the verb "to help" to a noun: "the Help" (Fordham 2013b).

86. Douglas 1972. See also Lévi-Strauss 1966; Dumont 1970.

87. Douglas 1972, 61.

88. Tatum 1997.

89. This was especially true of the Black kids who were identified and self-identified as "biracial." Others did not sit at the table because they brought food from home and/or they did not share the hegemonic values of the group. Nonetheless, the Black students who strongly identified with a Black identity tended to sit at the table most days.

90. See Low 2003, 2009; C. Harris 1993.

91. See C. Alexander 1996.

92. Tompkins 2012.

93. Traditionally, anthropologists sought to do fieldwork in exotic, strange, and unfamiliar cultures hoping to minimize the impact of prior knowledge. The anthropologist's attempt to be "deliberately naive" was designed to construct a similar strangeness in a familiar (not strange) social context.

94. It is important to remember that there were only three Black professional adults employed at the school: the secretary/receptionist, a Black female counselor, and one classroom teacher. Unlike the White females, who were surrounded by a plethora of same-gender adults, in this strange institutional setting, these (Black) teenage girls had virtually no adults whose identity they thought mirrored their own.

95. Holland and Eisenhart 1990, 86.

96. In order to get to what I identify here as the Red-Light District (RLD), one enters the front door of the building, walks past the main sentry station outside the main office, through a set of double doors and past the cafeteria on the right, then turns left at the first intersection. One is then officially in the RLD, which, paradoxically, includes the school library. The first indication that one is in the RLD are the rows of institutional gray lockers on both sides of the corridor and the virtual absence of light—even in the hallways.

97. The student participants' diaries are referenced sparingly here for several reasons: (1) Participation rates were low. (2) The documents written in pencil in cursive were almost indecipherable. (3) Most of the sub-

mitted entries revealed the importance of money in fueling this segment of the study. I plan to explore this and other components of my study in a future monograph.

98. Adams and Bettis 2003, 1–7.

99. Merten 1996. See also Adams and Bettis 2003. The Black girl who did not fit the stereotypical image did not internalize the cheerleader image or what I have labeled elsewhere "racelessness" (Fordham 1991, 54–85). My incomplete analysis suggests that she was instead "admitted, but left out" (Anderson 2012). Moreover, my findings parallel Merten's claims regarding the life of a "Burnout" who becomes a cheerleader at the high school he studied (Merten 1996, 51–70).

100. Field notes, 12 October 2004.

101. See, for example, Chagnon 1990; Foley 1994; Moss 2003; Ogbu 1974.

102. For example, Dickar 2008; MacLeod 2009.

103. C. Harris 1993.

104. While the methodology is divided into three distinct phases in keeping with the Euro-American preference for linear, orderly thinking (see, for example, D. Lee 1987), in fact, like most of social life, the research stages reported here often overlapped and were messy and nonlinear, compelling me to revisit an earlier stage or to fast-forward to a stage that was supposed to come much later in the research process.

105. I am no longer as naive as I was earlier in my professional life, misrecognizing niceness and politeness for acceptance and sincerity. Their willingness to interact with the anthropologist was a professional responsibility, and they did not take that lightly.

106. Field notes, 25 March 2004.

107. See, for example, Lareau (2003) 2011; Levine 2008; and Ostrander 1984.

108. The problem of getting in touch with parents prior to talking with students was made worse between the spring and fall semesters of 2004 because although the administration gave the anthropologist an official list of the phone numbers for students identified as potential participants during the spring semester, many of them moved during the summer break. She was reluctant to ask for an updated list—not just because they would have to copy the information again, but also because she worried about how they would see her inability to get the desired twenty students.

109. Field notes, 12 October 2004.

110. Ibid.

111. For a full discussion of how "jobs below the job ceiling" differ from "jobs above the job ceiling," see Ogbu 1974, 1978.

112. In her efforts to contact the parents of Black students, the anthropologist talked with only one male parent. The overwhelming majority of the parents she interacted with via phone and/or in person were female.

113. During this initial stage of her research project, the anthropologist did not have a cell phone and did not have access to a phone while at the school. (There was a pay phone near the main office that she could use by having the correct change—fifty cents per call.) It was not until almost a year later that the university allowed her to use a portion of her small start-up account to pay for a cell phone. While getting a phone did not completely solve the problem, it enabled students to call her, which ultimately meant that she succeeded in obtaining the students required for the study.

114. While all of the parents were asked to participate in this part of the study, the bar was lower in that she was only seeking a population of ten of the twenty parents to sign this form.

115. When discussing this intrusive process with friends, they often referred to it as the bureaucratic equivalent of the "helicopter parent," with the major difference being that these faceless but powerful bureaucrats had a lot more power than any individual parent.

116. Numerous studies have been done regarding how "linguistic profiling" influences the perception of the intelligence, motivation, and class status of people of African ancestry. Some of the most compelling evidence can be found in the work of John Baugh and William Labov (1999, 19), who detail how the linguistic practices of African Americans are continually stigmatized, historically and contemporarily.

117. At this school (and in the larger American society), acknowledging that students of African ancestry had more than one racial identity was problematic on many levels. Consequently, students of African ancestry who participated in the study and who self-identified as biracial or of mixed heritage were generally denied that identity and consigned, against their wishes, to the racial category Black. Elsewhere (Fordham 2010, 4–10) I have described this practice historically, especially as it was portrayed in the "one-drop rule," concluding that virtually all Americans of African ancestry are compelled to pass for Black.

118. Field notes, 17 February 2004.

119. Here I am referencing only my experience. When I talk with people outside the discipline and identify myself as an anthropologist, I am understood to be an archaeologist, primarily because this subdivision

of the discipline is more recognizable in the public domain due to such popular-culture vehicles as the Indiana Jones movies. When I attempt to correct this misrecognition by pointing out that archaeology is a subdiscipline of anthropology and that I am a cultural anthropologist, the initial interest often appears to wane.

120. W. E. B. Du Bois coined the term "dual consciousness" in 1903 (Du Bois [1903] 1994).

121. See Crick and Grotpeter 1995; Simmons 2002.

122. Waters 2004.

123. Wiseman 2002.

124. Simmons 2002.

125. Kochman and Mavrelis 2009; Sandberg 2013.

126. Mauss (1950) 1990.

127. This was a new experience for me. In all my earlier ethnographic work in school settings, it had never been difficult to get students to participate.

128. Field notes, February 2005.

129. Formal student interview, 14 March 2005.

130. Looking back, I am convinced that this is in part a function of the labor force participation of the adult females in this community. Many of these women were stay-at-home moms and had children who were now in school, leaving them free to spend time "giving back to the community."

131. It is important to remember that this is taking place between 2004 and 2006, when technologies such as software applications that simulate whiteboards were not as widely used as they are today.

132. The extent of fear and surveillance at UGRH in the wake of 9/11 cannot be overstated.

133. This parent's concerns had particular resonance for the anthropologist, who sensed her distrust and fear of betrayal. The parent responded to the anthropologist as if she were the embodiment of the historical legacy of inappropriate research practices.

134. Field notes, 21 May 2004.

135. Fordham 1985, 1993; Fordham and Ogbu 1986.

136. The anthropologist knew both experientially and from the research literature that teachers are overloaded with massive requests for reports and other written paperwork. Against that background, she tried to assure them that if they could find a moment to talk with her about the student, that would be sufficient. She did not want them to feel that she was adding to their already stressed-out professional lives.

3. Nadine

1. I have struggled here with these two powerfully stigmatizing words: "nigger" and "bitch," words that strike enormous fear in the minds of persons raced Black, and individuals—regardless of race—gendered female. Unquestionably intended to harm, these words and the images they evoke are both powerfully stigmatizing and mind-altering. I have meandered—back and forth, back and forth—trying to decide whether I should include the actual words these young girls spoke or whether I should alter them to comport with the new sensibilities (we should never use the n-word, even if it is actually what the speaker said; this is particularly applicable when referencing the n-word). I want to stress here that I have negotiated an uncomfortable compromise with myself: I have opted to use the actual words—"bitch" and "nigger"—that the girls spoke because (1) their usage and understanding across race and gender lines among these rookie adults suggest that these specific words embody the antebellum period of American social life; (2) the words the members of a culture speak are only a small smidgen of their language; stated differently, language is so much more than the words we speak or utter; and (3) these were the actual words these girls, sixteen, seventeen, and eighteen years old, used repeatedly when talking among themselves and about each other, especially in their diaries. And even though the data in their diaries are sparingly included in this book, I have to admit that even a cursory analysis shockingly reveals how often the words "bitch" and, to a little lesser extent, "nigger" were routinely and repeatedly used when referring to other women and each other. I admit that I was surprised to learn that these teenagers, whose identities were shaped in the wake of the physical violence (terrorism) of 9/11 and at the commencement of the twenty-first century, routinely used this kind of language, despite claims to the contrary. Sadly, I do not believe that as young working adults and college students they stopped using these words and/or this kind of language. Indeed, as recently reported in the *Washington Post*, "the modern n-word—a shifty organism that has managed to survive on these shores for hundreds of years by lurking in dark corners, altering its form, splitting off into a second specimen and constantly seeking out new hosts, all the while retaining its basic and vile DNA— . . . defies black-and-white interpretations and hard-and-fast rules" (Sheinin and Thompson 2014).

2. Field notes, 15 February 2005.

3. Douglas 1966; Fordham cited in White 2007. See also Palmer 1989.

4. Nadine would later change her mind—at the last minute—and go to the prom with a group of female friends, not with her current dating partner, the White boy.

5. When I asked why the pizza from this particular chain was the only pizza option offered every day at the school, I was told that the company had a contractual agreement with the Rodman school system, including UGRH.

6. Field notes, 27 May 2005.

7. Formal interview, 22 June 2005.

8. Field notes, 26 May 2005.

9. The anthropologist was unable, despite repeated attempts, to get Mr. Kanker to talk to her about the thought process used in dismissing Nadine for the physical fight described here. For some disconcerting reason, he always had an excuse for why he could not talk with her about the policy issues involved in this case. After trying unsuccessfully to talk with him about the issue, she concluded that he was determined not to talk to her about why it was appropriate to suspend Nadine, but not Kirstin, for the fight chronicled here.

10. Formal interview, 22 June 2005.

11. Du Bois (1903) 1994.

12. Formal interview, 22 June 2005.

13. Just to clarify: I do not mean to suggest that I am talking about the institution where I currently work. My reference here is to institutions with both undergraduate and graduate programs where I taught multiple sections of introductory anthropology.

14. Ferguson 2001.

15. Gwaltney 1980.

16. Bourdieu 2004, 339–42.

17. Farmer 2004, 281–89.

18. Sullivan 2000.

19. Cited in Coloroso 2003, 28–29.

20. Kirstin's refusal was not unconditional (her little sister followed the plan of her big sister). She said she would consider participating if the anthropologist altered the research protocol and limited interactions to interviewing her and observing her in some of her classes. She made it crystal clear that she would not be willing to participate in the study if the anthropologist did not jettison the component devoted to observing her after school and/or in nonschool contexts, which would inevitably have entailed seeing her interactions with her (Black) boyfriend.

21. As I describe in "Keyshia," chapter 5 in this volume, I was waiting in the office for Nadine and Keyshia to complete their long-planned lunch in the cafeteria. I was waiting to make formal interview appointments with each of them.

22. There are many versions of this old saying. One of the first is said to have been in the *Christian Recorder,* March 1862.

23. Simmons 2002; Coloroso 2003; L. Brown 1998, 2003; Pipher and Ross 1994; Lamb 2001.

24. Rosenberg 1997.

4. Brittany

1. Field notes, 4 February 2005, 2, 4.

2. Willie 2003; Young 2007.

3. James Loewen (2005) does not offer information on "illegal" night life in which Black bodies played a primary role. His only reference, for example, to prostitution is to the building locations in different parts of the country. Interestingly, his focus appears to be on disabusing many Americans of the wrongheaded assumption that the degrading, humiliating segregation that is widely reported in the Southern states was not found in the North. He identifies specific states and towns (e.g., Anna, Illinois, which he asserts was shorthand for "Ain't No Niggers Allowed") were actively engaged in this practice—in the nation's vaunted Heartland.

4. Loewen 2005. See also Blackmon 2008; Berlin 1998, 2003; Griffin (1961) 1989; Wilkerson 2011; C. Woodward 1955.

5. Rosaldo 1980, 1989a, 1989b; Slotkin 1973; Dew 2016.

6. Low 2009.

7. Evans 1988; Fordham 1993.

8. Morris 2006.

9. Kochman and Mavrelis 2009.

10. Fordham 2013a.

11. In their anthology, Helen Longino and Valerie Miner (1987) offer essays from a variety of authors who chronicle in great detail the myriad ways females have traditionally competed, the goal of which, they argue, is to learn to lose. The essay that embodies what Brittany notes here was written by Daphne Muse (1987).

12. Phillips 2013; Fordham 2012b, 2013b; 2014; Smith, personal communication; C. Harris 1993.

13. I am paraphrasing what Brittany told me during one of our many

informal chats. We completed formal interviews, but she seemed to talk more freely and openly when taking brief walks outside or while waiting to find a room for a planned interview. She was much more open when the tape recorder was not on, as I repeatedly note in my field notes.

14. Grant 1984.

15. Size (that is, being small) matters for females primarily because the traditional, gender-specific hegemonic norm rewards females who have no voice (do not speak), are invisible (are silent), and occupy little space (are very thin). Admittedly many social and cultural practices have changed, but so much remains unchanged. For example, Ally, another participant in the study reported here (see chapter 7), is anorexic and spent more than three months in a hospital struggling to come to grips with her "too tall and too big body." Convinced that she gets more attention and, ironically, more protection from males when she is thin, she struggles with the idea of being weak and protected or being healthy and reasonably strong but alone. Fordham 2012a, Hossfeld 1994.

16. Morris 2006, 55–78.

17. Ibid, 107–28.

18. Bass 2001, 219–30.

19. Not only are bystanders not neutral or benign observers, they are essential to the conflict (Sullivan 2000, 35–38).

20. Kelly 2006.

21. Brittany's diary, 15 March 2005.

22. "Bantustan"—a term first used to describe the impoverished Black enclaves in South Africa during the official reign of apartheid—is used here in a pejorative sense. Its meaning is inverted to apply to this privileged research site that is best characterized by its monochromatic racial identity: Whiteness and privilege. See, for example, Lewis-McCoy 2014.

23. Again, in order to honor the promised confidentiality, this is not her actual birthday.

24. Field notes (date omitted for confidentiality).

25. Brittany's diary, 4 March 2005.

26. Larsen 1929; Piper 1992; W. White 1948.

27. C. Harris 1993.

28. Bourdieu 2004.

29. Ibid., 272; Grant 1984.

30. Heath 1983; Delpit 1988.

31. Das 2004, 327–33.

5. Keyshia

1. I do not mean to imply here that these two students are in any way closeted. Indeed, I think they are what they profess to be: heterosexual. What I do wish to point out in this discussion is that this was one of only a few instances when any of the "key informants" made reference to the idea of gay being a social category in their school. None of the female participants acknowledged or implied that she was gay or that there was a gay population in the school. I was baffled by the almost total taboo about this population but realized that I observed gay students at the school every time I was there. Apparently, none of the gay students who self-identified as female were willing to participate in my study or, alternatively, none of the gay or lesbian participants were willing to claim that identity when interacting with me.

2. What only a few brave souls would dare say, in hushed tones, but what the anthropologist was supposed to infer from what they did say, was that the academic life of this intellectually gifted middle-class Black female student had been hijacked by the drug culture, turning her into a person that none of them recognized. Even more critical here is that none of the school officials were willing to help her (using her family support system) find a way out of this cesspool. Did they avoid confronting her because they feared her parents' reactions? Or, alternatively, did her rapid descent into a social space where she was not distinguished from their dominant perception of the typical Black student at the school reinforce unvoiced beliefs of incompetence? The answer is not clear.

3. This statement caused the anthropologist to wonder why she was not an appropriate escort. Fortunately, in this instance, she was wise enough to pretend that she did not notice this contradiction.

4. Field notes, 8 March 2005.

5. Keyshia's girlfriend (and all the other students at the table) laughed and gave the anthropologist a knowing look that she understood to mean what everyone there knew: Keyshia had no intention of providing the requested information the next day or any other day. The body language of all the other students at the table indicated that they, too, knew she was having fun at the anthropologist's expense. Her face burned cold with the humiliation that she could not acknowledge.

6. Field notes, 8 March 2005.

7. Formal interview, 7 June 2005.

8. This is an interesting twist to the argument made by Ann Ferguson

(2001) and others. (See for example, Julie Bettie's descriptions of the oppositional, gender-specific cultural performances of the Chicas and the Preppies at Waretown High [Bettie 2003].) Ferguson argues that at the school she studied—Rosa Parks Elementary School—Black students, especially Black males, are routinely "adultified": compelled to be adults when they are only children, with the gender-specific emotional immaturity affiliated with young children.

9. Formal interview, 7 June 2005.

10. Formal interview, 7 June 2005. Keyshia was revealing her perception of the youth and inexperience of the teachers at UGRH. I share her perception. However, unlike at Capital High, where, for my earlier study, I was not only invited to attend the regularly scheduled faculty meetings and assigned a mailbox where notices to the faculty and staff were placed every day (including daily attendance sheets), these courtesies were not extended to me at UGRH. I was not on the e-mail list of daily announcements, and I was never invited and never attended a full faculty meeting. Nonetheless, my perceptions of the age (and gender) of the teachers at the school and in the classrooms I observed in connection with the key participants in my study support Keyshia's claim that the teachers lack extensive teaching experience because most of them were at the beginning of their professional careers, with many of them having the primary responsibility for the nurturing and care of their evolving families.

11. I was unable to independently verify or validate this claim because I did not have access to the academic files of the students. As part of trying to get past the difficulties noted earlier in getting approval from the RSRB at the institution where I was employed, I opted out of this level of access in order to obtain what is generally known as an "expedited review." Even with this "rushed" process, it took almost nine months to obtain the necessary approval (see chapter 2).

12. Fordham 1985, 1988; Fordham and Ogbu 1986.

13. Boyd 1997.

14. These teenage girls' arguments regarding authentic and unauthentic fueled my evolving interest in race as a social construction, leading me to publish "Passin' for Black: Race, Identity, and Bone Memory in Postracial America" (Fordham 2010). See also Piper 1992, 546–55.

15. Raybon 1997.

16. This word—"drama" (as in performance)—is most often used contemptuously, especially when applied to Black people (and women—regardless of race or ethnicity) and their cultural practices. The enormous

pain affiliated with enslavement—official and unofficial—merged to Jim Crow incarceration appears to have engendered an emotional cultural response that evokes the enduring contempt of the larger society. This response is not limited to high school students but extends, more critically, to their parents, peers, relatives, and friends.

17. Formal interview, 28 April 2004.

18. Parker 1999.

19. Formal interview, 7 April 2005.

20. As noted in the case study devoted to Nadine (chapter 3 in this volume), the fight between these two females occurred the year prior to the commencement of the study reported here. Therefore, I did not witness their interactions and am reporting the memory of the incident as told to me by the students and adults a little more than a year later. Based on what they told me, I would characterize the fight not so much as a physical event, although there was some physical contact, but more along the lines of the relationship violence that is the centerpiece of the study reported here. They berated each other both during the initial fight and continuously for more than six months, slowly tapering down to the point that they were willing and able to use their mutual friends to get them to the point where they were willing to meet for lunch to talk about reclaiming their friendship.

21. I am deliberately being vague here because if I were to identify the specific sport (one that Black females do not engage in very often), I fear that this student's identity would be revealed and I would be in violation of the confidentiality clause I agreed to. In addition, I must acknowledge that there was a real bias against girls who were either cheerleaders or athletes at the school. Cheerleaders were seen as fake athletes, and girls who participated on "real" sports teams were routinely patronized and their achievements underappreciated. For example, the first time I went to a basketball game to see one of the females in my study, I assumed that, like what I had experienced when I went to one of the male students' games, I would have to purchase a ticket. When I went to the same school official to inquire about purchasing a ticket to the game, she told me that tickets were not sold to the girls' games. My facial response must have indicated my private thoughts. Apparently, the only people who typically went to the female games (at that time) were parents and other close family members. Put differently, the widespread lack of interest in the girls' games would be further eroded by the need to buy tickets.

22. According to Barbara Coloroso (2003), Dan Olweus (1993), and

Keith Sullivan (2000), bystanders are neither neutral nor innocent. They are, instead, absolutely essential to the fight or conflict.

23. Formal interview, 7 June 2005.

24. Ibid.

25. I must admit that I did not fully appreciate the distinction Keyshia was making here between the words "stupid" and "nigger." Some would argue that at the core of the slur "nigger" is the idea of being "stupid," even inhuman. Nonetheless, Keyshia saw a big difference in the meaning of the two terms and refused to see how Nadine could be genuinely infuriated by being identified as embodying either of the words "stupid" or "nigger."

26. Formal interview, 7 June 2005.

27. Ibid.

28. Ibid.

29. My colleague Faye Harrison labels them "human mascots" (2008 and personal communication). See also V. Woodward 2014.

30. Fordham 2010; Gatewood 2000; Kerr 2006; Larsen 1929. The "brown-paper-bag principle" is a reference to the idea that only people with skins lighter than a brown-paper bag were acceptable.

31. There were rumors among the staff and students that Keyshia wore color contacts. When asked, she assured the anthropologist that that was not true.

32. I did not question the probability of this having occurred because I have heard (and friends have shared with me their version of) this and similar stories throughout my life.

33. Fordham 2007a.

34. I have to admit that I had no direct evidence of this assertion, though it was widely reported not just among the students in my study (some of the students in my study would repeatedly point out to me and/or tell me about [White] girls who had had breast implants) but also among the adults, especially the counselors and administrators. In striking contrast, one student in my study, Genevieve, had breast-reduction surgery just prior to the end of the school year and strategically planned it so that she would have sufficient time to heal and be able to participate in the graduation ceremony and the long-planned graduation party that her parents and grandparents were giving her as a graduation gift.

35. "Junk in the trunk" is both a compliment, when used *within* the Black community, and a derisive phrase when appropriated and used to describe the Black female body by outsiders. Moreover, adolescent Black female bodies are widely believed to be more developed physically than

those of their White female counterparts and to develop at a younger age (some researchers insist that Black females experience puberty earlier than White females; see, for example, Herman-Giddens et al. 2012). Even when they were observing UGRH's rules regarding the length of skirts and shirts and the tightness of the ubiquitous jeans, their bodies' configuration made them appear to be in violation of the established, hegemonic rules, leading to higher rates of suspension for violation of this rule among Black female students than White female students.

36. Bass 2001, 219–30.

37. Oddly, at the time of the study, I was told that Cam'ron, an emerging superstar of hip-hop, had begun wearing pink, and it now appears to be some males' favorite color; more than one person told me that that was because this celebrity had broken the no-pink color taboo for males. See a more detailed discussion regarding male aversion to pink in Alter 2013.

38. M. Alexander 2010.

39. Richard Majors and Janet Billson (1992) make the case that Black males embrace a "cool pose," refusing to appear frightened or disoriented by any issue confronting them in the public sphere. They teach their sons to respond in this manner as well.

40. I remember my surprise at hearing Keyshia's story since I had heard a similar story years earlier from a colleague, Enoch H. Page, at a meeting of the American Anthropological Association in Washington, D.C.; see Page 2000.

41. She preferred to interact with Ms. Redding rather than Ms. Long because Ms. Redding was, as she constructed her, more of a Christian and more likely to mask her disapproval by acknowledging and being deferential to the status differences between teachers and members of the school's staff, not to mention that she was also just a tad bit more likely to embrace the Black–White status difference. In striking contrast, Ms. Long was far less likely to mask her disapproval of Ms. Gilderhead's practices and to respond to her request less than favorably.

42. Delpit 1988, 1996; Delpit and Dowdy 2002.

43. This is how Ferguson (1996, 2001) frames the academic problems of Black children at the research site she studied. What I would add to this critical narrative is the consistent practice of making Black children adults and infantilizing their parents. Prior to the institutionalization of affirmation action for Black people, an unlabeled affirmative-action program was aggressively enforced for White Americans, with Roosevelt's New Deal policies the exemplar of this practice. See Katznelson 2005 for a detailed

chronicling of this misrecognized program of affirmative action for White Americans.

6. Chloe

1. Nader 1972, 284–311; Scheper-Hughes and Bourgois 2003, 1–31.

2. Depression, obesity, alcoholism, and the like are often framed as social rather than medical issues, and sometimes both. Much has been written about the medicalization of social issues. Conrad 2007 and Conrad and Schneider 1980 and 1983, for example, are widely known and cited. Other writers have dealt specifically with how the bodies of African American females are routinely commoditized and raped, compelling them to be (in)animate possessions in the service of science, hospitals, medical schools, and individual medical professionals. See, for example, Washington 2006. For a more global look at this practice, see Patton 1996.

3. By "zebra-striped families" I mean families not limited to the hegemonic normality and nuclear family.

4. Chloe's journal, 8 May 2005.

5. See, for example, M. Alexander 2010; Blackmon 2008; Du Bois (1903) 1994; Frazier 1939; Spivey 1978; Wilkerson 2011.

6. Blackmon 2008.

7. Section 1 of the Thirteenth Amendment to the U.S. Constitution reads: "Neither slavery nor involuntary servitude, except as a punishment for crime whereof the party shall have been duly convicted, shall exist within the United States, or any place subject to their jurisdiction."

8. Parsell 2006.

9. See Kohl 1995.

10. Murray (1956) 1999.

11. As suggested by many linguists, including Lisa Delpit and Kilgour Dowdy (2002), the way people talk is not limited to the words they speak but is, instead, a combination of speech, images/symbols, and language broadly defined. See also Baugh and Labov 1999.

12. See Fordham 2010.

13. See Davis 2001.

14. Parker 1999.

15. Parker 2000.

16. Ibid.

17. Fordham 2007a, 146–48.

18. See Alter 2013.

19. Dowling 2000.

20. Chloe does not fully appreciate the fact that her mother and extended family members—on both her mother's and her father's sides—gravitate toward the social and cultural behaviors and practices that are rewarded, not punished.

21. There are many books about mixed raced, including Ragusa 2006; Williams 1995; Johnson 2015; Nichols 2014, to name a few.

22. Ragusa 2006.

23. Williams 1995.

24. See, for example, Newitz and Wray 1996; Wray 2006; Hartigan 1997, 1999; Perry 2001, 56–91; Bucholtz 2011; Vance 2016.

25. Newitz and Wray 1996; Wray 2006.

26. Chloe's journal, 17 May 2005.

27. For example, anthropologist Evelyn Newman Phillips (personal communication) describes a painful language encounter she had with her gynecologist as she was undergoing an annual exam. Unexpectedly, in the middle of a discussion of her particular health issues, this doctor suddenly asked her, "Why is it that you never changed your accent?" Her response: "Should I have?" Encounters like Phillips's are not uncommon and are reported in such disparate sources as Gonzales 2001; Delpit and Dowdy 2002; Baugh and Labov 1999; Smitherman (1977) 1988; Heath 1983; and Ragusa 2006.

28. For a compelling description of the draconian efforts of "other" Black people—that is, Jamaicans, Haitians, Dominicans, Nigerians, and others in the African diaspora, including the intragroup and in-group demarcations based on class and skin color (what I have described elsewhere as "skinship"; Fordham 2010, 9–12)—to distance themselves from the stigmatized identity of African Americans, see Matory 2015.

29. Matory 2015.

30. Formal interview, 26 May 2005.

31. Matory 2015.

32. Anderson 2012.

7. Ally

1. Murray Webster and James Driskell Jr. (1983) make the argument that in our society, beauty operates in ways that parallel race and gender, making it a status with similar rewards and consequences. See also Judge and Cable 2011.

2. Formal interview, 19 April 2005.

3. During her tenth- and eleventh-grade years of schooling, Ally had struggled with anorexia. She had regained a lot of the weight she lost prior to the time I met her.

4. Formal interview, 8 June 2005.

5. When thinking about body image between Black and White women, it is very important to consider their different historical legacies. Food deprivation was a prominent component of enslaved Africans, leading to inadequate nourishment. And as some anthropologists have noted, in some cultures, bigger bodies are equated with greater access to food and less poverty.

6. Formal interview, 27 May 2005.

7. Formal interview, 26 May 2005.

8. Margaret Mead, a student of Franz Boas, the founder of American anthropology, popularized anthropology in America in the 1960s and 1970s, especially regarding sexual mores and practices, and was not well liked by her professional colleagues for doing so. There is also a real possibility that gender played a major role in their response to her popularity.

9. Here I am opting to leave unnamed the university where her mother was or is employed. Again, this is intended to minimize the possibility that the student's identity will be revealed.

10. Formal interview, 27 May 2005.

11. Nichter 2001. See also N. Wolf 1991; Hesse-Biber 1996; Bordo 1993.

12. Admittedly, while Webster and Driskell (1983) insist that beauty is "a status," that is, that it is critical throughout the life course for both males and females—especially females—I am arguing here that it is particularly important for females during high school and early adolescence, not only because it fuels desire and the attendant reproduction but also because during this life stage, females are so anxious to embody the hegemonic, gender-specific cultural script—whatever it is—in order to maximize their dating and reproduction options.

13. Ally does not cite nor does she give any indication that she consciously knows about the huge advantages and disadvantages powerfully linked to smaller women. However, research by Karen Hossfeld (1994) on immigrant women suggests that in many of the world's workplaces, including Silicon Valley, the race, gender, class, and other forms of subordination in these settings mirrors and "reproduces(s) the racially [and genderedly] structured labor market and class structure that discriminates against minorities and immigrants" in the larger societies outside the workplace (90).

14. Formal interview, 27 May 2005.

15. In your teenage logic, being "pleasantly plump" is acceptable for a fifty-something married mother of two. If Ally were fifty-something, it is unlikely that she would be having the problems with food and body image that she is currently experiencing—at least not to the same degree. Ally rationalizes her position on this issue, not conscious of its connection to her stage in life. She is a rookie adult, at the beginning rather than the ending stage of her reproductive life.

16. Field notes, 27 May 2005.

17. Formal interview 19 April 2005.

18. It was clear to me that Ally did not mean she really disliked her friends, that is, defined them as her enemies, including her BFF. I interpreted her statement that she "disliked her friends" as meaning that she wanted them to accept her unconditionally—her weight, height, and other idiosyncrasies notwithstanding. She did not think they did because they were often guilty of teasing her, criticizing her for being overweight and for being too tall, and so on, compelled to live outside the idealized, gender-specific normality.

19. William Pollack (1998, 50) insists that the powerful "boy code" that forces males to value fitting in compels them to suppress a range of emotions, especially sadness. The only emotion that males can express unconditionally, he insists, is anger. This means that for many boys, sadness is a taboo emotion. In light of this claim, this is an area of study that is especially needed in understanding Black males and other males of color.

20. Field notes, 27 May 2005.

21. Although Ally does the right thing, that is, she supports her BFF and her other girlfriends, her anger and envy toward her friend(s) remains underground, fueling her latent hostility and resentment. She believes there are moral laws that are absolute truths. One of her teachers suggested that she thought Ally's peer relationships (not her family relationships) were the source of her eating disorder.

22. Field notes, 27 May 2005. Tuition remission or remittance is an increasingly common practice in academia nationwide. Admittedly, this practice is not limited to the children of low-status workers. State employees at state institutions, employees of both public and private institutions, the children of faculty members and academic officials, including presidents, provosts, deans, and other high-ranking officials, are also eligible for at least partial (or complete) tuition remission. But most kids whose parents, especially the children of single parents, are employed in low-status

jobs are eligible for this kind of compensation—but only if they are able to meet the stringent admission requirements. Arguably, in the latter case, tuition remission could be a kind of delayed raise or, more accurately, "the gift" (Mauss [1950] 1990) that compels these workers to display gratitude for the anticipated gift their children will receive when they become eligible for college. Anecdotal rather than empirical evidence suggests that these workers, especially low-status workers gendered female, endure lack of raises and promotions so that their kids can go to college for free or almost free. Typically, they've worked for a pittance, but they get reimbursed for it, in a way, by having this tuition remission or reduced tuition available to their offspring, as is the case in the institution where I work.

23. Knowing how sensitive Ally was about her weight, I have to admit that I was very uncomfortable asking her to tell me exactly how much she weighed; I could never make myself ask her that question directly. Her counselor told me that she was fairly certain that Ally weighed about 175 pounds, but Ally deemed that to be extremely overweight.

24. In a seminal article written more than thirty years ago, anthropologists were urged to broaden the lens of their analyses by discontinuing the practice of focusing exclusively on the deficiencies and weaknesses of the powerless. It was suggested that we study, instead, power and the powerful (Nader 1972, 284–311).

25. In their book *Social Suffering* (1997), Arthur Kleinman, Veena Das, and Margaret Lock assemble a group of researchers who do more than simply report the existence of suffering; rather, they define it as a dynamic social process that has powerful lasting consequences. See also Fordham 2013a, 206–28.

26. This misrecognition is a common cultural, gender-specific misunderstanding. Gender emotions—male and female—are often misrecognized and misunderstood. Stated differently, when males appear angry, often they are really sad; when females appear sad, they are in actuality angry (Pollack 1998).

27. See the description by Ben Rothenberg (2015) of the way the idealized female body image compromises the winnings of female tennis players.

Conclusion

1. Henry 1963, 1971.
2. Henry 1973.

3. See also Freire and Ramos 1993 for a parallel but at the same time dissimilar analysis.

4. See the introduction to this volume.

5. Kimmel 2002. See also Kimmel and Ferber 2014.

6. Kimmel 2002, 42.

7. Normality is not a static concept. It is, instead, freighted with fluidity, contestations, and dynamic changes over time, leading to what John Fiske ([1989] 2011, 20) identifies as "nomadic subjectivities."

8. Chesler 2009.

9. Crenshaw 1991; Fiske (1989) 2011.

10. See, for example, exceptions to this claim in Chesler 2009; Simmons 2002; Fordham 2010, 2013a; L. Brown 1998, 2003.

11. Bourdieu 2004, 339–42; Choi, Callaghan, and Murphy 1995, 97–112.

12. There are multiple versions of this quotation in the public domain. The most common feature of most versions is that acknowledgment of a problem precedes its change or amelioration.

13. I am in no way suggesting that this impact of race is not an issue in the lives of Black male students (and many of the other self-identified demographic groups, including White females) at the school. Black male students were not a part of this study population. I am therefore unable to make empirically based claims regarding their experiences at the school. For greater elucidation of the claims made here, see, for example, Lewis-McCoy 2014; Sullivan 2000; Pollock 2004.

14. As Dan Olweus (1993) asserts, bystanders are not neutral or objective observers. This was manifestly evident, for example, in the efforts to desegregate schools in the South. Several of the Little Rock Nine and other "warriors" for social justice reveal how difficult it was to be soldiers in an undeclared war, especially one specifically designed to block racial desegregation. See Bates and Carson 2007; Beals 2007; Hunter-Gault 1993; Fulwood 1997.

15. I embrace the word "violence" here because, as documented in this book, actions intended to harm another embody what is here known as violence—by another name. See Farmer and Sen 2005; Spender and Sarah 1988.

16. In her article "Nurturing Anger: Race, Affect, and Transracial Adoption" (2015), Jacqueline Ellis, a White woman, reveals that she was compelled to teach her Black daughter to suppress her anger. At UGRH, only the biracial girls were eligible for and/or received some level of accep-

tance. The evidence I have presented here suggests that their willingness to mask their anger was pivotal in their success. Nonetheless, even when presenting themselves as willing to assimilate—unequivocally—the girls socially identified as unadulterated Black (that is, those "passin' for Black"; Fordham 2010) were not granted total admittance to the core of this gated academic habitus.

17. In the same article, Ellis insists that, like caring for her young daughter, nurturing anger is not a part-time or trivial job (J. Ellis 2015).

18. Perry 2001, 2002. See also Bucholtz 2011.

19. Edward Morris (2006, 129) also notes this, making the following claim in his book in describing the Black–White divide today: "The current normative, dominant form of whiteness in our society is built on attaining social and spatial distance from nonwhites."

20. Bucholtz 2011, 211.

21. Fiske (1989) 2011.

22. Griffin (1961) 1989.

23. See, for example, Blackmon 2008. See also M. Alexander 2010.

24. See, for example, Moody 1976; Angelou (1969) 2009.

25. Fanon cited in Kebede 2001, 539. The Black Panthers and the advocates of Black Power, including Stokely Carmichael and Ekwueme Michael Thelwell (Carmichael 2005), H. Rap Brown (2002), Eldridge Cleaver (1999), Elaine Brown (1993), Kathleen Cleaver (1998), and Kwame Ture and Charles Hamilton (1992), resisted the tenets of nonviolence, seeking instead retribution, an eye for an eye.

26. See Bourgois and Schonberg 2009.

27. These inadequacies run the gamut, including intellectual inferiority, inadequate family structure and parenting, cultural deprivation, and lack of interest in schooling and education.

28. See Castile and Kushner 1981, in which the various authors argue persuasively that the influence and impact of collective symbols on the "enclavement" of certain human populations has many parallels to Bourdieu's claims regarding the persistence and impact of habitus. Building on the work of Edward Spicer (1971), each of the contributors makes a case for the persistence of certain peoples that defies the widely accepted idea of the necessity of a homeland, a language, and the like in order for a demographic to see themselves as a people. For example, Vera Green, in her contribution to the anthology (Green 1981, 69–77), argues that African Americans' struggle against racial discrimination promoted their ability to

survive the horror of racism and racial discrimination and, by extension, to become a people, as Castile and Kushner define it. See also Jackson 2012.

29. Faulkner 1951.

30. Moone 1981, 228–42.

31. See Fordham 2013a.

32. Here I do not mean to suggest that most of the students at the school are unaware of the disjuncture between the dominating norms and their experiential lives and knowledge. They are—often keenly—but incompletely. Indeed, it is often the crippling awareness of the distance between what is supposed to be and what actually exists that compels them to embrace social practices and behaviors that, paradoxically, further marginalize them, ensuring their lack of academic achievement.

33. It goes without saying that males are compelled to eschew practices and behaviors identified with females and femininity if they want to be identified with heterosexual masculinity. Since most of our traditional cultural rules and practices were put in place by persons who self-identified as males, this is in no way unexpected or surprising.

34. For example, today's unemployed or partially employed married-with-children woman is not known by the 1950s term "housewife." In today's world, she is known as a "stay-at-home mom" rather than a "housewife."

35. I have sought to limit my use of the four-letter word "mean." Why? Because I have come to see it as gender-specific, limited primarily to the interactions of females. Instead, I have opted to substitute "violent" for "mean."

36. Page 2000, 111–28.

37. As I pointed out in chapter 1, demands (tone) often make the powerful uncomfortable (comfort is the first marker of privilege) and are reserved for conversations between individuals in asymmetrical relationships, such as worker and boss, master and slave, police officer and driver, or prison guard and inmate.

38. Nunley 2004, 221–41.

39. C. Harris 1993, 1726.

40. See Fordham 2010.

41. Bucholtz 2011. See also Hall 2000.

42. Bucholtz 2011.

43. Ibid. See also Heath 1983.

44. Delpit 1988, 1996; Fordham 2010.

45. This is indeed fascinating in that she was completely aware of her father's socially constructed identity: Black. In this book, I am focusing not on skin color, not on the perceived degree of Blackness, but on how individuals identify themselves culturally. See Fordham 2010, 4–30; Dache-Gerbino and Mislan 2015. See also Larsen 1929; Hobbs 2014.

46. I am aware that what we typically mean when we say females are "conflict averse" is connected to physical, not symbolic, violence. See, for example, Bourdieu 2004.

47. I am not making a biological argument here, and I am certainly not claiming that gender is an uncontested, static concept. As John Fiske ([1989] 2011) asserts, "nomadic subjectivities" are both the social norm and omnipresent. The narratives of Keyshia and Nadine, class-differentiated Black girls in this book, is applicable here.

48. See, for example, Bucholtz 2011, 164–86; Perry 2001, 2002. This total distancing of the "unadulterated" Black girls from the friendship networks of the White girls was not completely applicable to the girls who self-identified as biracial; they were at least partially accepted in that they often had at least one—and sometimes more—White female friend. See, for example, Raybon 1997.

49. Bourdieu 2004, 339–42.

50. Bettie 2003.

Bibliography

Adams, Natalie Guice, and Pamela J. Bettis. 2003. *Cheerleader! Cheerleader! An American Icon.* New York: Palgrave Macmillan.

Ainsworth-Darnell, James W., and D. B. Downey. 1998. "Assessing the Oppositional Culture Explanation for Racial/Ethnic Differences in School Performance." *American Sociological Review* 3, no. 4: 536–53.

Alexander, Claire E. 1996. *The Art of Being Black: The Creation of Black British Youth Identities.* Oxford: Oxford University Press.

Alexander, Michelle. 2010. *The New Jim Crow: Mass Incarceration in the Age of Colorblindness.* New York: New Press.

Alter, Adam. 2013. *Drunk Tank Pink: And Other Unexpected Forces That Shape How We Think, Feel, and Behave.* New York: Penguin Books.

AAUW (American Association of University Women). 1995. *How Schools Shortchange Girls: The AAUW Report.* New York: Marlowe.

Anderson, Jenny. 2012. "Admitted, but Left Out: For Minority Students at Elite Private Schools, Admittance Doesn't Bring Acceptance." *New York Times,* October 21.

Angelou, Maya. (1969) 2009. *I Know Why the Caged Bird Sings.* Reissue. New York: Ballantine Books.

Bachrach, Peter, and Morton Baratz. 1962. "Two Faces of Power." *American Political Science Review* 56, no. 4: 947–52.

Baldwin, James. 1985. "Every Good-Bye Ain't Gone." In *The Price of the Ticket: Collected Nonfiction 1948–1985,* 641–47. New York: St. Martin's Press.

Barlow, Kathleen, and Elaine Dunbar. 2010. "Race, Class, and Whiteness in Gifted and Talented Education: A Case Study." *Berkeley Review of Education* 1, no. 1: 63–85.

Barrett, Paul M. 2000. *The Good Black: A True Story of Race in America.* New York: Plume.

Bass, Margaret. 2001. "Being a Fat Black Girl in a Fat-Hating Culture." In *Recovering the Black Female Body: Self-Representations by African*

American Women, edited by Michael Bennett and Vanessa D. Dickerson, 219–30. New Brunswick, N.J.: Rutgers University Press.

Bates, Daisy, and Clayborne Carson. 2007. *The Long Shadow of Little Rock: A Memoir.* Fayetteville: University of Arkansas Press.

Baugh, John. 1983. *Black Street Speech: Its History, Structure, and Survival.* Austin: University of Texas Press.

Baugh, John, and William Labov. 1999. *Out of the Mouths of Slaves: African American Language and Educational Malpractice.* Austin: University of Texas Press.

Baumrind, Diana B. 1972. "An Exploratory Study of Socialization Effects on Black Children: Some Black–White Comparison." *Child Development* 43: 261–67.

Beals, Melba P. 2007. *Warriors Don't Cry: A Searing Memoir of the Battle to Integrate Little Rock's Central.* New York: Washington Square Books.

Bellafante, Ginia. 2013. "A Favor Economy in Which Kind Acts Come with Expected Reciprocity." *New York Times,* December 22.

Berlin, Ira. 1998. *Many Thousands Gone: The First Two Centuries of Slavery in North America.* Cambridge, Mass.: Harvard University Press.

———. 2003. *Generations of Captivity: A History of African-American Slaves.* Cambridge, Mass.: Harvard University Press.

Bettie, Julie. 2003. *Women without Class: Girls, Race, and Identity.* Berkeley: University of California Press.

Blackmon, Douglas A. 2008. *Slavery by Another Name: The Re-Enslavement of Black Americans from the Civil War to World War II.* New York: Doubleday.

Bolick, Kate. 2015. *Spinster: Making a Life of One's Own.* New York: Crown.

Bolles, A. Lynn. 2005. "One Love, One Heart, and Skin-Teeth: Women Workers in Negril, Jamaica." In *Caribbean Tourism: People, Service, and Hospitality,* edited by Chandana Jayawardena, 136–47. Kingston, Jamaica: Ian Randle.

Bolton, Sharon C. 2005. *Emotion Management in the Workplace.* New York: Palgrave MacMillan.

Bordo, Susan. 1993. *Unbearable Weight: Feminism, Western Culture and the Body.* Berkeley: University of California Press.

Bourdieu, Pierre. 1977. *Outline of a Theory of Practice.* Vol. 16. New York: Cambridge University Press. doi:10.1590/S0103-20702013000100001.

———. 1984. *Distinction: A Social Change of the Judgment of Taste.* London: Routledge.

———. 1985. "The Forms of Capital." In *Handbook of Theory and Research for the Sociology of Capital,* edited by J. G. Richardson, 241–58. New York: Greenwood Press.

———. 2004. "Gender and Symbolic Violence." In *Violence in War and Peace: An Anthology,* edited by Nancy Scheper-Hughes and Philippe Bourgois, 339–42. Malden, Mass.: Blackwell.

Bourdieu, Pierre, and Richard Nice. 2000. *Pascalian Meditations.* Stanford: Stanford University Press.

Bourdieu, Pierre, and Loïc Wacquant. 2004. "Symbolic Violence." In *Violence in War and Peace: An Anthology,* edited by Nancy Scheper-Hughes and Philippe Bourgois, 272–75. Malden, Mass.: Blackwell.

Bourgois, Philippe. 2004. "U.S. Inner-City Apartheid: The Contours of Structural and Interpersonal Violence." In *Violence in War and Peace: An Anthology,* edited by Nancy Scheper-Hughes and Philippe Bourgois, 301–7. Malden, Mass.: Blackwell.

———. 2007. "Intimate Apartheid: Ethnic Dimensions of Habitus among Homeless Heroin Injectors." *Ethnography* 8, no. 1: 7–31.

Bourgois, Philippe, and Jeffrey Schonberg. 2009. *Righteous Dopefiend.* Berkeley: University of California Press.

Bowick, Theresa Lou. 2013. *Collard Green Curves: A Fat Girl's Journey from Childhood Obesity to Healthy Living.* Bloomington, Ind.: AuthorHouse.

Boyd, Todd E. 1997. *Am I Black Enough for You?: Popular Culture from the 'Hood and Beyond.* Bloomington: Indiana University Press.

Brettell, Caroline B., ed. 1996. *When They Read What We Write: The Politics of Ethnography.* Westport, Conn.: Bergin and Garvey.

Brown, Elaine. 1993. *A Taste of Power: A Black Woman's Story.* New York: Doubleday.

Brown, H. Rap [Jamil Abdullah Al-Amin]. 2002. *Die Nigger Die!: A Political Autobiography of Jamil Abdullah Al-Amin.* Chicago: Chicago Review Press.

Brown, Lyn Mikel. 1998. *Raising Their Voices: The Politics of Girls' Anger.* Cambridge, Mass.: Harvard University Press.

———. 2003 *Girlfighting: Betrayal and Rejection among Girls.* New York: New York University Press.

Bucholtz, Mary. 2011. *White Kids: Language, Race, and Styles of Youth Identity.* Cambridge: Cambridge University Press.

Butler, Judith. 2011. *Gender Trouble: Feminism and the Subversion of Identity.* New York: Routledge.

Carmichael, Stokely. 2005. *Ready for Revolution: The Life and Struggles of Stokely Carmichael (Kwame Ture).* With Ekwueme Michael Thelwell and with an introduction by John Edgar Wideman. Reprint ed. New York: Scribner.

Castile, George P., and Gilbert Kushner, eds. 1981. *Persistent Peoples: Cultural Enclaves in Perspective.* Tucson: University of Arizona Press.

Chagnon, Napoleon. 1990. *The Yanomamo: The Legacy Edition.* Belmont, Calif.: Wadsworth.

Chesler, Phyllis. 2009. *Woman's Inhumanity to Woman.* Brooklyn, N.Y.: Lawrence Hill Books.

Chisom, Ronald, and Michael Harrington. 1997. *Undoing Racism: A Philosophy of International Social Change.* 2nd ed. Vol. 1. New Orleans: People's Institute for Survival and Beyond.

Choi, Jung Min, Karen A. Callaghan, and John W. Murphy. 1995. *The Politics of Culture: Race, Violence, and Democracy.* Westport, Conn.: Praeger.

Chua, Amy. 2011. *Battle Hymn of the Tiger Mother.* New York: Penguin Books.

Clark, Reginald. 1983. *Family Life and School Achievement: Why Poor Black Children Succeed or Fail.* Chicago: University of Chicago Press.

Cleaver, Eldridge. 1999. *Soul on Ice.* New York: Delta.

Cleaver, Kathleen. 1998. *Memories of Love and War.* New York: Random House.

Clifford, James. 1986. "Introduction: Partial Truths." In *Writing Culture: The Poetics and Politics of Ethnography,* edited by James Clifford and George Marcus, 1–26. Berkeley: University of California Press.

Coates, Ta-Nehisi. 2015a. *Between the World and Me.* New York: Spiegel and Grau.

———. 2015b. Interview by Terry Gross. *Fresh Air,* NPR, July 13.

Collins, Patricia Hill. 1991. *Black Feminist Thought: Knowledge, Consciousness, and the Politics of Empowerment.* New York: Routledge.

Coloroso, Barbara. 2003. *The Bully, the Bullied, and the Bystander: From Preschool to High School—How Parents and Teachers Can Help Break the Cycle of Violence.* New York: HarperCollins.

Conrad, Peter. 2007. *The Medicalization of Society: On the Transformation of Human Conditions into Treatable Disorders.* Baltimore: The Johns Hopkins University Press.

Conrad, Peter, and Joseph W. Schneider. 1980. *Deviance and Medicalization: From Badness to Sickness.* Edited by Joseph W. Schneider. Philadelphia: Temple University Press.

———. 1983. *Having Epilepsy: The Experience and Control of Illness.* Philadelphia: Temple University Press.

Cook, Phillip J., and Jens Ludwig. 1997. "Weighing the 'Burden of Acting White': Are There Race Differences in Attitudes toward Education?" *Journal of Policy Analysis and Management* 16, no. 2: 256–78.

———. 1998. "The Burden of Acting White: Do Black Adolescents Disparage Academic Achievement?" In *The Black–White Test Score Gap*, edited by Christopher Jencks and Meredith Phillips, 375–400. Washington, D.C.: Brookings Institution Press.

Cosby, Bill, and Alvin F. Poussaint. 2007. *Come On, People: On the Path from Victims to Victors*. Nashville, Tenn.: Thomas Nelson.

Crenshaw, Kimberlé. 1989. "Demarginalizing the Intersection of Race and Sex: A Black Feminist Critique of Antidiscrimination Doctrine, Feminist Theory, and Antiracist Politics." *University of Chicago Legal Forum* 140, no. 1: 139–67.

———. 1991. "Mapping the Margins: Intersectionality, Identity Politics, and Violence against Women of Color." *Stanford Law Review* 43, no. 6: 1241–99.

———. Crenshaw, Kimberlé. 2015. *Black Girls Matter: Pushed Out, Overpoliced, and Underprotected*. With Priscilla Ocen and Jyoti Nanda. African American Policy Studies, Center for Intersectionality and Social Policy Studies. New York: Columbia University.

Crick, N. R., and J. K. Grotpeter. 1995. "Relational Aggression, Gender, and Social-Psychological Adjustment." *Child Development* 66: 710–22. doi:10.1111/j.1467-8624.1995.tb00900.x.

Dache-Gerbino, Amalia, and Cristina Mislan. 2015. "Passin' for Latin@ and the Politics of Black-imiento." Unpublished paper presented at the Critical Race Theory annual conference, May.

Das, Veena. 2004. "Language and Body: Transactions in the Construction of Pain." In *Violence in War and Peace: An Anthology*, edited by Nancy Scheper-Hughes and Philippe Bourgois, 327–33. Malden, Mass.: Blackwell.

Das, Veena, Arthur Kleinman, Margaret M. Lock, Mamphela Ramphele, and Pamela Reynolds, eds. 2001. *Remaking a World: Violence, Social Suffering, and Recovery*. Berkeley: University of California Press.

David, F. James. 2001. *Who Is Black? One Nation's Definition*. University Park: Penn State University Press.

de Button, Alain. 2004. *Status Anxiety*. New York: Vintage Books.

DeCuir-Gunby, Jessica T. 2006. "'Proving Your Skin Is White, You Can Have Everything': Race, Racial Identity, and Property Rights in

Whiteness in the Supreme Court Case of Josephine DeCuir." In *Critical Race Theory in Education: All God's Children Got a Song,* edited by Adrienne D. Dixson and Celia K. Rousseau, 89–112. New York: Routledge.

Delpit, Lisa. 1988. "The Silenced Dialogue: Power and Pedagogy in Educating Other People's Children." *Harvard Educational Review* 58, no. 3: 280–98.

———. 1996. *Other People's Children: Cultural Conflict in the Classroom.* New York: New Press.

Delpit, Lisa, and Joanne Kilgour Dowdy, eds. 2002. *The Skin We Speak: Thoughts on Language and Culture in the Classroom.* New York: New Press.

Demerath, Peter. 2009. *Producing Success: The Culture of Personal Advancement in an American High School.* Chicago: University of Chicago Press.

Detherage, Katherine. 2014. Foreword to *Global Health Systems: Comparing Strategies for Delivering Health Systems,* by Margie Lovett-Scott and Faith Prather, xv–xvi. Burlington, Mass.: Jones and Bartlett Learning.

Dew, Charles B. 2016. *The Making of a Racist: A Southerner Reflects on Family, History, and the Slave Trade.* Charlottesville: University of Virginia Press.

Diamond, Jared M. 1997. *Gun, Germs, and Steel: The Fates of Human Societies.* New York: W. W. Norton.

DiAquoi, Raygine C. 2015. "Colorblind and Colorlined: African American Parents Talk with Their Adolescent Sons about Racism." PhD diss., Harvard Graduate School of Education.

Dickar, Maryann. 2008. *Corridor Culture: Mapping Student Resistance at an Urban High School.* New York: New York University Press.

Douglas, Mary. 1966. *Purity and Danger: An Analysis of Concepts of Pollution and Taboo.* London: Routledge.

———. 1972. "Deciphering a Meal." In *Myth, Symbol, and Culture,* ed. Clifford Geertz, 61–82. New York: Routledge.

———. 1990. "Forward: No Free Gifts." In *The Gift: The Form and Reason for Exchange in Archaic Societies,* by Marcel Mauss, trans. W. D. Halls, viii–xviii. New York: Routledge.

Dowling, Colette. 2000. *The Frailty Myth: Redefining the Physical Potential of Women and Girls.* New York: Random House.

Du Bois, W. E. B. (1903) 1994. *The Souls of Black Folk.* New York: Dover.

Dumont, Louis. 1970. *Homo Hierarchicus: The Caste System and Its Implications.* Chicago: University of Chicago Press.

Dyson, Michael Eric. 2005. *Is Bill Cosby Right? Or Has the Black Middle Class Lost Its Mind?* New York: Basic Civitas Books.

Early, Gerald. 1993. *Lure and Loathing: Essays on Race, Identity, and the Ambivalence of Assimilation.* New York: Penguin Books.

Eilberg-Schwartz, Howard, and Wendy Doniger, eds. 1995. *Off with Her Head! The Denial of Women's Identity in Myth, Religion, and Culture.* Berkeley: University of California Press.

Ellis, Carolyn. 2004. *The Ethnographic I: A Methodological Novel about Autoethnography.* California: AltaMira Press.

Ellis, Carolyn, and Arthur P. Bochner. 2000. "Autoethnography, Personal Narrative, Reflexivity: Researcher as Subject." In *The Handbook of Qualitative Research,* edited by Norman K. Denzin and Yvonna S. Lincoln, 2nd ed., 733–68. Thousand Oaks, Calif.: Sage.

Ellis, Jacqueline. 2015. "Nurturing Anger: Race, Affect, and Transracial Adoption." *Women's Studies Quarterly* 43, nos. 1–2: 213–27.

Emanuel, Ezekiel. 2007. "Unequal Treatment." Review of *Medical Apartheid,* by Harriet A. Washington. *New York Times,* February 18.

Evans, Grace. 1988. "Those Loud Black Girls." In *Learning to Lose: Sexism and Education,* edited by Dale Spender and Elizabeth Sarah, 183–90. London: Women's Press.

Falcone, Jessica Marie. 2013. "The Hau of Theory: The Kept-Gift of Theory Itself in American Anthropology." *Anthropology and Humanism* 38, no. 2: 122–45.

Fanon, Frantz. 2008. *Black Skin, White Masks.* Rev. ed. New York: Grove Press.

Fanon, Frantz, and Richard Philcox. 2005. *The Wretched of the Earth.* Repr. ed. New York: Grove Press.

Farmer, Paul. 2004. "On Suffering and Structural Violence: A View from Below." In *Violence in War and Peace: An Anthology,* edited by Nancy Scheper-Hughes and Philippe Bourgois, 281–89. Malden, Mass.: Blackwell.

Farmer, Paul, and Amartya Sen. 2005. *Pathologies of Power: Health, Human Rights, and the New War on the Poor.* Berkeley: University of California Press.

Faulkner, William. 1951. *Requiem for a Nun.* New York: Random House.

Ferguson, Ann. 1996. "Can I Choose Who I Am? And How Would That Empower Me? Race, Gender, Identities, and the Self." In *Women, Knowledge, and Reality,* edited by Ann Garry and Marilyn Pearsall, 2nd ed., 108–26. New York: Routledge.

———. 2001. *Bad Boys: Public Schools in the Making of Black Masculinity.* Ann Arbor: University of Michigan Press.

Fincher, Leta Hong. 2014. *Leftover Women: The Resurgence of Gender Inequality in China.* London: Zed Books.

Fiske, John. (1989) 2011. *Understanding Popular Culture.* 2nd ed. London: Routledge.

Foley, Douglas. 1994. *Learning Capitalist Culture in Tijuana: Deep in the Heart of Tejas.* Philadelphia: University of Pennsylvania Press.

Ford, Iris. 2010. "Postrace: Every Good-Bye Ain't Gone." *Harvard Educational Review* 80, no. 1: 53–61.

Fordham, Signithia. 1982. "Cultural Inversion and Black Children's School Performance." Paper presented at the Eighty-First Annual Meeting of the American Anthropological Association, Washington, D.C., November.

———. 1985. "Black Student School Success: Coping with the Burden of 'Acting White.'" Paper presented at the Eighty-Fourth Annual Meeting of the American Anthropological Association, Washington, D.C., November.

———. 1988. "Racelessness as a Factor in Black Students' School Success: Pragmatic Strategy or Pyrrhic Victory?" *Harvard Educational Review* 58, no. 1: 54–85.

———. 1991. "Racelessness in Private Schools: Should We Deconstruct the Racial and Cultural Identity of African-American Adolescents?" *Teachers College Record* 92, no. 3: 470–84.

———. 1993. "'Those Loud Black Girls': (Black) Women, Silence, and Gender 'Passing' in the Academy." *Anthropology and Education Quarterly* 24, no. 1: 3–32. doi:10.1525/aeq.1993.24.1.05x1736t.

———. 1996. *Blacked Out: Dilemmas of Race, Identity, and Success at Capital High.* Chicago: University of Chicago Press.

———. 1998a. "Correspondence by Fordham, Signithia, and Joseph Hawkins." *Harvard Educational Review* 58, no. 3: 420–25.

———. 1998b. "Speaking Standard English from Nine to Three: Language as Guerrilla Warfare at Capital High." In *Kids Talk: Strategic Language Use in Later Childhood,* edited by Susan M. Hoyle and Carolin Temple Adger, 205–16. Oxford: Oxford University Press.

———. 1999. "Dissin 'The Standard': Ebonics as Guerrilla Warfare at Capital High." *Anthropology and Education Quarterly* 30, no. 3: 272–93.

———. 2005. "Revisiting Ogbu and Fordham's [*sic*] Hypothesis." Closing remarks at "Acting White," the Second Annual Youth and Race Conference, Chapel Hill, N.C., October.

———. 2007a. "My Love Affair with My Arrogant Hair." *Transforming Anthropology* 15, no. 2: 146–48.

———. 2007b. "You Can Do Better Than That: John Ogbu (and Me) and the Nine Lives Peoples." In *Minority Status, Oppositional Culture, and Schooling*, ed. John U. Ogbu, 130–45. New York: Routledge.

———. 2008. "Beyond Capital High: On Dual Citizenship and the Strange Career of 'Acting White.'" *Anthropology and Education Quarterly* 39, no. 3: 227–46.

———. 2009. "Write-Ous Indignation: Black Girls, Dilemmas of Cultural Domination, and the Struggle to Speak the Skin We Are In." In *Anthropology Off the Shelf: Anthropologists on Writing*, edited by Alisse Waterston and Maria D. Vesperi, 79–92. Chichester, U.K.: John Wiley and Sons.

———. 2010. "Passin' for Black: Race, Identity, and Bone Memory in Postracial America." *Harvard Educational Review* 80, no. 1: 4–30.

———. 2012a. "Ally: Size Matters. Too Fat and Too Tall for (Male) Attention." Paper presented at the 111th Annual Meeting of the American Anthropological Association. San Francisco, 18 November.

———. 2012b. "*The Help* as Indebted Bodies." "Symposium. Fabricating the Body III: Indebted Bodies. Exploring the Effects of Economy, Obligation, and Exchange in Contemporary Literature." Fifty-Fourth Annual Convention of the Midwest Modern Language Association (MMLA), Cincinnati, Ohio, 10 November.

———. 2013a. "Competing to Lose: (Black) Female Success as Pyrrhic Victory." In *The Social Life of Achievement*, edited by Nicholas J. Long and Henrietta Moore, 206–28. London: Berghahn.

———. 2013b. "Fabricating Indebted Bodies: *The Help, The Gift*, and Reciprocity." "Symposium. Religion, Exchange, and Blackness." 112th Meeting of the American Anthropological Association, Chicago, 23 November.

———. 2013c. "Mirror, Mirror on the Wall: Beauty Competition and School Achievement between (and among) Black and White Girls at [Underground Railroad] High." Paper read at the conference Diversity in Pedagogy/Teaching 2013, Rochester, N.Y.

———. 2013d. "What Does an Umbrella Do for the Rain? On the Efficacy and Limitations of Resistance." In *Youth Resistance Research and*

Theories of Change, edited by Eve Tuck and K. Wayne Yang, 97–106. New York: Routledge.

———. 2014. "Gifting and Indebted Bodies; or, alternatively, Is It Violence—By Another Name?" Paper presented at the Diversity Conference at the University of Rochester, Rochester, N.Y., 28 March.

Fordham, Signithia, and John U. Ogbu. 1986. "Black Students' School Success: Coping with the 'Burden of "Acting White."'" *Urban Review* 18, no. 3: 176–206.

Foster, Michele. 1989. "It's Cookin' Now: A Performance Analysis of the Speech Events of a Black Teacher in an Urban Community College." *Language and Society* 18: 1–29.

Foucault, Michel. 1977. *Discipline and Punish: The Birth of the New Prison.* New York: Random House.

———. 2000. "Polemics, Politics, and Problematizations." In *Essential Works of Foucault, 1954–1984.* Vol. 1, *Ethics.* Edited by Paul Rabinow. London: Penguin Books.

Frazier, E. Franklin. 1939. *The Negro Family in the United States.* Chicago: University of Chicago Press.

Freire, Paulo, and Myra Bergman Ramos. 1993. *Pedagogy of the Oppressed.* 20th anniv. ed. New York: Continuum.

Fryer, Roland, and Steven D. Leavitt. 2004. "Understanding the Black–White Test Score Gap in the First Two Years of School." *Review of Economics and Statistics* 86, no. 2: 447–64.

Fulwood, Sam, III. 1997. *Waking from the Dream.* New York: Anchor Books.

Gadsden, Vivian L. 1994. "Understanding Family Literacy: Conceptual Issues Facing the Field." *Teachers College Record* 96, no. 4: 837–59.

Galtung, Johan. 1969. "Violence, Peace, and Peace Research." *Journal of Peace Research* 6, no. 3: 167–91.

Gandhi, Arun. 2012. *Passive Violence.* Interview on *All Things Considered,* National Public Radio, September 1, 2012.

Gatewood, Willard. 2000. *Aristocrats of Color: The Black Elite, 1880–1920.* Fayetteville: University of Arkansas Press.

Gee, James P. 2004. *Situated Language and Learning: A Critique of Traditional Schooling.* New York: Routledge.

Gladwell, Malcolm. 2011. *Outliers: The Story of Success.* Reprint ed. New York: Back Bay Books.

Goffman, Erving. 1990. *The Presentation of Self in Everyday Life.* New York: Anchor Books.

Gonzalez, Norma. 2001. *I Am My Language: Discourses of Women and Children in the Borderlands*. Tuscan: University of Arizona Press.

Goodwin, Marjorie Harness. 2006. *The Hidden Life of Girls: Games of Stance, Status, and Exclusion*. Malden, Mass.: Blackwell.

Grant, Linda. 1984. "Black Females' 'Place' in Desegregated Classrooms." *Sociology of Education* 57, no. 2: 98–111.

Green, Vera. 1981. "Blacks in the United States: 'The Creation of an Enduring People?'" In *Persistent Peoples: Cultural Enclaves in Perspective*, edited by George P. Castile and Gilbert Kushner, 69–77. Tucson: University of Arizona Press.

Griffin, John Howard. (1961) 1989. *Black Like Me*. Cutchogue, N.Y.: Buccaneer Books.

Guinier, Lani, and Gerald Torres. 2009. *The Miner's Canary: Enlisting Race, Resisting Power, Transforming Democracy*. Cambridge, Mass.: Harvard University Press.

Gwaltney, John. 1980. *Drylongso: A Self-Portrait of Black America*. New York: Random House.

Hacker, Andrew. 2003. *Two Nations: Black and White, Separate, Hostile, Unequal*. New York: Scribner.

Hall, Julia. 2000. "It Hurts to Be a Girl: Growing Up Poor, White, and Female." *Gender and Society* 14, no. 5: 630–43. http://gas.sagepub.com/content/14/5/630.full.pdf+html.

Harris, Angel. 2011. *Kids Don't Want to Fail: Oppositional Culture and Black–White Achievement Gap*. Cambridge, Mass.: Harvard University Press.

Harris, Cheryl I. 1993. "Whiteness as Property." *Harvard Law Review* 106, no. 8: 1707–95.

Harris, Marvin. 1975. *Cow, Pigs, Wars, and Witches: The Riddle of Culture*. New York: Vintage Books.

———. 2001. *Cultural Materialism: The Struggle for a Science of Culture*. Lanham, Md.: AltaMira Press.

Harris, Ruth. n.d. Independent scholar, personal communication.

Harrison, Faye. 2008. *Outsider Within: Reworking Anthropology in the Global Age*. Chicago: University of Illinois Press.

Hartigan, John, Jr. 1997. "Unpopular Culture: The Case of White Trash." *Cultural Studies* 11, no. 2: 316–43.

———. 1999. *Racial Situations: Class Predicaments of Whiteness in Detroit*. Princeton: Princeton University Press.

Heath, Shirley Brice. 1983. *Ways with Words: Language, Life, and Work in Communities and Classrooms.* London: Cambridge University Press.

Henry, Jules. 1963. *Culture against Man.* New York: Random House.

———. 1971. "Is Education Possible?" In *Anthropological Perspectives on Education,* edited by Murray L. Wax, Stanley Diamond, and Fred O. Gearing, 156–62. New York: Basic Books.

———. 1973. *On Sham, Vulnerability, and Other Forms of Self-Destruction.* New York: Vintage Books.

Herman-Giddens, Marcia, et al. 2012. "Secondary Sexual Characteristics in Boys: Data from the Pediatric Research in Office Settings Network." *Journal of the American Academy of Pediatrics* 130, no. 5: 1058–68. doi:10.1542/peds. 2011-3291.

Hesse-Biber, Sharlene Nagy. 1996. *Am I Thin Enough Yet? The Cult of Thinness and the Commercialization of Identity.* New York: Oxford University Press.

Hill, Lawrence. *Someone Knows My Name: A Novel.* 2007. New York: W. W. Norton.

Hine, Darlene C. 1993. "In the Kingdom of Culture: Black Women and the Intersection of Race, Gender, and Class." In *Lure and Loathing: Essays on Race, Identity, and the Ambivalence of Assimilation,* edited by Gerald Early, 337–51. New York: Allen Lane, Penguin Press.

Hobbs, Allyson. 2014. *A Chosen Exile: A History of Racial Passing in American Life.* Cambridge, Mass.: Harvard University Press.

Hochschild, Arlie. 1979. "Emotion Work, Feeling Rules, and Social Structure." *American Journal of Sociology* 85, no. 3: 551–75.

———. 1983. *The Managed Heart: The Commercialization of Human Feeling.* Berkeley: University of California Press.

Holland, Dorothy C., and Margaret A. Eisenhart. 1990. *Educated in Romance: Women, Achievement, and College Culture.* Chicago: University of Chicago Press.

Horvat, Erin McNamara, and Carla O'Connor. 2006. *Beyond Acting White: Reframing the Debate on Black Student Achievement.* Lanham, Md.: Rowman and Littlefield.

Hossfeld, Karen J. 1994. "Hiring Immigrant Women: Silicon Valley's 'Simple Formula.'" In *Women of Color in U.S. Society,* edited by Bonnie T. Zinn and Maxine B. Dill, 65–94. Philadelphia: Temple University Press.

Hull, Gloria T., Patricia Bell Scott, and Barbara Smith, eds. 1982. *Some of Us Are Brave: All the Women Are White, All the Blacks Are Men.* New York: Feminist Press at City University of New York.

Hunter-Gault, Charlayne. 1993. *In My Place*. Reprint ed. New York: Vintage Books.

Hurston, Zora Neale. 1965. *Their Eyes Were Watching God*. New York: HarperCollins.

Hwang, Suein. 2005. "The New White Flight." *Wall Street Journal*, November 19.

Illich, Ivan. 1971. *Deschooling Society*. London: Marion Boyars.

Jackson, Jason B. 2012. *Yuchii Indian Histories before the Removal Era*. Lincoln: University of Nebraska Press.

Jewell, K. Sue. 1993. *From Mammy to Miss America and Beyond*. London: Routledge.

Johnson, Mat. 2015. *Loving Day*. New York: Penguin Random House.

Jones, James H. 1981. *Bad Blood: The Tuskegee Syphilis Experiment*. Revised ed. New York: Free Press.

Judge, T. A., and D. M. Cable. 2011. "When It Comes to Pay, Do the Thin Win? The Effect of Weight on Pay for Men and Women." *Journal of Applied Psychology* 96, no. 1: 95–112.

Karlsson, Evie Tornquist. 2006. "Evie and RSJ Help Women Celebrate Being God's Gals." *TRAA News*, January 11.

Katznelson, Ira. 2005. *When Affirmative Action Was White: An Untold History of Racial Inequality in Twentieth-Century America*. New York: W. W. Norton.

Kebede, Messay. 2001. "The Rehabilitation of Violence and the Violence of Rehabilitation: Fanon and Colonialism." *Journal of Black Studies* 31, no. 5: 539–62.

Kelly, R. 2006. "Slow Wind." Lyrics at http://www.metrolyrics.com/slow -wind-lyrics-r-kelly.html.

Kendall, Diana. 2002. *The Power of Good Deeds: Privileged Women and the Social Reproduction of the Upper Class*. Lanham, Md.: Rowman and Littlefield.

Kerr, Audrey Elisa. 2006. *The Paper Bag Principle: Class, Complexion, and Community in Black Washington, D.C.* Knoxville: University of Tennessee Press.

Kimmel, Michael. 2002. "Toward a Pedagogy of the Oppressor." *Tikkun*, December, 42–44.

Kimmel, Michael, and Abby L. Ferber, eds. 2014. *Privilege: A Reader*. 3rd ed. Boulder, Colo.: Westview Press.

Kleinman, Arthur, Veena Das, and Margaret M. Lock, eds. 1997. *Social Suffering*. Berkeley: University of California Press.

Kochman, Thomas. 1972. *Rappin' and Stylin' Out: Communication in Urban Black America*. Champaign: University of Illinois Press.

———. 1983. *Black and White Styles and Conflict*. Reprint ed. Chicago: University of Chicago Press.

Kochman, Thomas, and Jean Mavrelis. 2009. *Corporate Tribalism: White Men/White Women and Cultural Diversity at Work*. Chicago: University of Chicago Press.

Kohl, Herbert R. 1995. *I Won't Learn from You: And Other Thoughts on Creative Maladjustment*. 2nd ed. New York: New Press.

Lamb, Sharon. 2001. *The Secret Lives of Girls: What Good Girls Really Do— Sex Play, Aggression, and Their Guilt*. New York: Free Press.

Lareau, Annette. (2003) 2011. *Unequal Childhoods: Class, Race, and Family Life*. Berkeley: University of California Press.

Larsen, Nella. 1929. *Passing: A Novel*. New York: Knopf.

Larson, Joanne. 2014. *Radical Equality in Education: Starting Over in U.S. Schooling*. New York: Routledge.

Lee, Carol D., Margaret Beale Spencer, and Vinay Harpalani. 2003. "'Every Shut Eye Ain't Sleep': Studying How People Live Culturally." *Educational Researcher* 32, no. 5: 6–13.

Lee, Dorothy D. 1987. *Freedom and Culture*. Long Grove, Ill.: Waveland Press.

Leek, Clifford. 2013. "Whiter Shades of Pale: On the Plurality of Whiteness." In *Privilege: A Reader*, 3rd ed., edited by Michael S. Kimmel and Abby L. Ferber, 211–25. Boulder, Colo.: Westview Press.

Levi, Primo. 2004 "The Gray Zone." In *Violence in War and Peace*, edited by Nancy Scheper-Hughes and Philippe Bourgois, 83–90. Malden, Mass.: Blackwell.

Levine, Madeline. 2008. *The Price of Privilege: How Parental Pressure and Material Advantage Are Creating a Generation of Disconnected and Unhappy Kids*. New York: HarperCollins.

Lévi-Strauss, Claude. 1966. *The Raw and the Cooked: Mythologiques*. New York: Harper and Row.

Lewis, Amanda. 2001. *Race in the Schoolyard: Negotiating the Color Line in Classrooms and Communities*. New Brunswick, N.J.: Rutgers University Press.

Lewis-McCoy, R. L'Heureux. 2014. *Inequality in the Promised Land: Race, Resources, and Suburban Schooling*. Stanford: Stanford University Press.

Loewen, James. 2005. *Sundown Towns: A Hidden Dimension of American Racism*. New York: Touchstone.

Long, Nicholas J. 2007. *Political Dimensions of Achievement Psychology: Perspectives on Selfhood, Confidence, and Policy from a New Indonesian Province.* Oxford: Berghahn Books.

Long, Nicholas J., and Henrietta L. Moore. 2013a. "Introduction: Achievement and Its Social Life." In *The Social Life of Achievement,* edited by Nicholas J. Long and Henrietta L. Moore, 1–30. Oxford: Berghahn Books.

———, eds. 2013b. *The Social Life of Achievement.* Oxford: Berghahn Books.

Lovett-Scott, Margie, and Faith Prather. 2014. *Global Health Systems: Comparing Strategies for Delivering Health Systems.* Burlington, Mass.: Jones and Bartlett Learning.

Low, Setha. 2001. "The Edge and the Center: Gated Communities and the Discourse of Urban Fear." *American Anthropologist* 103, no. 1: 45–58.

———. 2003. *Behind the Gates: Life, Security, and the Pursuit of Happiness in Fortress America.* New York: Routledge.

———. 2009. "Maintaining Whiteness: The Fear of Others and Niceness." *Transforming Anthropology* 17, no. 2: 79–92.

Lutz, Catherine. 1995. "The Gender of Theory." In *Women Writing Culture,* edited by Ruth Behar and Deborah A. Gordon, 249–66. Berkeley: University of California Press.

Lyotard, Jean-François. 1984. *The Postmodern Condition: A Report on Knowledge.* Minneapolis: University of Minnesota Press.

MacLeod, Jay. 2009. *Ain't No Makin' It: Aspirations and Attainment in a Low-Income Neighborhood.* 3rd ed. Boulder, Colo.: Westview Press.

Majors, Richard, and Janet Mancini Billson. 1992. *Cool Pose: The Dilemmas of Black Manhood in America.* New York: Lexington Books.

Malinowski, Bronislaw. 1932. *Argonauts of the Western Pacific: An Account of Native Enterprise and Adventure in the Archipelagoes of Melanesian New Guinea.* London and New York: George Routledge and Sons.

Maslow, Abraham H. (1943) 2013. *A Theory of Human Motivation.* Eastford, Conn.: Martino Fine Books.

Massey, Douglas S., and Nancy A. Denton. 1998. *American Apartheid: Segregation and the Making of the Underclass.* Cambridge, Mass.: Harvard University Press.

Matory, J. Lorand. 2015. *Stigma and Culture: Last-Place Anxiety in Black America.* Chicago: University of Chicago Press.

Mauss, Marcel. (1950) 1990. *The Gift: The Form and Reason for Exchange in Archaic Societies.* New York: W. W. Norton.

McCall, Nathan. 1994. *Makes Me Wanna Holler: A Young Black Man in America*. New York: Vintage Books.

Merten, Don E. 1996. "Burnout as Cheerleader: The Cultural Basis for Prestige and Privilege in Junior High School." *Anthropology and Education Quarterly* 27, no. 1: 51–70.

———. 1997. "The Meaning of Meanness: Popularity, Competition, and Conflict among Junior High School Girls." *Sociology of Education* 70, no. 3: 175–91.

Messerschmidt, Donald A., ed. 1992. *Anthropologists at Home in North America*. New York: Cambridge University Press.

Milner, Murray, Jr. 2006. *Freaks, Geeks, and Cool Kids: American Teenagers, Schools, and the Culture of Consumption*. New York: Routledge.

Miner, Valerie, and Helen E. Longino, eds. 1987. *Competition: A Feminist Taboo?* New York: Talman.

Mitchell, Margaret. 1936. *Gone with the Wind*. New York: Macmillan.

Moody, Anne. 1976. *Coming of Age in Mississippi*. New York: Dell Bantam.

Moone, Janet R. 1981. "Persistence with Change: A Property of Sociocultural Dynamics." In *Persistent Peoples: Cultural Enclaves in Perspective*, edited by George P. Castile and Gilberte Kushner, 228–42. Tucson: University of Arizona Press.

Morris, Edward W. 2006. *An Unexpected Minority: White Kids in an Urban School*. New Brunswick, N.J.: Rutgers University Press.

Morrison, Toni. 1994. *The Bluest Eye*. New York: Plume.

Moss, Kirby. 2003. *The Color of Class: Poor Whites and the Paradox of Privilege*. Philadelphia: University of Pennsylvania Press.

Murphy, John W., and Jung Min Choi. 1997. *Postmodernism, Unraveling Racism, and Democratic Institutions*. Westport, Conn.: Praeger.

Murray, Pauli. (1956) 1999. *Proud Shoes: The Story of an American Family*. Boston: Beacon Press.

Muse, Daphne. 1987. "High Stakes, Meager Yields: Competition among Black Girls." In *Competition: A Feminist Taboo?*, edited by Valerie Miner and Helen E. Longino, 152–60. New York: Talman.

Nader, Laura. 1972. "Up the Anthropologist—Perspectives Gained from Studying Up." In *Reinventing Anthropology*, edited by Dell Hymes, 284–311. New York: Pantheon.

National Geographic Society. 1994. *Yanomami Homecoming*. Video. Washington, D.C.: National Geographic Society.

Neal-Barnett, Angela M. 2001a. "Being Black: New Thoughts on the Old Phenomenon of Acting White." In *Forging Links: African American*

Children Clinical Developmental Perspectives, edited by Angela M. Neal-Barnett, Josefina M. Contreras, and Kathryn A. Kerns, 75–88. New York: Praeger.

———. 2001b. Introduction to *Forging Links: African American Children Clinical Developmental Perspectives,* edited by Angela M. Neal-Barnett, Josefina M. Contreras, and Kathryn A. Kerns, xv–xvii. New York: Praeger.

Neal-Barnett, Angela M., Josefina M. Contreras, and Kathryn A. Kerns, eds. 2013. *Forging Links: African American Children Clinical Developmental Perspectives.* New York: Praeger.

Newitz, Annalee, and Matt Wray. 1996. *White Trash: Race and Class in America.* New York: Routledge.

Newman, Louise Michele. 1999. *White Women's Rights: The Racial Origins of Feminism in the United States.* New York: Oxford University Press.

Nichols, Edward A. 2014. *Fade to White: A Memoir.* Bloomington, Ind.: iUniverse.

Nichter, Mimi. 2001. *Fat Talk: What Girls and Their Parents Say about Dieting.* Cambridge, Mass.: Harvard University Press.

Norwood, Kimberly Jade. 2007. "BlackThink's Acting White Stigma in Education and How It Fosters Academic Paralysis in Black Youth." *Howard University Law Journal* 50, no. 3: 711–54.

Nunley, Vorris. 2004. "From the Harbor to Da Academic Hood: Hush Harbors and an African American Rhetorical Tradition." In *African American Rhetoric(s): Interdisciplinary Approaches,* edited by Elaine B. Richardson and Ronald L. Jackson II, 221–41. Carbondale: Southern Illinois University Press.

Nunoo-Quarcoo, Frank. n.d. Personal communication.

Oakes, Jeannie. 2005. *Keeping Track: How Schools Structure Inequality.* 2nd ed. New Haven: Yale University Press.

Obama, Barack. 1995. *Dreams from My Father: A Story of Race and Inheritance.* New York: New York Times Books.

———. 2006. *The Audacity of Hope: Thoughts on Reclaiming the American Dream.* New York: Crown.

Ogbu, John U. 1974. *The Next Generation: Ethnography of Education in an Urban Neighborhood.* New York: Academic Press.

———. 1978. *Minority Education and Caste: The American System in Cross-Cultural Perspective.* New York: Academic Press.

———. 1981. "On the Origins of Human Competency: A Cultural Ecological Perspective." *Child Development* 52: 413–29.

———. 2004. "Collective Identity and the Burden of 'Acting White' in Black History, Community, and Education." *Urban Review* 36, no. 1: 1–35.

———. 2008. *Black American Students in an Affluent Suburb: A Study of Academic Disengagement.* New York: Routledge.

Olweus, Dan. 1993. *Bullying at School: What We Know and What We Can Do.* Cambridge: Blackwell.

O'Neal, Ryan. 2012. *Both of Us: My Life with Farrah.* New York: Crown.

Orenstein, Peggy. 1993. *School Girls: Young Women, Self-Esteem, and the Confidence Gap.* New York: Doubleday.

Ostrander, Susan. 1984. *Women of the Upper Class.* Philadelphia: Temple University Press.

Page, Enoch H. 2000. "No Black Public Sphere in White Public Space: Racialized Information and Hi-Tech Diffusion in the Global African Diaspora." *Transforming Anthropology* 8, no. 1: 111–28.

Palmer, Phyllis. 1989. *Domesticity and Dirt: Housewives and Domestic Servants in the United States, 1920–1945.* Philadelphia: Temple University Press.

Parker, Lonnae O'Neal. 1999. "White Girl? Cousin Kim Is Passing. But Cousin Lonnae Doesn't Want to Let Her Go." *Washington Post,* August 8. http://www.washingtonpost.com/lifestyle/style/white-girl/2014/12/30/b292a3ec-9059-11e4-a412-4b735edc7175_story.html.

———. 2000. "'White Girl?': The Story, and Dialogue, Continue." *Seattle Times,* January 4.

Parsell, T. J. 2006. *Fish: A Memoir of a Boy in a Man's Prison.* New York: Carroll and Graf.

Patton, Adell, Jr. 1996. *Physicians, Colonial Racism, and Diaspora in West Africa.* Gainesville: University Press of Florida.

Perry, Pamela. 2001. "White Means Never Having to Say You're Ethnic: White Youth and the Construction of 'Cultureless' Identities." *Journal of Contemporary Ethnography* 30, no. 1: 56–91.

———. 2002. *Shades of White: White Kids and Racial Identities in High School.* Durham, N.C.: Duke University Press.

Phillips, Evelyn Newman. 2013. "Gifting the Indebted Body? A Tangled Web in Black Beauty Culture." Paper presented at the 112th Annual Meeting of the American Anthropolgical Association, Chicago, 20–24 November.

Piper, Adrian. 1992. "Passing for White, Passing for Black." In *Out of Order, Out of Sight,* vol. 1, 275–308. Cambridge: MIT Press, 1996.

Pipher, Mary, and Ruth Ross. 1994. *Reviving Ophelia: Saving the Selves of Adolescent Girls.* New York: Berkeley Publishing Group.

Pollack, William. 1998. *Real Boys: Rescuing Our Sons from the Myths of Boyhood.* New York: Henry Holt.

Pollock, Mica. 2004. *Colormute: Race Talk Dilemmas in an American School.* Princeton: Princeton University Press.

Poussaint, Alvin F. 1972. *Why Blacks Kill Blacks.* New York: Emerson Hall.

Ragusa, Kym. 2006. *The Skin between Us: A Memoir of Race, Beauty, and Belonging.* New York: W. W. Norton.

Raybon, Patricia. 1997. *My First White Friend: Confessions on Race, Love, and Forgiveness.* New York: Penguin Books.

Reed-Dahanay, Deborah E. 1997. *Auto/Ethnography: Rewriting the Self and the Social.* Oxford: Berghahn Books.

Rimm-Kaufman, Sara, and Ilonna Rimm. 1999. *See Jane Win: The Rimm Report on How 1,000 Girls Became Successful Women.* New York: Hyperion.

Robbins, Alexandra. 2006. *The Overachievers: The Secret Lives of Driven Kids.* New York: Hyperion.

Rosaldo, Renato. 1980. *Ilongot Headhunting, 1883–1974: A Study in Society and History.* Stanford: Stanford University Press.

———. 1989a. *Culture and Truth: The Remaking of Social Analysis.* Boston: Beacon Press.

———. 1989b. "Memory and Counter-Memory." *Representations* 26: 107–22.

———. 2004. *Grief and the Head Hunter Rage: On the Cultural Forces of Emotions.* Reissue. Edited by Edward Brunner. Long Grove, Ill.: Waveland Press.

Rosenbaum, James E. 1976. *Making Inequality: The Hidden Curriculum of High School Tracking.* Hoboken, N.J.: John Wiley and Sons.

Rosenberg, Pearl M. 1997. "Underground Discourse: Exploring Whiteness in Teacher Education." In *Off White: Readings on Race, Power, and Society,* edited by Michelle Fine, Lois Weis, Linda C. Powell, and L. Mun Wong, 79–89. New York: Routledge.

Rothenberg, Ben. 2015. "Tennis's Top Women Balance Body Image with Ambition." *New York Times,* July 10. http://www.nytimes.com/2015/07/11/sports/tennis/tenniss-top-women-balance-body-image-with-quest-for-success.html?_r=0.

Sandberg, Sheryl. 2013. *Lean In: Women, Work, and the Will to Lead.* New York: Knopf.

Sartre, Paul-Jean. 2005. Preface to *The Wretched of the Earth*, by Frantz Fanon. New York: Grove Weidenfeld.

Scheper-Hughes, Nancy. 1993. *Death without Weeping: The Violence of Everyday Life in Brazil*. Berkeley: University of California Press.

Scheper-Hughes, Nancy, and Philippe Bourgois. 2003. Introduction to *Violence in War and Peace: An Anthology*, edited by Nancy Scheper-Hughes and Philippe Bourgois, 1–31. Malden, Mass.: Blackwell.

Scheurich, James Joseph, and Michelle D. Young. 1997. "Coloring Epistemologies: Are Our Research Epistemologies Racially Biased?" *Educational Researcher* 26, no. 4: 4–16.

Schofield, Janet Ward. 1982. *Black and White in School: Trust, Tension, or Tolerance?* New York: Teachers College Press.

Schoolman, Morton, and Christian Potholm. 1979. *The Theory and Practice of African Politics: The Colonial Overlay and the African Response*. Upper Saddle River, N.J.: Prentice Hall.

Scott, James C. 1990. *Domination and the Arts of Resistance: Hidden Transcripts*. New Haven: Yale University Press.

———. 1999. *Seeing Like a State: How Certain Schemes to Improve the Human Condition Have Failed*. New York: Vail-Ballou Press.

———. 2009. *The Art of Not Being Governed: An Anarchist History of Upland Southeast Asia*. New Haven: Yale University Press.

Scott, Kesho Y. 1990. *The Habit of Surviving: Black Women's Strategies for Life*. New Brunswick, N.J.: Rutgers University Press.

Sheinin, Dave, and Krissah Thompson. 2014. "Redefining the Word: Examining a Racial Slur Entrenched in American Vernacular That Is More Prevalent Than Ever." With Lonnae O'Neal Parker. *Washington Post,* November 9. http://www.washingtonpost.com/sf/national/2014/11/09/the-n-word-an-entrenched-racial-slur-now-more-prevalent-than-ever/.

Shockley, William A. 1970. "Try Simplest Cases Approach to the Heredity–Poverty Crime Problem." In *Psychological Factors in Poverty*, edited by Vernon L. Allen, 141–46. Chicago: Markham.

Shumar, Wesley. 2004. "Making Strangers at Home: Anthroplogists Studying Higher Education." *Journal of Higher Education* 75, no. 1: 23–41.

Simmons, Rachel. 2002. *Odd Girl Out: The Hidden Culture of Aggression in Girls*. New York: Random House.

———. 2009. *The Curse of the Good Girl: Raising Authentic Girls with Courage and Confidence*. New York: Penguin Press.

Skloot, Rebecca. 2010. *The Immortal Life of Henrietta Lacks*. New York: Broadway.

Slotkin, Richard. 1973. *Regeneration through Violence: The Mythology of the American Frontier, 1600–1860.* Norman: University of Oklahoma Press.

Smith, Arlette Miller. n.d. St. John Fisher College, personal communication.

Smitherman, Geneva. (1977) 1988. *Talkin and Testifyin: The Language of Black America.* Detroit: Wayne State University Press.

Spencer, Margaret, J. Dobbs, and Dena Swanson. 1988. "African American Adolescents: Adaptational Processes and Socioeconomic Diversity in Behavioural Outcomes." *Journal of Adolescence* 11, no. 2: 117–37.

Spender, Dale, and Elizabeth Sarah, eds. 1988. *Learning to Lose: Sexism and Education.* London: Women's Press.

Spicer, Edward H. 1971. "Persistent Cultural Systems: A Comparative Study of Identity Systems That Can Adapt to Contrasting Environments." *Science* 174, no. 4011: 795–800.

———. 1980. *The Yaqui: A Cultural History.* Tucson: University of Arizona Press.

Spillers, Hortense. 1987. "Mamma's Baby, Pappa's Maybe: An American Grammar Book." *Diacritics* 17, no. 2: 65–81.

Spivey, Donald. 1978. *Schooling for the New Slavery: Black Industrial Education.* Westport, Conn.: Greenwood Press.

Staiger, Annegret. 2004. "Whiteness as Giftedness: Racial Formation at an Urban High School." *Social Problems* 51, no. 2: 161–81.

———. 2011. "Hoes Can Be Hoed Out, Players Can Be Played Out, but Pimp Is for Life—The Pimp Phenomenon as Strategy of Identity Formation." *Symbolic Interaction* 28, no. 3: 407–28. doi:10.1525/si.2005.28.3.407.

Steele, Claude. 2010. *Whistling Vivaldi and Other Clues to How Stereotypes Affect Us.* New York: W. W. Norton.

Stockett, Kathryn. 2010. *The Help: A Novel.* New York: Penguin Group.

Stockman, Farah. 2015. "The Outcast Effect." *Boston Globe,* November 13. https://www.bostonglobe.com/opinion/2015/11/12/the-outcast-ef fect/45yFNPzDcsOmECYankHzVM/story.html.

Stoler, Ann L. 2000. *Race and the Education of Desire: Foucault's History of Sexuality and the Colonial Order of Things.* Durham, N.C.: Duke University Press.

Stoller, Paul. 1989. *The Taste of Ethnographic Things: The Senses in Anthropology.* Philadelphia: University of Pennsylvania Press.

Sullivan, Keith. 2000. *The Anti-Bullying Handbook.* Oxford: Oxford University Press.

Swanson, Dena P., Malik Edwards, and Margaret B. Spencer. 2010. *Adolescence: Development during a Global Era.* Waltham, Mass.: Academic Press.

Talbot, M. 2002. "Mean Girls and the New Movement to Tame Them." *New York Times,* 24 February.

Tannen, Deborah. 1990. *You Just Don't Understand: Women and Men in Conversation.* New York: HarperCollins.

———. 1994. "How to Give Orders Like a Man." *New York Times,* September 18.

———. 1995. *Talking from 9 to 5: How Men's and Women's Conversational Styles Affect Who Gets Heard, Who Gets Credit, and What Gets Done at Work.* New York: Virago Press.

Tatum, Beverly Daniel. 1997. *"Why Are All the Black Kids Sitting Together in the Cafeteria?" A Psychologist Explains the Development of Racial Identity.* New York: Basic Books.

Tizon, Alex. 2014. *Big Little Man: In Search of My Asian Self.* New York: Houghton Mifflin Harcourt.

Tompkins, Kyla Wazana. 2012. *Racial Indigestion: Eating Bodies in the 19th Century.* New York: New York University Press.

Tough, Paul. 2004. "The 'Acting White' Myth." *New York Times,* December 12. http://www.nytimes.com/2004/12/12/magazine/acting-white-myth-the.html.

Touré. 2012. *Who's Afraid of Post-Blackness? What It Means to Be Black Now.* With a foreword by Michael Eric Dyson. New York: Atria Books.

Ture, Kwame, and Charles V. Hamilton. (1967) 1992. *Black Power: The Politics of Liberation.* New York: Vintage Books.

Tyson, Karolyn. 2002. "Weighing In: Elementary-Age Students and the Debate on Attitudes toward School among Black Students." *Social Forces* 80, no. 4: 1157–89.

———. 2011. *Integration Interrupted: Tracking, Black Students, and Acting White after Brown.* New York: Oxford University Press.

Tyson, Karolyn, William Darrity, and Domini R. Castellino. 2005. "It's Not 'A Black Thing': Understanding the Burden of Acting White and Other Dilemmas of High Achievement." *American Sociological Review* 70, no. 4: 582–605.

Vance, J. D. 2016. *Hillbilly Elegy: A Memoir of a Family and Culture in Crisis.* New York: Harper Collins.

Wang, Wendy, Kim Parker, and Paul Taylor. 2013. "Breadwinner Moms." Pew Research Center Social and Demographic Trends. http://www.pewsocialtrends.org/2013/05/29/breadwinner-moms/.

Ward, Martha, and Monica Edelstein. 2005. *A World Full of Women*. 4th ed. New York: Pearson Education.

Washington, Harriett A. 2006. *Medical Apartheid: The Dark History of Medical Experimentation on Black Americans from Colonial Times to the Present*. New York: Doubleday.

Waters, Mark. 2004. *Mean Girls*. Movie. America: Paramount Home Media.

Webster, Murray, and James E. Driskell Jr. 1983. "Beauty as Status." *American Journal of Sociology* 89, no. 1: 140–65.

Weems, Renita J. 2004. "Sanctified and Suffering: Women and Victimization." *Essence*, December.

Weil, Elizabeth. 2012. "Puberty before Age 10: A New 'Normal'?" *New York Times*, March 30.

Weitz, R., and L. Gordon. 1993. "Images of Black Women among Anglo College Students." *Sex Roles* 28, nos. 1–2: 19–33.

White, Deborah Gray. 1985. *Ar'n't I a Woman: Female Slaves in the Plantation South*. New York: W. W. Norton.

———. 2007. "'Matter Out of Place': *Ar'n't I A Woman*? Black Female Scholars and the Academy." *The Journal of African American History* 92, no. 1: 5–12.

White, Walter. 1948. *A Man Called White: The Autobiography of Walter White*. Athens: University of Georgia Press.

Wilder, Craig S. 2013. *Ebony and Ivy: Race, Slavery, and the Troubled History of America's Universities*. New York: Bloomsbury Press.

Wilkerson, Isabel. 2011. *The Warmth of Other Suns: The Epic Story of America's Great Migration*. New York: Random House.

Williams, Gregory. 1995. *Life on the Color Line*. New York: Penguin Group.

Willie, Sarah S. 2003. *Acting Black: College, Identity, and the Performance of Race*. New York: Taylor and Francis.

Wise, Tim. 2011. *White Like Me: Reflections on Race from a Privileged Son*. Rev. ed. Berkeley, Calif.: Soft Skull Press.

Wiseman, Rosalind. 2002. *Queen Bees and Wannabes: Helping Your Daughter Survive Cliques, Gossip, Boyfriends, and the New Realities of Girl World*. New York: Three Rivers Press.

Wolf, Eric. (1982) 2010. *Europe and the People without History*. Berkeley: University of California Press.

Wolf, Naomi. 1991. *The Beauty Myth: How Images of Beauty Are Used against Women*. New York: Anchor Books.

Woodson, Carter G. 1933. *The Mis-Education of the Negro*. Trenton, N.J.: Africa World Press.

Woodward, C. Vann. 1955. *The Strange Career of Jim Crow.* New York: Oxford University Press.

Woodward, Vincent. 2014. *The Delectable Negro: Human Consumption and Homoeroticism within US Slave Culture.* New York: New York University Press.

Wray, Matt. 2006. *Not Quite White: White Trash and the Boundaries of Whiteness.* Durham, N.C.: Duke Univeristy Press.

Young, Vershawn. 2007. *Your Average Nigga: Performing Race, Literacy, and Masculinity.* Detroit: Wayne State University Press.

Index

SIGNITHIA FORDHAM is associate professor of anthropology at the University of Rochester, where she was a Susan B. Anthony Professor of Gender and Women's Studies from 2002 to 2007. She is the author of *Blacked Out: Dilemmas of Race, Identity, and Success at Capital High.*